LAND USE PLANNING MADE PLAIN

Second Edition

D1294641

LAND USE PLANNING
MADE PLAIN

2nd Edition

by

Hok-Lin Leung

UNIVERSITY OF TORONTO PRESS
Toronto Buffalo London

© University of Toronto Press Incorporated 2003
Toronto Buffalo London
Printed in Canada

Reprinted 2003

ISBN 0-8020-8552-0

Printed on acid-free paper

First published by Ronald P. Frye and Company, 1999
ISBN: 0-8020-8552-0 (paper)

National Library of Canada Cataloguing in Publication

Leung, Hok Lin, 1944–
    Land use planning made plain / Hok Lin Leung. – 2nd ed.

Includes bibliographical references and index.
ISBN 0-8020-8552-0

1. Land use – Planning.   2. City planning.   I. Title.

HD108.6L48 2002   307.1′2   C2002-905172-X

The University of Toronto Press acknowledges the financial assistance to its publishing program of the Canada Council for the Arts and the Ontario Arts Council.

University of Toronto Press acknowledges the financial support for its publishing activities of the Government of Canada through the Book Publishing Industry Development Program (BPIDP).

TABLE OF CONTENTS

Chapter Five   ANALYSIS 89

List of Tables

LIST OF FIGURES

PREFACE TO THE SECOND EDITION

Since the first edition of this book came out in 1989, reader response has been very encouraging. After ten years and four reprints, it is time to revamp the book to accommodate new theoretical development and changes in professional practice. In particular, there has been a resurgence of the physical dimension in city planning.

This edition follows very much the philosophy and format of the first, emphasizing informed practice, plain speaking, and easy reference. Most of the new materials and changes are concentrated in Chapters Four (information), Five (Analysis) and Six (Synthesis). I have brought in new sections on infrastructure and transportation planning, philosophies about "the good city", strategic choices in plan making, and planners and city future. I hope readers will find these a worthwhile effort.

ACKNOWLEDGMENTS

I wish to thank my students for their support and inspiration, critics of my first edition for their insight and suggestions, Janet Neves and Terence Leung for their assistance in research, and Jo-Anne Williamson and Jackie Bell for the typing and proofreading.

Most of all, I wish to acknowledge my intellectual debt to Kevin Lynch, whose professional work and personal life exemplified an unwavering faith in human reason and generous celebration of the human spirit.

To my mother for her faith in me.

To my wife for her encouragement.

PREFACE TO THE FIRST EDITION

This is a book about how to make and implement land use decisions. It seeks to develop a set of coherent planning principles by drawing out useful and generally applicable elements from the various systems and approaches. It makes assumptions about what land use planning is supposed to do and what elements in existing theories and practices can be useful in this pursuit. It is not a report or a critique but a guide for practice.

The focus is on planning at the city level. It is addressed to planners who make and implement plans, to politicians and administrators who legitimize and supervise them, to developers and property owners whose actions and decisions are conditioned by them, and to specific groups and the general public whose welfare and quality of life are affected by them. Through a shared understanding of the purpose, analytic skills and substantive considerations of plan-making, and the ways and means of plan-implementation, both the planner and the planned may become more responsible and responsive in using our land to satisfy the many human needs.

In writing this book, I borrowed heavily, both in style and substance, from four sources: Lewis Keeble's Town Planning Made Plain, Sebastian Loew's Local Planning, Chapin and Kaiser's Urban Land Use Planning, and Kevin Lynch's Site Planning. I hope the authors consider my effort has been worthwhile.

WHY PLAN?

. . . .

To ask the question "why plan?" is like asking "why be concerned about the future?" Hans Blumenfeld observed that "there is no such animal as planners," suggesting that making plans is a basic human trait, at least in the contemporary western culture. But then he hastens to add that "some are more planners than others," intimating that some are more thoughtful and skillful in this than others.

A land use plan is a conception about the spatial arrangement of land uses, with a set of proposed actions to make that a reality. Land use planning is, therefore, the process of identifying and analysing problems, defining goals and refining objectives, and developing and evaluating the options available to a community in pursuit of these goals and objectives.

The classic statement about the land use plan is perhaps offered by Kent (1964:18): "The official statement of a ... legislative body which sets forth its major policies concerning desirable future physical development." Therefore, in practical terms a land use plan should, as Chapin and Kaiser (1979:63) suggest, "indicate the distribution and intensity of development of industry, the wholesale, supplier and trans-shipment functions, centers for retail and related functions, and residential areas relative to open space, transportation systems, and other community functions." Planning decisions and actions can be long-term or short-term, city-wide or site-specific, and involving all or any particular type of land use.

In this book, land use planning is defined as the process of protecting and improving the living, production and recreation environments in a city through the proper use and development of land. Human behaviour is very adaptable and human beings can sustain great environmental stress before breaking down, but the chief aim of good planning is to strain this adaptability as little as possible. By carefully matching human activities to the physical environment, planning tries to minimize this stress, although there will always be greater stress to some members of the society than others. Any sensible plan will try to maximize the potential of the environment for the use and enjoyment of the community as a whole, safeguard all users from unacceptable environmental hardship, and share out the gains and losses to different users of land in an equitable manner. In this way, a planned environment will enhance the quality of life and impose less strain on human adaptability than an environment created by nonplanned development.

Typically, land use decisions are about the type, amount and location of uses of land. That is, "What?", "How much?" and "Where?" These questions about "siting" and "sizing" can be asked in a variety of ways: "Is this use appropriate on this site?" "Where is this use most suitably located?" "Are the uses located on the same site or on adjacent sites compatible with one another?" "How much land is needed for this particular use?" and so on. How these questions are answered is not only important to professional planners but also to public and private developers and users of land, and that includes just about everybody. While this book is intended to serve a wide range of audience, it is pitched at an introductory level with an emphasis on practice. It covers the range of scales from a site to a neighbourhood, and to a whole city.

Figure 1-1: Classical Explanations of the Urban Spatial Structure

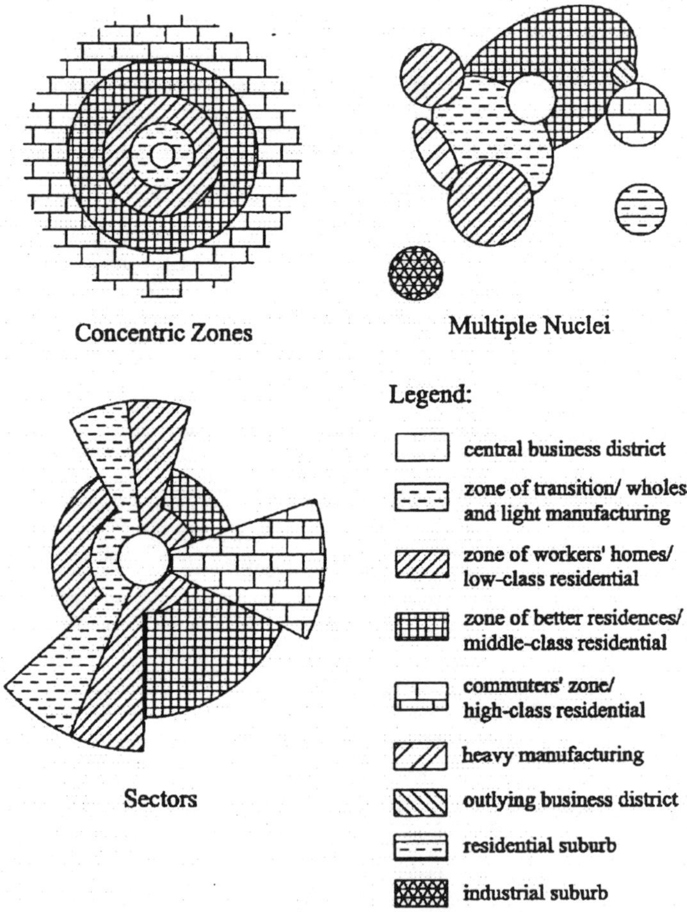

Concentric Zones

Multiple Nuclei

Sectors

Legend:

central business district
zone of transition/ wholesale and light manufacturing
zone of workers' homes/ low-class residential
zone of better residences/ middle-class residential
commuters' zone/ high-class residential
heavy manufacturing
outlying business district
residential suburb
industrial suburb

Source: Adapted from Harris and Ullman (1945)

This book focuses on urban land use in cities and towns, encompassing the whole spectrum of urban settlements smaller than a conurbation and larger than a village. There is usually little doubt about whether an urban settlement is a village or a town. On the other hand, a conurbation is a more or less continuous urban development expanded over a large area where one city merges into another. National and regional policies on population, employment, environment, agriculture, resources, parks and highways will be considered as exogenous factors. Each city usually carries out its planning function within its political administrative boundaries, although these do not always correspond to the social, economic and visual boundaries. One useful rule-of-thumb is that people seem unwilling to accept a commuting time of more than 45 to 60 minutes in any one direction, irrespective of the mode of transportation. This is a crude but realistic way to think about the functional boundaries of a city for land use planning purposes.

This book draws upon U.S., Canadian and British experience which has a general application. These countries share a similar history in the development of their modern land use planning theories and have always had a tradition of learning and borrowing from one another. While physical and cultural distinctions must have influenced the development of theory and practice, this book is concerned with shared experiences and generic principles of land use planning. In making the choice, the following criteria have been used.

- Principles and techniques that can be used readily by practitioners who do not have the time to go to First Causes every instance a decision has to be made and yet who are trained to make intelligent enquiry into the fundamentals if need be.

- Analytic and design methods that can be used at different levels of technical sophistication. Techniques and methods that can be employed in most planning offices which are usually small and have limited resources.

- Techniques and methods that do not intimidate or mystify the ordinary person, or can at least be made clear and straightforward.

LAND USE AND LAND USE PLANNING

In a city one sees buildings of various shapes and sizes; roads and streets with vehicles, people and sometimes animals; trees and parks and benches; shop windows and market stalls; traffic signs, shop signs, posters and billboards; hydrants, lamp posts and bus stops; monuments and pigeons; and, if we are lucky, the distant mountains, sea and sky. All these serve the activities of individuals, households, businesses, and institutions. The order and relationship among these have been brought about and are continually being transformed through the interaction between landowners, developers, consumers, financial intermediaries, and public agencies. There are some classic descriptions and explanations of the urban spatial structure.

Burgess (1925) describes the urban land use pattern of the city as a series of concentric rings. Hoyt (1939) observes that the location of different income classes can be found in the form of sectors of a circle centred on the core business district of the city. McKenzie (1933), and later Harris and Ullman (1945) note that urban land uses tend to be organized in a number of nuclei rather than a single, central core. Hawley (1950), on the other hand, applies a human ecology perspective and sees land use pattern as the result of market-driven competition for space, in which land users settle on locations that they can best adapt.

Alonzo (1960 and 1964) provides the first coherent explanation of the city land use pattern. He suggests that the urban land use pattern, that is, the way in which similar land uses and densities are grouped, is derived from the interaction between consumer demand, which is a function of income and preferences, and the locational quality and spatial quantity of the supply of land. Wingo (1961) provides yet another explanation which is based on the concept of accessibility. Introducing transportation and focusing on the "journey to work," the central idea of his theory is that the distribution of residential location is a result of the trade-off between transportation cost (measured in terms of time and out-of-pocket costs) and space cost. This explains the smaller quantity of space consumed by households in the more accessible locations and, therefore, the higher density.

These views about the political-economic processes as the determinants of urban land use patterns have not changed much, although the analytic modelling techniques have become much more sophisticated and have included the effects of public sector intervention. As suggested by Rudel (1989), there are essentially two sets of variables: market (demographic and market forces) and politics (stakeholders and constituents). They combine to produce the land use pattern on the ground. For instance, growth of the urban population, which creates demand for more housing, combined with consumer preference for single-detached houses, lead to urban expansion into rural agricultural areas. Then, the new inhabitants in the rural areas exercise their political powers to obtain restrictive controls to protect their residential environment from agricultural uses. The resultant land use pattern is low-density sprawl. Then, there is Webber's (1964) extreme view which considers land only as a residual part of the interaction among people. For him, urban-ness may have little to do with urban places, hence his concept of non-place urban realm.

Land use planning theory, somewhat different from the land use theories, has an overtly normative view of how land should be used. Land use theories aim at discovering "what is." Land use planning theories pursue the question of "what ought to be." The essential justification for land use planning is the public interst.

It is not the intention of this book to debate about how the "public interest" should be established or even about the questionable existence of a unified public interest. Rather, we will examine those public interest justifications that have come to be generally accepted as the mandate for land use planning.

PUBLIC INTEREST ELEMENTS IN PLANNING

Before we discuss the different elements of the public interest it is perhaps necessary to lay out some of the current trends that may influence the definition of the public interest.

Since the 1980s we have seen a growing awareness of an aging population, aging suburbs and aging infrastructure, as well as a renewed interest in quality of life issues and equity of access to housing and services. There is, on the one hand, the entrenchment of identity politics and proliferation of special interests and, on the other, a retreat from the welfare state, from environmental action, and from public intervention. The new emphases are fiscal responsibility, public accountability, performance efficiency, and reliance on market solutions to social problems.

> (i) Fiscal responsibility has come to mean the "downloading" of government functions from senior to local levels, the abscondment of long-term of investment (especially on infrastructure) in favour of short-term fixes, and the proliferation of fees and charges on what were once considered "free" public services.

> (ii) Public accountability has come to mean the devolution of powers (but not necessarily funds) from senior to local governments and a definite increase in public meetings, public hearings and public enquiries.

> (iii) Performance efficiency has come to mean the promotion of simplified, streamlined and expedited development control processes as well as the establishment of performance-based standards and best-management practices.

> (iv) Reliance on market solutions to social problems has produced a new mind-set in government, which sees its citizens as clients, customers and even shareholders and has led to a big push for privatization (usually restricted to the more profitable functions or assets), corporatization (the creation of quasi-public, arms-length corporations to carry out certain public function, such as airport authorities and public land corporations), deregulation, de-control, and a reliance on financial and fiscal incentives.

Many of these trends represent social values that are different from those of environmentalism, pluralism and optimism in governments of the 1960s and 1970s. In fact, these may well be reaction to the earlier excesses. As well, many of these new trends are not compatible among themselves. This tug of war among the different "ways of doing things" has created uncertainty in planning practice.

The public interest elements discussed here have been more or less sanctioned by law as legitimate public purposes to be pursued through land use planning. These include the core elements of health, safety, and convenience; the ever-present considerations of economic efficiency and social equity; the entrenched concerns over environmental quality and energy conservation; the controversial question of visual amenity; and other emerging and reemerging issues. Many of them are contradictory and an essential planning task is to prioritize them in a specific situation. We will now examine these one by one.

Health and Safety

Health and safety have always been the first justifications of land use planning. In fact, modern planning legislation has its roots in late 19th century legislation regarding sunlight, water supply, fire protection, sewage disposal, and housing conditions for the working class. The adequate and sanitary provisions of these services were considered essential in tackling the problem of epidemic disease and urban congestion. Therefore, one of the basic principles of modern planning is the prevention or amelioration of conditions injurious or hazardous to the physical well-being of people and property. Health and safety considerations have been extended to include mental and emotional well-being, and to stress the enhancement or improvement of well-being rather than just the prevention of hazards and accidents.

The following list used by the Committee on the Hygiene of Housing of the American Public Health Association is indicative of what is considered to be the minimum requirement:

- protection against accident hazards;
- protection against contagion and provisions for maintenance of cleanliness;
- provision of adequate daylight, sunshine and ventilation;
- protection against excessive noise;
- protection against atmospheric pollution; and
- protection from fatigue and provision of adequate privacy.

It is from principles such as these that health, sanitation, housing, and building codes are drawn up to regulate and control individual buildings or specific activities in order to protect the users and the community at large. These may range from the requirement of a flush toilet and a bath with hot and cold running water for each dwelling unit to the requirement of fire escapes in hotels and places of public assembly, and from the control over food handling to the minimum size of window area for daylight.

In land use planning the controls over the location, density, use, bulk, forms of construction, and occupancy are aimed at ensuring a healthy and safe environment for the user and the public. A particularly important consideration is vehicular and pedestrian safety. In fact, the careful channeling or segregation of vehicular and pedestrian traffic has been considered a major achievement in modern planning. Another consideration is safety against the natural elements and security against crimes. As people are rediscovering that city streets are not only a means of circulation but also the living and breathing area for the community, more thought is now given to making streets safe, secure, and pleasant. In particular, safety for women, the elderly, children and the handicapped has emerged as a significant planning issue.

Planning for health and safety can also take the form of action-oriented measures such as public works improvement and urban redevelopment. In such undertakings other public interest elements are usually involved, such as the provision of social housing, the revitalization of an area, or the recovery of land value increases which the community has helped to create.

Convenience

There are two kinds of convenience: (i) the adequacy and suitability of a space for the activities to be carried out in it; and (ii) the accessibility and choice of services and facilities at a location. The former can be achieved through such measures as efficient site layouts, adequate floor areas, and parking provisions. The latter can be achieved through reduction in time and distance between such points as home and work, home and school, work and recreation, home and shopping, and shopping and work; or, in the case of movement of goods, through reduction in time and distance between wholesale and retail areas, retail and industrial areas, and so on.

Land use planning is concerned with the time and distance relationships between locations. Convenience is affected by the density, or compactness, of land development. The higher the density of land use the shorter the time and distance between uses. But this also means more constricted sites and more built-up areas with less adequate and suitable space for the users and perhaps greater health and safety problems. Discovering the balance is one of the essential tasks of land use planning.

Efficiency

Efficiency in land use planning is commonly thought of in terms of public cost, especially municipal government expenditures (fiscal efficiency). This is a particularly significant consideration in the case of new development at locations where new infrastructure has to be provided and maintained.

Developers and the public view cost differently. There has been growing consensus on requiring new development to pay the "real" cost of the infrastructure it uses. There is also growing consensus about the efficient use of serviced land, which is usually translated to mean more compact and higher density development. This is attractive to both the municipal government and developer, but existing neighbours often do not like it.

An emerging efficiency issue is the redevelopment or reuse of abandoned, idled, or under-used commercial, industrial and institutional facilities (land) which have been contaminated. These "brownfield sites" are usually located on prime land which is often adequately serviced, but the environmental problems can be serious.

Convenience and efficiency are frequently linked. The former relates to expenditure of time and money by the users, the latter raises questions about the cost to the public. In both cases the key issues are location and density of the development. For example, a haphazard and low density land use pattern would involve more roads and greater lengths of utility lines. This would cost more money to build, operate and maintain, but balanced against this are health and sometimes environmental quality benefits. What is important to keep in mind is the overall efficiency of the city and the balance between present and future costs and savings. For this purpose, we need to have long range plans which coordinate urban development with the provision of infrastructure.

Equity

Two issues are involved: fairness and choice. The first deals with the question of who pays and who benefits; the second, with the question of who is being kept out.

The upgrading of a road may improve the access of many people living and working along it but others may be adversely affected by the increased traffic volume and noise. Still others may be forced to relocate because of the road work. Also, the siting of enterprises such as pubs, funeral homes, and gas stations may provide needed service to some but may cause stress to neighbours. In such cases, someone's gain is another's loss. Good planning ensures that decisions are taken to foster the greatest good of the community without local or individual biases.

Social equity is also concerned with equal opportunities to the necessities of life such as work, shelter, education and medical care. Controls of densities of residential areas and locations of community facilities have direct consequences on choice. For instance, by insisting on large lot sizes, lower income people may be excluded from an area. In fact, planning should not only take a preventive role to avoid unequal opportunity but should actually take on an affirmative role to make up for past deficiencies and lack of access, especially regarding housing and community facilities. Since the 1960s there has been a steady societal recognition of the multicultural context of planning and a continual increase in the number of advocacy groups of various kinds to articulate the conditions, needs, and aspirations of the underprivileged and minority groups (racial groups, aboriginal groups, elderly, handicapped, etc.). These include affordable and appropriate housing for the poor, accessible services for the handicapped, safe environment for women, equitable distribution of the costs and benefits of public improvements, and so on. There is also the feminist reaction to the existing urban environment which is seen from this viewpoint as discriminating against women in the vital areas of "access, equality of treatment, dominance and power" (Andrew and Milroy, 1988:1). However, it is ironic that the advocacy approach is now also used by powerful interests to protect the status quo or to advance their cause.

The Environment

A broad based environmental movement emerged during the 1970s. Land use planning now incorporates a much broader view of the relationship between land use action and environmental protection and enhancement. The detrimental effect of economic and population growth on the environment has made many communities rethink their past stance for all-out growth, and to adopt growth management policies.

Traditionally, environmental hazards such as flooding, landslides, soil erosion, and the like are well recognized in land use planning. However, environmental degradation such as air and water pollution, excessive noise levels in cities, and the destruction of fragile habitats now also receive a great deal of attention. The more current issues include the siting of waste treatment facilities, landfill sites and the transportation of toxic, inflammable or other harmful materials.

It is perhaps in the area of remedial and preventive actions regarding air and water quality that environmental protection legislation has made the greatest strides. Land use planning must now take into consideration environmental protection guidelines concerning air quality when deciding on the location of transportation facilities and the distribution of different land uses. This applies not only to the location of traditional smoke-stack industries but also to non-industrial uses such as regional shopping centres, "big-box" retail, universities, and even apartment complexes where the volume of traffic is likely to increase air pollution levels significantly.

With respect to water quality, clean water standards define the capacities of river and stream systems to absorb effluence from waste disposal facilities along the shoreline. This, together with the increasing public demand for the protection of habitats and sensitive areas, has restricted the development capacity of waterfront land.

Another new issue is the quantity and quality of urban runoff. In addition to the traditional concerns of erosion and flooding, the health and environmental effects of the runoff on the receiving waters are emerging as a major planning problem.

Protection of Agricultural Land and Other Resources

The emphasis is on protection against urban uses. There are two main reasons for the protection of agricultural land from non-agricultural uses. (i) Many cities are located on, or next to, prime agricultural land. Urban expansion consumes valuable agricultural land. (ii) Urban uses (users) often conflict with agricultural uses (users). Urban expansion disrupts and displaces surrounding agricultural operations and lands.

Land use planning and regulations are needed to manage urban growth at the fringe areas of the city in order to halt the encroachment on agricultural land and to protect the rural ambience enjoyed by the existing residents. If an urban use is unavoidable, lot sizes and separation distances are controlled to minimize the impact.

Mineral resources (e.g. aggregates, minerals and petroleum) may need to be protected from urban activities that could preclude or hinder their extraction or use. Also, sites have to be rehabilitated after the extraction in order to accommodate subsequent land uses.

Energy

Energy conservation as an element of the public interest emerged at about the same time as environmental protection. For thousands of years, energy conservation has been achieved through careful siting and orientation of buildings. Modern land development and building technology based on the plentiful supply of cheap energy have ignored many of the simple and commonsense lessons of energy conservation. When the energy crunch came in the 1970s, the importance of an energy efficient land use pattern was "rediscovered," but our cities had already been locked into a land use pattern of low-density sprawl dependent on the automobile.

In North America we use four times the energy per capita in our transportation sector than in Europe. Much of that has to do with our lower overall population density. In the last 10 years, gasoline consumption has not gone down in spite of more fuel-efficient cars. Also, transit ridership is down everywhere. There have been very significant changes in commuting patterns. Instead of the traditional suburb-to-centre commutes there are many suburb-suburb commutes, and the nine-to-five workday is not longer the norm.

It should be noted that although energy conservation points to higher density land use, contiguous and compact development may not be incompatible with the need to protect and enhance environmental quality, as suggested by conventional thinking. Environmentally sensitive development does not necessarily mean low density and spaced-out development. In fact the reverse is true. High-density cluster development is not only energy efficient but takes up less land and leaves environmentally hazardous and sensitive areas untouched.

Heritage

Heritage conservation must be appreciated within the general climate of preservation and conservation of the environment, energy and our past. There are several reasons for the shift from urban redevelopment and renewal to heritage conservation. First, a very large proportion of the worst housing is now gone. Second, urban renewal and redevelopment has acquired a bad name for itself, especially as the villain responsible for breaking up communities and creating high-rise ghettos. Third, the old building stock which has been left untouched by urban renewal has acquired a scarcity value and is considered a status symbol. The comparatively well-to-do have now moved into areas previously occupied by the relatively poor.

Heritage conservation can apply to a single building or to a whole area. The usual requirement is that the building or buildings should have special architectural or historic merit, worthy of conservation or enhancement. In practice it is the building facade which will be kept. The interior or even the structure itself is changed to serve a need totally different from that for which the building was originally designed. The artificiality and high cost of conservation have begun to cause concern.

There is also the protection of "natural heritage" features and areas from incompatible development and alteration. These include "significant" wetlands, and endangered and threatened species. Some habitats are also protected. Sometimes, even development of adjacent land is not allowed if that will bring about negative impacts on the natural features or on the ecological functions of the natural area.

Transportation

Traffic problems such as congestion were tackled in the past by road widening, road construction, and realignment. Such improvements attracted more cars and caused more congestion. The last 30 years have seen a realization of the folly of allowing the unrestrained growth of private automobile use. Very diverse segments of society have now started to react and campaign against this unfettered growth. They are particularly concerned about the inequalities perpetuated by the private automobile and the negative effect it has on the environment.

There is a new push for public transit and other modes of transportation. Traffic consideration has loomed large again in land use planning, from reducing pollution to avoiding accidents, and from improving pedestrian comfort to increasing transit ridership. We may yet see a renewed effort to integrate transportation/traffic planning with land use planning, especially in reducing dependence on the private automobile and increasing the viability of public transit, cycling and walking.

Telecommuting is an emerging issue. This, together with teleshopping, may have profound effects on transportation (volume, direction, time, etc.) as well as land use (where people work and what supporting facilities and services they will need).

Infrastructure

Most of the "modern" infrastructure such as storm and sanitary sewers, highways and roads, was built between 30 to 50 years ago. It is now middle-aged. Through neglect, overuse and abuse over the years, the physical infrastructure in many cities, especially in the older parts, has deteriorated so much that it has become a health and safety concern. Much of it needs replacement and major overhauls, not just minor repairs and patch-up works. Tremendous cost will be involved in such remodernization.

A number of planning issues are involved: the choice between demand management and capacity expansion, and between rehabilitation and replacement; the programming of repairs and replacement so that urban life will not be drastically disrupted and that public funds are used in the most effective way; the incorporation of other public interests such as energy conservation, environmental protection and enhancement; and the exploitation of this opportunity to reorganize land use to reflect new living and working patterns.

Affordable Housing

This is one of those public interest elements which have changed from their original idea or have reemerged after a period of dormancy. The planning profession has its roots in the problem of "workers' housing" and the provision of housing has always been at the centre of planners' preoccupations.

There are several directions. One is the improvement and better use of the existing housing stock, and the enhancement of community facilities and neighbourhood environment. The challenge to the planner is the identification and definition of the boundaries of areas suitable for improvement while devising the regulatory controls and affirmative actions needed to improve these areas without relocating the population.

Another direction is the provision of housing for special groups. The traditional concern of housing for low-income families is now giving ground to the provision of suitable and affordable housing for such disadvantaged groups as the elderly, the handicapped and single-parent households. The locational and spatial requirements of these population groups present new challenges to the planner.

A third direction is to influence housing costs by designating and servicing land for higher density housing (intensification). The logic is to reduce housing costs by reducing land consumption and increasing infrastructure efficiency. However, this approach is aimed essentially at moderate and lower income households rather than the hard-core needy. The planning challenge is to forecast market demand for affordable housing, translate this demand into land (location and size), and distribute the land and infrastructure requirements equitably across the different municipalities within a region.

Visual Amenity

This refers to the pleasantness of the urban environment as a place in which to live, work, and spend one's leisure time. As an element of public interest, this aesthetic dimension of the city has generated much controversy. It is generally assumed that it is not possible to secure a consensus of tastes. Therefore, it is difficult to develop control measures to achieve an attractive and pleasant urban environment. In most cases, visual amenity is used in conjunction with other more "established" public interest elements.

However, it is increasingly being realized that amenity is an important dimension of public health and mental well-being. Unfortunately, although city planning was once closely associated to architecture, it is now highly social-science oriented. Consequently, most planners are poorly equipped to give good advice on urban design or to appreciate and analyze collective perceptions about the built-environment.

Citizens often object to a development proposal because they do not like the look of it or because they prefer the existing look. But nobody dares say so because there is the preconception that aesthetic judgements are arbitrary and whimsical. We may be surprised to find that our tastes are not altogether arbitrary and that there are common perceptions about an environment, which are shared by a large number of people. It is unfortunate that people cannot deal with aesthetic perceptions openly, and that they usually become hidden in debates about such things as building heights, shadow effects, traffic volume, and other items which may appear more "objective" but are really not the "real" concerns.

Other Elements of the Public Interest

Here are some secondary elements or emerging issues of the public interest.

1. Planning decisions have been based on the protection of public morals. The assumption is that public morals can be protected through controlling the location of such establishments as casinos and adult entertainment shops. There are two approaches: to concentrate such establishments into one location so that their collective impacts can be contained or to disperse them throughout the community so that their individual impact can be minimized.

2. The prevention of bankruptcy has been used as the basis of planning decisions. For example, application for the development of a gas station in close proximity to a number of existing ones may be refused on the grounds that it has a high risk of commercial failure. This is a highly controversial public interest element. Some argue that the public has no business to interfere with someone who is willing to make an unwise commercial location decision (assuming that the planner is indeed wiser). Others point out that if the business fails the building would be left empty, changed to another use, or demolished and redeveloped. To have allowed the development to go ahead may result in waste. Commercial failures

occurring in large numbers and in close proximity to one another can also contribute to urban blight. Therefore, the argument goes, good planning should prevent this from happening. Of course, an often hidden consideration is the pressure brought on by competitors in the business, such as the operators of the existing gas stations in the above example.

3. Planning has been justified on its money-making potential for the municipal government. This may take the form of sales of development rights, exaction of development fees, imposition of conditions on development, land banking by municipal development corporations, and so on. Depending on the ambition of the government, planning has been justified on such grounds that it protects the community from unwittingly subsidizing private development; recaptures for the community the increases in land values which it helps to create; and ensures the community's share of the profit of new (especially large scale) development. This element of the public interest, and the prevention of bankruptcy, are usually subsumed under the economic efficiency argument.

4. An emerging issue which has captured the public's attention is the land use implication of economic restructuring. People speak of post-industrial growth, its influence on urban life and city form, and the role of local government in economic restructuring. There are two separate but related lines of thought. Economic restructuring, often fueled by the development of high technology industries or sophisticated services and businesses, represents an opportunity for local economic growth. The land use planner's job is to attract and retain these industries and businesses through proper land use allocation and improvement of physical and social infrastructure. But economic restructuring can also mean that certain industries/businesses or production/marketing methods have become obsolete or non-competitive. This results in underuse or abandonment of physical plants and job loss. The effects can be localized or widespread. Local governments want to arrest the decline, revitalize the area, or retrain the workers. The land use planner is called in to develop schemes for urban renewal or beautification, the adaptive reuse of the building stock, and the siting of job training and counselling centres.

5. The last decade of government downsizing has rendered many public buildings and land "surplus". They often locate at strategic sites. Their future use can have very significant effects on the property market and urban land use pattern. Different levels of government may need to work together to ensure orderly reuse, disposal or development/redevelopment.

THE ACTORS IN LAND USE PLANNING

The planning process begins with the desire on the part of some person, organization, or government to carry out planning. Today, it is usually the government which initiates the process, because both the legal powers and resources required are so great. The first thing that is done, of course, is to pass the appropriate legislation. In North America, the powers given by planning legislation are exercised by the local government as well as the provincial government in Canada, and the state government in the United States. Generally speaking, plan making and development control powers are entrusted to local governments, while senior governments retain a supervisory role in the exercise of these powers and an adjudicating role in the event of disputes.

In this book, we focus on planning at the municipal government level, while treating senior level government policies and actions as exogenous factors in local planning. These can range from environmental protection and resource use policies to national/regional transportation and employment location policies, from industrial strategies to energy conservation, and from housing programmes to regional development programmes. The layering of policies channelled down from the above will create continuing tensions as municipal governments seek to reconcile these policies with their own philosophy in coordinating and harmonizing the infrastructure and land use systems within the city. However, the substantial amount of aid which usually accompanies senior level government programmes tends to influence or even distort local priorities. For instance, since 1994 the Canadian federal government has implemented an Infrastructure Works Programme aimed at creating jobs. It uses a tri-partied funding formula in which the federal, provincial and municipal government each pays one-third. The 33 cent-dollar is so seductive that municipalities have only been too willing to adjust their infrastructure programme to fit the federal government's job creation agenda.

Higher level governments set out policies, standards, and guidelines in various sectors such as transportation, the environment, parks, and housing as well as procedural and management requirements for their programmes. All of these affect plan making and development control at the local level. At the same time, the cumulative results of these policies and programmes will have significant impact on the cost of private development and the nature and magnitude of user demand.

At the municipal level, the land use planning and development control function is usually handled by a planning department but this function is affected by the policies and actions of other local governmental departments and agencies who pursue their own mandates, such as public works, parks and recreation, education, public transit, and roads. The uneven distribution of powers and resources among departments and agencies, interagency rivalry, or simply the ignorance of what each other is doing will influence how planning is carried out.

Then there are local constituencies such as the residents who work and live in the community, the industries which operate there, the firms which do business there, and organized interest groups. These groups may be locally based such as ratepayers' groups, merchant associations, real estate boards, and chambers of commerce. They may have a more global base as is often the case with environmental groups, trade and industrial associations, ethnic and minority groups, and special population groups such as the elderly and the handicapped. Individual citizens are particularly concerned about the "rights" of ownership. People feel very strongly and react very violently if they feel their ownership rights are threatened by public controls or by proposals on other properties which affect them. For them, there is always too much restriction on the use and development of one's own land and too little restriction on other properties. As far as the business community's influence is concerned, most cities will continue to pursue policies aimed at attracting new firms. The assumption that growth is good and that growth is best measured by how a city attracts and retains new firms will continue to influence local land use decisions for some time to come. Special interest groups, both the new "rights" groups and the traditional property and business interests, have diversified and intensified pressure on land use decisions. All the above have led to a proliferation of participatory devices in order to bring all the different viewpoints into land use deliberations. Unlike the impact by senior level governments, influences of local constituencies come from very diffuse sources and are much less formalized and more difficult to coordinate.

Nothing will happen without the developers. A typical development process consists of five stages: conceptualizing, feasibility study, design, contract and construction, and marketing, management and disposal. Developers play crucial roles in each of these stages: as promoter and negotiator with regulatory and approved authorities as well as other parties with an interest in the proposed development; as market analyst and marketing agent; as securer of financial resources; as employer and overall manager of the professional team engaged on the project; and as entrepreneur in the production of a property and then selling it for a profit. Developers commit their equity, equipment, labour force, and managerial talents to the conversion of land from one use to another. To them, a land development is justified when the present value of the expected benefits is equal to, or greater than, the cost of obtaining those benefits. They are risk bearers, including interest rate risk, business risk, market risk and financial risk. But developers are often regarded by other actors in the development process as purely profit-seekers. There are tensions between developers and public officials. For instance, developers are driven by financial incentives and are particularly sensitive to the length of the regulatory process, whereas public officials who have a mandate to safeguard the public interest would want to move more cautiously and deliberately. Most developers think there are more regulations and controls than are really necessary. There are also tensions between some developers and citizens. In the suburbs as well as inner city areas, where significant development pressure exists, residents want stability and protection of property values, and environmental and heritage groups want to protect the status quo. They see developers as threats. Planners often find themselves involved in negotiations between developers, government and citizens.

Public opinions are important, in the political sense. But planners, in their professional capacity, must retain a clear perspective of the characteristics of this "public," whether it is the citizenry, the business community, or the special interest groups. This "public" is often quite ignorant about land use planning. It knows it wants the countryside preserved, safe and uncongested roads, sufficient and well-located schools and public open spaces, good housing and the preservation of fine buildings, and so on, but it often knows, or cares, little about how these wants can be satisfied, and what obstacles and sacrifices are involved in attaining them. The exercise of planning powers, especially in the form of development control, often provokes campaigns which are usually closely connected with self-interest. The situation is not helped by petty tyranny, inflexibility, and even cynicism on the part of bureaucrats, including planners.

The public can be biased. Today's objector is tomorrow's developer. Sometimes, there is blatant bigotry and discrimination. An excerpt from Thomas Sharp's paper read to the Town Planning Institute is as appropriate today as it was in 1937: "One reads of bitter protests from London suburbs when a policeman or a bus driver goes to live in a street occupied by bank clerks and their like. Protests in which the suggestion is quite seriously made that the mere fact of a bus driver's coming home in his uniform may depreciate the value of a whole street to the tune of £l0 or £100 a house. We all know of the opposition that is regularly raised to the building of municipal houses anywhere near estates of so-called 'better class property'" (Keeble, 1983: 149). This kind of social discrimination continues. As a matter of fact, planners have helped to entrench such biases through the requirement of large lots in certain areas and the rigid exclusion of "incompatible" uses.

There are also religious prejudices and racial biases. Racial discrimination in planning has already been extensively documented in the United States (e.g., Myrdal, 1944; Muth, 1969; Yinger, 1979; Squires, 1994; and Blakely and Deka, 1996). Lewis Keeble tells us of his experience of religious prejudice in Northern Ireland: "One of the cases which I determined in Belfast in the 1960s ... related to the proposed establishment of a Catholic youth centre in a disused cinema which formed part of quite a well grouped neighbourhood shopping centre. It was opposed quite blatantly on the grounds that it overlooked part of the route of a traditional Orangemen's march and so constituted provocation. I determined in favour of the proposal" (1983: 149). Then there is the question of "unfair competition" where planning powers are used to forestall competition by preventing business competitors from locating near one's own establishment, such as a gas station, a pub, or a shopping mall. This is really nothing more than "jealousy with a halo."

Planners have to work within these local and supralocal contexts in interpreting the land use implications of the various public interest elements and the goals the community wants to pursue. Only then can plans be made and tools devised to carry them out.

Forester talks about "to be rational, be political" (1989:25). He points out that effective planning in the face of conflict requires a shift from adversarial to collective problem-solving; voluntary development controls and agreements; improved city-developer-neighbourhood relationships; more effective neighbourhood voice; and joint-benefits for the municipality, neighbours, and developers alike. To achieve this, planners have a dual mandate to demonstrate substantive knowledge and to foster a participatory process (Forester, 1989).

THE DEBATE ABOUT THE MANDATE OF LAND USE PLANNING

Physical Planning

There is a desire among land use planners for their activities not to be labelled as "mere physical planning" (Keeble, 1983: 60). Physical planning is considered bad because it has been equated with physical determinism. To wit:

> In the beginning was design and for a long time after it remained design. The traditional approach to planning was based on the "blueprint concept" itself based on the assumption that if we design the right city (or environment), we shall obtain a good community ... It was assumed that predictions could be made about how society would behave in a number of years and that the proper environment could be designed for it. Because of this casual attitude of this approach and its parallel with physical sciences, it was called "physical determinism (Loew, 1979: 98-99).

This indictment of physical planning, or rather of planning which focuses on the physical dimension, was a reaction to the socially insensitive plans produced by some land use planners. However, it is quite irresponsible to insist, as Herbert Gans (1968) did, that land use planners are enamoured of two environmental or physical fallacies: first that the physical environment is a major determinant of society and culture; and second that only an environment based on professional planning principles can deliver the good life.

It is true that the early planners did believe that the physical environment could have an overwhelming influence on our well-being. But this has to be understood in terms of the conditions at the turn of the century when urban congestion and overcrowded living conditions were closely associated with epidemic diseases, devastating fires, and generally poor health of the citizenry. No planner worthy of the name ever believed that "human beings for whom architects and planners create their designs are simply molded by the environment which is provided for them" (Broady, 1968:1) Critics such as Jane Jacobs insist that planners were misguided to try to design "beautiful" cities in order to achieve happy communities (Jacobs, 1972). But Jacobs also suggests that planners should provide diversity and small scale development because that is what people want. That certainly is physical planning. It seems that the problem is not physical planning as such but rather physical planning that the critics do not like.

The label of "physical determinism" is a game of "reduction to absurdity." It is neither true nor necessary. The physical environment will certainly affect people's well-being but it is not the only factor, although a very important one. Land use planning should always focus on the physical dimension of land, that is: what? where? how much? and when? But the rationale and justification for planning is the satisfaction of the social, economic and psychological needs of the community. The planner's task, therefore, is to find out how the physical environment can contribute to the satisfaction of these needs.

The invention of the fiction of "physical determinism" and the condemnation of it is perhaps a catharsis for the planning profession for its two related failures.

First, an acknowledged aim of planning is to achieve a pleasant environment, but after 50 years of post-World War II planning and development control there is not much evidence to show that planning has made any great achievement in this area. Indeed, the main criticism that the general public has against planning is the low aesthetic quality of new development. The invention and then rejection of "physical determinism" absolves the planners' incompetence. Second, planners had always wanted to be seen not only as socially responsible and sensitive in planning the physical environment but also as politically astute and effective in organizing social priorities. They wanted to argue the wisdom, or otherwise, of the social policies adopted by governments, rather than just focusing on dealing with the impact of such policies on land use. This merging of professional mandate and political activism has brought about disappointment and frustration. The invention and then rejection of "physical determinism" help to ease the planners' conscience about their frustrated ambition and absolve their inadequacy in influencing public social policies.

Positive Planning

It has also been fashionable for a time to consider the practice of planning, especially development control, as negative and reactive as opposed to what some writers call positive and proactive planning. There are some truths and some myths about these perceptions.

It is fallacious to say that planning control is negative simply because it is a control measure. Planning control is often time-consuming and frustrating for everybody involved but it is only negative to the extent that it prevents some people from doing things they would have been able to do, had there been no control. But planning is positive because by saying "no" to undesirable development the use of land is guided and directed toward a desirable pattern. However, control itself is not planning. Without the guidance of a clear plan, control is only an arbitrary exercise of government power. Unfortunately, many land use plans are too vague and ambiguous to give good guidance. Worse still, development control is sometimes used without the guidance of any plan.

Another more serious condemnation is that most planning is reactive. Plans are made in an ad hoc and piecemeal fashion to respond to crisis instead of being guided by a vision of the future. "Reactive planning" is a contradiction in terms, but this indictment is correct. Planning, at least as it is practiced now, has lost much of the sense of purpose and mission that infused the pioneers, and has become a deadening bureaucratic function. We see reaction to this in the more recent rush to do "strategic planning" and "visioning". This is very unfortunate because modern planning was first embraced precisely because it gave hope and showed the possibility that urban living can be significantly improved through planning. Maybe it is a reflection of our society at large that the present is considered more important than the future. Without an emphasis on the future, planning is no more than management without an objective, which is neither exciting nor justifiable.

Comprehensive Planning

Comprehensive planning has conventionally been taken to mean planning which covers the whole city area and all different types of land use. Such planning takes into consideration the various factors which affect the congruence between user activities and land. However, there has been an ambitious attempt to make "comprehensive" planning mean planning of every conceivable government function, from education to defence and from land use to employment.

There are at least two reasons to explain this. First, the social, economic and environmental problems and goals tackled by land use planning are often tackled by other government departments as well. Also, land use implementation may be handled by government departments other than the planning department, as in the case of capital works and social facilities. The comprehensive "corporate" approach is advocated, arguing for multi-departmental teams but always assuming that the planner heads the team. Second, able and ambitious planners seeking to become chief among chiefs are tempted to suggest that their planning skills are needed in all the activities of local government and that the skills and experience in city (land use) planning guarantee skills in all other kinds of planning. Underlying this argument is the assumption that all planning is much the same and is really just decision making, so planners should only be trained in the art of decision making rather than in land use and design.

This tug-of-war between what planners can do and should do has been going on for a long time and the titles of these two provocative articles, written some years ago, really sum up the essence of the dilemma: "If Planning Is Everything, Maybe It Is Nothing" (Wildavsky, 1973); "If Planning Isn't Everything, Maybe It's Something" (Alexander, 1981). Some of the skills in land use planning are useful to anyone concerned with the good city. Likewise, land use planning can benefit tremendously from the skills of other disciplines, from economics to architecture and from accounting to engineering. However, there are clearly land use planning functions in government that need to be done and only trained planners should undertake such functions. So far, our performance has not been outstanding.

The Debate about the Mandate of Land Use Planning

Hok-Lin Leung

A PLAN FOR PLANNING

here are two related elements in any plan for planning: the logical process and the substantive components. Perhaps the most famous dictum about logical planning practice is Patrick Geddes' prescription of survey, analyze, and plan. A rather comprehensive and detailed discussion is provided by Chapin and Kaiser (1979: ch.3). It has the following sequence:

LOGICAL PLANNING PRACTICE

Setting the plan for planning: This is the determination of basic parameters which include the agenda and priorities for the community, the role of land use planning, resources that can be devoted to it, and the programme for planning.

Building the information system base: This includes the designing, building, and maintenance of "intelligence" for planning.

Problem analysis and goal specification: This is the translation of perceived problems into facts and estimates, and the establishment of the relationship between problems and goals.

Advanced formulation of policies/plans: This includes a policy framework fromwhich a 20 to 25 year land use plan is developed, which in turn serves as the basis for a set of five to six year land development plans and one year improvementprogrammes. Also included is a guidance system plan for day-to-day administration. At this stage, the implications of the planning goals are examined and alternative scenarios are developed, leading from the long-term and general land use plan to the medium-term and short-term plans and programmes.

Action Planning: This is ongoing decision making, problem solving, and impact assessing as opposed to advanced planning.

A much less comprehensive and detailed scheme but one which has incorporated some administrative and practical considerations of plan making is suggested by Loew (1979). Although it deals primarily with planning for a smaller local area within a metropolitan area, the logic of the scheme can be generalized. It has the following sequence. Through an analysis of the physical, social, economic, administrative contexts, and public participation, community goals are defined.

These goals then serve as a guide for the analysis of the characteristics, opportunities, and constraints of the situation to be tackled. This leads to refinement of the goals or a redefinition of the problems with further public participation. From this stage will emerge a set of specific objectives to be pursued by the plan. Different strategies are then generated. Through a combination of technical evaluations and consultation with the public and other interested parties, a choice is made among the strategies. Implementation measures are then established, which will be monitored and the results serve as feedback to the reformulation of goals, objectives, and strategies.

There is no lack of prescriptions about the logical process for plan making. They are usually based on a "rationalist" model (meaning totally rational and considering all possibilities) and on goal satisfaction. However, real-life planning decisions are made differently. There may be three reasons for this. Most planning decisions are made about a much shorter time horizon and a much smaller scale than those tackled in a long-range plan. Logically, these decisions should be guided by a long-range comprehensive plan. In fact, most planning legislation requires an explicit demonstration that this is indeed the case. But the usually rather vague and motherhood statements of a long-term comprehensive plan can be construed easily to justify any specific decision. Most of the time, this presents no problem because an experienced planner will have internalized the essence of the comprehensive plan and have a good sense about the specific issues at hand. But this may lead to intellectual laziness and unintentional slips may be made, resulting in appeals, public outcry and administrative or judicial censure.

A second reason for not using the rationalist approach in making planning decisions is the lack of resources. There is also the feeling that, since it is not possible to be totally rational, why try? The academic debate about this boils down to two contending arguments. One argument asserts that it is better to be partially rational ("bounded rationality") than to be irrational. The other contends that it is impossible to draw a boundary to rationality, and any decision short of being "totally rational" cannot be logically defended as a better decision than any other.

The third reason for discarding the rationalist approach has to do with the nature of planning problems. Planning problems have been called "wicked problems" because they keep transforming themselves (Rittel and Webber, 1973). Any rigid adherence to a particular interpretation is neither realistic nor desirable. The earlier land use plans, with their very clearly spelled-out and concise statements about the future of a city, have been discredited as being physical deterministic and insensitive to change.

A number of alternative approaches have been suggested. The "incrementalists" believe that planning decisions are, and should be, made without any grand vision and plan; and that society as well as planners are just muddling through (Braybrooke and Lindblom, 1963). The advocates of "strategic planning" argue against comprehensiveness and opt for a systematic way to scan for, and focus on, critical issues (Bryson, 1988). The "critical theorists" emphasize the political nature of planning and focus on communication, critique and empowerment (Forester, 1989). The "transaction theorists" see planning as a process for articulation and negotiation among stakeholders, and they emphasize consensus building and dispute resolution (Susskind and Cruikshank, 1987).

Extreme positions provide interesting points of departure, from which academics can theorize and write about planning. No practicing planner will be dogmatic or naive enough to be totally rational or irrational, inclusive or exclusive, open or closed, in the sense that the terms are used in academic debates. Essentially, planners are enjoined to be more methodical about plan making, and yet be sensitive to changing needs and circumstances, whether for the whole city or for a specific site. Depending on the resources available, a planner may sometimes be able to go back to first principles, collect primary data, and do sophisticated analysis. Or he/she may have to rely on established norms, standards, and rules-of-thumb. In all, we have to be sensitive to reality with all of its constraints and opportunities, and have reasonable expectations about ourselves and other people. Then, we just do our professional best.

Regardless of resources and capabilities, I think planning always involves the following related components: goals, information, analysis, synthesis, and implementation, each of which can be the initiator of the planning process. Essentially, land use planning is the art of matching different users of land to the supply of land, that is, the attainment of congruence between user needs and land supply by the proper siting and sizing of land uses. By relating the substantive land use considerations to the analytic components of the planning process, we can develop "a plan for planning."

1. The goals of a plan reflect the ideological positions and social values of its makers. They can be an affirmation of an ideal or a response to a problem. The goals must either have land use consequence or can be pursuable through land use means. Since goals are subjective, in the sense that they are value-laden, they may change with time and with circumstances. A planner's job is not so much to debate these but to recognize, appreciate, interpret, and define these in terms of land use. Goals are what confer meaning and give guidance to all the other planning activities. Some planning has been done without a legitimate goal such as for securing funds from some senior levels of government for housing, transportation, or community facility projects. The idea of requiring a comprehensive land use plan for these funds is a very good one because it ensures that the projects are compatible with other land use elements or development strategies. But such a plan has the tendency to overemphasize the funding justifications and ignore, or even suppress, other legitimate goals or concerns. What is more unfortunate is that such a specific-purpose plan may later become the general land use plan, which has only a limited purpose, a biased purpose, a wrong purpose, or no purpose at all.

Land use planning is about using and developing land in such a way as to protect and enhance the public interest. We have discussed those elements of the public interest which have been recognized as legitimate concerns in land use planning. These will form the basis of planning goals. The determination of goals in a concrete situation and the degree to which they are to be pursued is a function of community values. This, in turn, is a function of the relative importance of the different user groups, the level of their expectations, and the way in which social costs and benefits should be distributed. Since prevailing social values and political ideologies change, we should also expect community goals about land use to change. This is particularly significant in long-range planning where some stability about goals is of primary importance. It is, therefore good practice to secure greater consensus for longer term goals.

2.   Information has to do with facts and estimates, that is, with what is and what will be. There is no "neutral" information. Information has to be relevant to the planning purpose, which means it must shed light on the nature and magnitude of the problems to be tackled and the conditions and causes underlying them. In the use of information, planners are prone to either extremes, irresponsible recklessness or paralyzing caution.

Although in most cases information gathering is guided by planning purposes and analytic needs, it can also serve to trigger a rethinking of such purposes and needs. New information or processing techniques can raise questions about conventional wisdom in analyzing and dealing with problems. The sophisticated socioeconomic indicators, satellite and remote sensing techniques, and computer manipulation of data have changed the way planners observe and think about issues.

We need three sets of information. First, we need to know about the users of land, their types, numbers, and characteristics, their activities in space, their level of satisfaction with the present situation, their perceived needs and preferences, and their ability and intention to satisfy them. From these we can work out their locational and space requirements as well as the environmental impact exerted. Second, we need information about the land, especially the suitability of its physical and economic characteristics for different existing and potential uses and its capacity both as an individual site and in aggregate form to accommodate different uses. Third, we need an inventory of existing policies and practices regarding land use location and allocation, as well as laws, regulations, and programmes which are used in implementing land use decisions. In short, we need information on existing and projected user needs, the supply of land to meet these needs, and the guidance system which governs the matching between needs and supply.

3.   Whereas information is about collecting facts and making estimates, analysis is about understanding and manipulating them. Analytic needs determine the kind and amount of information required and analytic findings provide the basis for planning decisions. The crux of land use analysis is the congruence between user needs and the quality and capacity of the physical environment to satisfy these needs. The focus of attention is the need gap, that is the discrepancy between what exists and what should be. Therefore, it is easy to see that while analysis follows logically from purpose and information and prepares the ground for synthesis, it can also stimulate a rethinking of planning purposes, a redirection of information gathering efforts, and a reevaluation of existing plans.

Planning analysis is about the identification and explanation of gaps, discrepancies, or incongruities between needs and supply. There are two ways to go about identifying these. First, land use norms and standards such as overcrowding indices, maximum walking distances, optimal gradients, and minimum lot sizes are used as benchmarks to identify problems or evaluate proposals. These norms and standards can take the form of general principles such as "avoidance of strip development" and "segregation of pedestrian and vehicular traffic," or detailed specifications such as road widths and lot sizes. The problem with using norms and standards is that these were often developed from physical, economic, cultural, and technological contexts which were very much different from those under which they are presently applied. A second but more expensive and time-consuming approach is to develop evaluative criteria from user and land surveys. This approach is used only in large scale planning exercises or when dealing with controversial situations. In most cases, a sensitive and careful use of norms and standards is sufficient.

Analysis should not only identify and measure problems but should also provide explanations about the causes of such problems. For this, planners make use of social, economic, and behavioural theories and their techniques to help them to locate the causes of problems. For instance, inadequate supply of housing can be explained by theory of market imperfection, urban blight by theory of social ecology, and cumbersome development approval process by theory of bureaucratic and organizational behaviour. Unfortunately, most of these theories do not see land use as a possible solution to the problem. Partly, this is because most of the theory builders lack an appreciation of the physical dimension of the problems they are dealing with, and partly because of the artificial separation between analytic disciplines. It is absurd to suggest that the way land is used and developed can explain everything about housing inadequacy, urban blight, development delay and other similar problems. But, it is equally absurd to suggest that nothing should be done to ameliorate pressing problems, simply because we do not yet have a perfect explanation for these problems. We have to apply theories intelligently and sensibly and to keep in mind that planning must lead to action.

4. Synthesis is that creative process of inventing solutions which are technically sound, economically viable, politically acceptable, and administratively feasible. Clear purposes, adequate information and logical analysis will combine to give good guidance and bases for synthesis.

Synthesis is about creating solutions that match user needs with land supply, and resolve conflicts and restore the proper relation among different land uses. Most academic discussions end with analysis, and most professional practices begin with synthesis. Synthesis deals with design, not only the design of schemes and policies but also organizations and procedures. It is at this stage that one may begin to lose sight of the purposes for which the planning is undertaken, especially when there is so much conventional wisdom and so many borrowed solutions in land use synthesis. It is especially important for planners to think both forward and backward at this stage: forward about the political acceptability, economic and financial viability, and administrative and technical feasibility of the proposal; and backward about the values, evidence, and analysis on which the proposal is based. Synthesis requires both creative thinking and critical judgement. It is the easiest and the most difficult.

But planning synthesis must begin the notion of the "good city". On a philosophical level, land use planning is the pursuit of truth, goodness and beauty in our cities. Our concepts about these ideals form the basis of all planning decisions, whether they are made by an individual or by the community. Mario Salvadori poses this observation: "The generosity and the cruelty, the beauty and the ugliness of architecture are a measure of the conscience of society...." (from Raskin, 1974:x). To this, Eugene Raskin's response is: "The cityscape is much more than a problem of design and planning. It is first of all a problem of human values, in goals and in the recognition of personal obligation... Look into their hearts, their souls and their minds. When these have become beautiful, the city will soon follow." (Raskin, 1974:154).

5.   Implementation is the execution of a planning scheme or a planning decision. It can be control-oriented, specifying what can and cannot be done, the determining conditions and criteria, and the way in which the control will be enforced. It can be action-oriented in that it directs private and/or public investment and resources towards the solution of problems. The planning process can actually begin again at the implementation stage, when new problems are uncovered or created. These force a reexamination of what exists and gives impetus for the search of new solutions.

A plan is only as good as its implementation. In practice, frequent failure at this stage highlights the fact that planners have not given sufficient attention to the implementability of plans. Planning without considering implementation is bad planning, and we are now discovering that there are many bad plans. This new awareness about implementation has brought about a renewed interest in monitoring and evaluation. Frequent implementation failure also points to the fact that planning has cut itself off from other governmental functions and has become so compartmentalized within itself that plan making is no longer related to plan implementation.

If the synthesis has been good, implementation should be straightforward. Control-oriented measures which regulate the siting and sizing of different land uses, and action-oriented measures which direct the preparation and release of land for the different uses, should be coordinated. But in practice they often work against each other. For instance, a city may have an effective property standards enforcement programme which removes substandard housing and an equally effective rent control programme which discourages the replenishment of the housing stock. It is important to monitor and evaluate land use implementation to see if what is happening in reality conforms with what was planned, to note new problems arising from, or brought forth by, the implementation, and to collect intelligence for the planning process. Bureaucracies and programmes have a desire to perpetuate themselves and can react violently to any effort to reorganize or terminate them; therefore monitoring and evaluation by any outsider are resented. It seems that given the existing bureaucratic structure in most local governments, "self" monitoring and evaluation may have a better chance to succeed. Implementation, monitoring, and evaluation should be part and parcel of the planning process.

Therefore, the proposed plan for planning in this book has five components or steps. Each is logically linked to the next and each can be used to initiate the planning process:

- Establishing goals which represent legitimate public interests and which recognize the relative importance of the users, their expectations, and the proper relationship among them;

- Getting information about the users, their activities, and their locational and space requirements as well as their environmental impact on others; about the suitability and capacity of the land supply, both developed and underdeveloped; and about the land use guidance systems;

- Analyzing the gaps, discrepancies and incongruences between user needs and the land supply, and the conflicts between different land uses;

- Making schemes and decisions, and devising administrative structures and procedures that match user needs to land supply and resolve the conflicts between different land used; and

- Implementing the scheme or decision through control-oriented and action-oriented measures, and constantly monitoring and evaluating the situation.

There are different types of plans: the long-range plan provides a vision for a 20- to a 25- year period; the medium-term (five to six years) development plan provides guidance to the programming of capital projects as well as for the regulation of development pressure; and the short-term plan provides coordination for current actions. A plan can also be general or particular, it can cover all land uses or address a particular type of land use. It can be comprehensive or specific, covering the whole city or a particular area or site. It can be a new plan, or an amendment to an existing plan. For all these different time horizons, degrees of specificity, and levels of detail, the same logic of the planning process applies, although the nature of goals, amount of information, depth of analysis, scope of synthesis, and choice of implementation measures will differ greatly. It is the planner's job to recognize and differentiate between what is, and is not, important. For this, it is good to begin with clear planning purposes.

Hok-Lin Leung

CHAPTER THREE

PURPOSE

. . . .

Planning goals can be elusive. More often than not a community relies on its planner to search for and articulate its aspirations. The early planning profession was characterized by its utopian, visionary, and reformist spirit. This gave the pioneers a sense of mission and challenge. The vitality of the profession has since suffered from what Brooks (1988) has called the quest for increased political efficiency, sanction and financial support from the government, academic respectability and, lately, recognition by the private sector as a facilitator in service to its activities. Many of these quests have proven injurious to the "soul" of the profession. The more thoughtful planners are calling for a return to the humanistic and utopian vision that should distinguish the profession (e.g., Brooks, 1988: Krueckeberg, 1983; and Perloff, 1980). The planner, when helping the community to find and express its goals, should provide leadership and inspiration in its search for the good city.

PROBLEM IDENTIFICATION

Planning is not just problem-solving but also problem-avoidance. In practice, planning is most frequently used to tackle perceived problems, and to ensure that such problems do not occur in the future. Whether it is problem-solving or problem-avoidance, the process invariably begins with problem identification. A problem is said to occur when there is a gap between expectations and reality. Therefore, problems are defined by reference to some expectations, or goals. But goals do not exist in a vacuum. They are an idealistic affirmation of certain values in specific situations. Without clear goals, problem identification is no more than a statement of "existing conditions" without any sense of why these conditions constitute a problem.

The problem statement that "there is an alarming number of substandard housing in a city neighbourhood" may have internalized values and assumptions that can be clarified as follows: the existing conditions show that a fifth of the houses have major structural defects, a third are unsafe against fire hazards, and half are poorly maintained. Based on these observations, a housing problem is diagnosed. The problem statement reveals: (i) a belief that the observed facts are a valid indication of substandard housing; (ii) a judgement that the proportion of substandard housing is unacceptably high; and (iii) an affirmation that adequate housing is an important public interest because most of us live in decent housing and think that it is a good thing for all people to have. It is further observed that most of the housing in question is rental housing and many units are owned by absentee landlords. From this an assumption is made that the problem is mainly caused by landlords who either refuse or are unable to maintain the rental units. So based on this combination of observations, values, and assumptions, a goal is established "to improve the maintenance of the physical environment so as to make it more livable." From this general goal statement, achievable objectives are set out. These are: (i) to eliminate the uninhabitable housing; and (ii) to upgrade the fire safety and to reduce undermaintenance to the average city level. Thus we see that problem-identification and goal-setting are interrelated. They are two sides of the same coin: a recognition of an unsatisfying reality and a diagnosis of its causes, and an affirmation of certain values and a call to action.

A word of caution may be useful here about the perennial search for the "real" cause of problems. It is easy to get carried away. Dilapidated housing is a symptom that anybody can see. Some say it is caused by vandalism; others say that the property tax structure does not give incentive to do repair; still others insist that the underlying cause is poverty and disenfranchisement. Soon it seems that nothing can be done short of changing the whole society. The government, in doing any repair work, is accused of cosmetic gestures which do not deal with the root of the problem. Such a debate is a recipe for inaction, while giving the illusion that some serious thinking is being done. Although we should never do anything rashly, we should not be incapacitated by excessive caution. While concern with such issues as poverty, disenfranchisement, discrimination and homelessness may be personally satisfying, one has also to ask what can be done within a professional context. Take, for instance, the issue of homelessness. There is a sociological argument which suggests that we should deal with the underlying poverty and disenfranchisement. Then there is the social action argument, which suggests that no effective solution is possible, unless the homeless are organized and demand their fair share. What should the land use planner do when a nonprofit group proposes to construct a shelter for the homeless and the neighbours object to it? By citing different studies and using various definitions of the homeless, the applicant can demonstrate that there are hundreds, even thousands, of people who need the shelter. On the other hand, the neighbours point out that there are really very few people who actually sleep on the street or in the parks. Are we to join the debate, or are we to examine the proposal in terms of its implications on traffic, noise, health, and so on, while assuming that a shelter for even a small number of homeless is serving a definite housing need? Treating the symptom is sometimes the only thing we can do, unless we do nothing. In fact, it may be the only thing we should do, because like the common cold, the cause may be intractable, but that does not make the symptom any more bearable. There are intellectual games where any reasonable argument can be pushed to its extreme and then demonstrated to be absurd. Any problem can be defined away and any reasonable and acceptable situation can be so defined as to become a problematic situation.

GOALS AND OBJECTIVES

According to Chapin and Kaiser (1979) goals are ends toward which the planning effort is directed. They are usually general in form, and express ideals. Objectives are intermediate milestones on the way toward a goal. They are expressed in a form that is measurable and achievable. A goal can be translated and divided into a number of objectives.

The appropriate level of generalization or detail of goals is difficult to decide. Statements such as "to make the area a better place in which to live and work" might have some value in a political campaign, but are of no use in planning terms. Practically any public action would achieve these vague aims and they, therefore, could not be used to test or compare alternative planning proposals. On the other hand, if the goals are too precise, they could preempt the consideration of other viable alternatives. So goals have to be general enough yet include some clear policy intentions.

Goals are translated into specific operational objectives such as "to provide indoor plumbing in every household" or "to avoid the intrusion of through traffic into the area." Unfortunately politicians and planners often want to avoid commitments and opt for objectives such as "to provide a high degree of accessibility for public transport." But how high is high? So the objective should be more specific, such as "to have a public transit stop at no more than three minutes' walk from each dwelling."

But not all problems and objectives can be quantified. In particular, those concerned with the aesthetic or sensory quality of the environment are essentially subjective and can be interpreted in different ways, such as "to achieve high standards of environmental design" and "to maintain and enhance the distinctiveness of the local streetscape." But it is difficult to make these objectives more precise.

The following is an example from Chapin and Kaiser (1979: 342-343) illustrating the difference between goals and objectives. The stated goal is "an emphasis on sites for work areas accessible to worker housing, energy-efficient in location, environmentally suitable for development, cost-effective to serve with infrastructure, and compatible with surrounding areas." From this general goal five objectives are set.

1. With respect to accessibility to worker housing, the objective is to locate work area sites so as to minimize worker travel.

2. For energy-efficiency in location the objective is to locate work area sites so as to minimize all travel to and from the sites.

3. With respect to the site being environmentally suitable for development, the objectives are to prohibit development in environmentally critical areas and to minimize destruction of natural systems and to prevent significant deterioration in air quality in the airshed or of water quality in the drainage basin.

4. The goal that the sites have to be cost-effective to serve with infrastructure is translated into the objective to minimize capital and maintenance costs ascribable to new work areas

5. With respect to the goal that the sites have to be compatible with surrounding areas, the objectives are to design work areas as small and medium size concentrations in park-like settings, to minimize traffic disruption, and to minimize noise and visual insults.

We can see that the various elements in the goal conflict with one another. For instance, locations which are cost-effective for infrastructure may not offer the best accessibility to worker housing. Also, an objective can be used to serve a number of goal elements. For instance, locations that minimize worker travel will maximize accessibility to worker housing, as well as provide for energy-efficient locations. Therefore, to relate the goals and objectives to one another, and to resolve the conflicts among them, can be a very complex exercise. The distinction between goals and objectives should not be pursued ad infinitum. Otherwise, the whole process degenerates into one big semantic confusion, contributing nothing to intelligent discussion about planning. While academics continue to argue over the definition of goals and objectives in the abstract, the practitioners fill out pro forma statements without the least concern about their theoretical relation and practical implications. I tend to agree with Lewis Keeble that "intentions" may adequately cover both.

However, it seems that terms such as goals, objectives, and strategies will continue to be used because they are now very much entrenched in planning literature and bureaucracies. The following hints are useful.

1. To rank the goals so that when they conflict with one another we have an idea of which one is more important.

2. To make explicit the relationship between goals and objectives, preferably in a table form.

3. To avoid the everything-is-related-to-everything syndrome which will make the above table too complex for any practical use. Only the most salient few objectives for a goal should be stated. This will allow for clear examination of the relationship between the goals which express general purposes, objectives which specify particular ends to be sought, and the means by which they are pursued.

PARTICIPATION

Public participation is a subject which has been discussed ad nauseam. Little is known about how the public feels about it, but for planners it is welcomed by a few, resisted by some, and carried out as a matter of form by most.

If real participation means sharing in the formulation of policies and proposals, then we have very little of it. Public meetings, exhibitions, handouts, interviews, are all exercises in participation but they do not add up to sharing in the decision-making process. Everybody talks about participation but nobody practices it. As one observer puts it, "instead of arguing endlessly about participation it would be better if all concerned recognized the futility of it and agreed to go back to its well-tried, time-honoured predecessor — confrontation" (Howard, 1976: 164) Taking Arnstein's (1969) classic ladder of citizen participation as a guide (which suggests that there are 12 steps of participation from manipulation to citizen control), we are probably at best at the step of consultation which means finding out from people what they would like. Consultation might take place before, during, and after a decision is made. It can involve the dispersal of information through such means as mass media, leaflets, exhibitions, and public meetings; the collection of information such as through surveys, study groups, forums and consultative groups; the enhancement of citizenship such as through forums and cooption on committees. Consultation must be both sincere and appear to be sincere, or no one will trust it or trust those who conduct it. It is important to remember that in consultation the planner does not often deal with the general public as a mass. More often, the planner mainly addresses the "elite" members of the general public. One problem in consultation, especially at the early stages, is the question of how representative is the participation for the area or the affected group as a whole. This is particularly difficult in local areas with a variety of activities and land uses. A planner will have to do his/her best to identify representative groups and involve them from the outset. As a guide, if people do not react against a particular group it may be reasonably assumed that they consider it as representative. In the case of local forums it is important to inform all interested parties of what is going on, otherwise they feel left out. Public involvement is never unbiased. In fact, the public is consulted because it has very specific interests. It is best to remember that none are less capable of giving reliable and unbiased opinion about a proposed development than those people who live in the immediate vicinity. So when we say local views are important, we must also realize that they are the most biased.

The circumstances under which questions are put to the public and the way people react to certain questions can influence the answers. Answers given at a public meeting where there is an audience can be quite different from those given in a questionnaire survey or a face-to-face interview. In all cases the interpretation of the answers will not be easy and it is important to listen to different kinds of comments from the people and not only those related to planning directly. For the members of the public, the local government is a unity and not a series of separate departments. Their comments and complaints are made to the government in general. The planner has to sort out those which are relevant to, and capable of being handled by, land use planning.

In order to elicit genuine responses there has to be a general belief among respondents that their opinion will have some effect. If alternative plans are put forward for public discussion it is important that the choice is real, and is seen to be so. Therefore, the exhibits used in public consultation should not be too slick or people may feel that a decision has already been reached and their participation is actually irrelevant. On the other hand, if the exhibits are too crude and the questions are too vague, then people will be annoyed at the sloppiness of the professionals. The location of an exhibition is also important. People will not make a special effort to go to it. It has to be conveniently located (such as at a shopping mall) so that people can find it "on their way." If any genuine and fruitful debate is to take place in a meeting it has to be comparatively small in size. This means that, if an overall planning scheme for the city is to be prepared, a meeting should be held at every neighbourhood level, if meaningful consultation is desired. Genuine consultation takes a long time and a lot of patience.

CHAPTER FOUR

INFORMATION

H ow much information is needed to make a planning decision? We can make a decision based on any amount of information. The question is how sure we are that it is the right decision and how convincing it is to the people who matter. Then, there are the questions of whether the information exists, and the cost and time required to acquire it.

Very important decisions have been made based on very little information, because the decision-maker is "convinced" that he is right and there is no pressure on him to justify himself to others. On the other hand, some decisions never get made and more and more "studies" are said to be needed because nobody wants to be convinced.

In land use planning there are "standard" items of information which have traditionally been considered essential to planning decisions. There is no "proof" that they are really the most appropriate and indispensable. However, they are generally accepted by the profession as relevant and important. Most of these are obtained readily from universal secondary sources such as the census or standard bureaucratic routines such as development control records. Custom-made information gathering is very costly and is usually avoided. Of course, the amount and detail of information is a function of the depth of the analysis required and the resources available to collect and process the data.

PLANNING AREA

The first decision to be made is "what is the planning area?" This, of course, depends on the planning issue at hand. It can be the nation, region, city, district or street block. At the theoretic level and the regional (national) scale, Pickard (1972) has used density and interaction to define major urban regions. Berry (1972) has used labour markets to construct commutersheds, and Friedmann (1973) has speculated about "urban fields."

Our focus, however, is the city and its constituent municipalities, wherever applicable. In most cases the planning area is the same as the municipal political boundary as defined by the provincial/state act, the municipal charter, or local ordinance. But in case of an annexation, amalgamation, or creation of a new jurisdiction, the boundaries of a planning area should be based on a combination of political, technical, and functional considerations (Chapin and Kaiser, 1979: 114-120).

1. Land use policies, regulations and public investment proposals must be congruent with those political jurisdictions which make these decisions. If the overall planning area is made up of smaller areas, the boundaries of these components should coincide with the jurisdictions of the relevant smaller political units (e.g., the central city, the constituent municipalities, etc.).

2. On technical grounds, a planning area should have the same boundaries as the areas used for census reporting, because the census is a fundamental source of information. However, as a city grows, there may be changes in the census boundaries as peripheral areas which meet the census criteria for inclusion are brought in as part of the city. This will affect the comparability of successive censuses. This is one of the reasons why it is better to have data on small census areas (as small as a street block if costs allow), which can always be aggregated to larger areas, and not vice versa.

3. For planning purposes functional relationships are important, and they are not necessarily accommodated in census boundaries. The delineation of the planning area may require a broader and more integrated approach. There might be boundaries based on shopping, social interaction, and recreation patterns; land development processes and land markets; and functionally related natural processes. These relationships can be revealed through the radius of coverage of a city newspaper, the extent of a system of transportation, the dependence on certain financial institutions, the network of telephone calls, and so on.

The city-wide planning area often needs to be broken down into local districts or zones for analytic purposes. Many such zones are already established in most urban areas, ranging from political districts (such as wards and townships) to locally determined analysis units (such as traffic analysis zones and neighbourhood areas). Some planners are attracted to geometric grid systems which break down the city into areas which are usually based on multiples of one thousand feet or meters to a side. These systems have the advantage of standardization, which allows for ready link-up with satellite data (LANDSAT) on land use and environment, easy analytic manipulation (such as density calculation), and computer graphic presentation. But grid systems have problems. Census areas and political jurisdictions are not in this form. Also, since grid lines often cut across areas that should be treated as economically, socially or environmentally functional units, they are not inherently suitable to deal with functionally integrated systems.

Lines on a map must be drawn with care. They have administrative and resource allocation implications. A building or a piece of land within the lines will be treated differently from outside of them. The following considerations may be used to delineate analysis zones or districts within the city-wide planning area.

1. The delineation of an analysis zone is best determined by referring to its role (existing as well as expected), the compatibility of physical or social characteristics within the zone, and the unity of planning problems found in the zone. A zone may function as a regional shopping centre, a dormitory housing development in the commuter belt, or an industrial park. Often, there is a multiplicity of roles: such as the combination of a central area, a tourist attraction, an entertainment centre, and a major inner-city housing redevelopment.

2. A zone may have a geographical unity and its boundaries can be established by referring to physical features such as a river, a railway embankment, or a highway. There may be some features throughout the zone, for example, a type of building (19th century terraced housing), a type of land use (industrial area or shopping centre), a natural characteristic (an area prone to flooding). The residents may have some common characteristic which identifies them within the context of a wider area, such as a ghetto inhabited by an ethnic minority. It is customary to draw the boundary line of a zone along the centre line of a street. But since the character of land use on both sides of the street is usually the same, it is more logical to include the block faces on both sides. However, this is not always possible, especially when the boundary is between two neighbouring municipalities. On one such boundary street in the Toronto region, there are 10-12 storey high commercial buildings on one side of the street, and single-detached houses on the opposite side.

3. A zone may be defined by a certain problem or a combination of problems, such as housing overcrowding, traffic congestion, derelict buildings, and the disappearance of a major employment generator. However, urban problems have an over-spill effect on adjacent areas which should be considered as well.

Should a zone be defined as the residents perceive it, or should the planner take a more "objective" point of view? There is no convenient answer. The involvement of the public, and the planner's greater knowledge of the district as the planning process progresses, will help to gradually define the boundaries more clearly. But, in the meantime, the planner cannot wait to have a perfect definition of the zone before he/she starts planning for it. The main thing is to retain a degree of flexibility in adjusting the boundaries, upon further knowledge of the area and the adjacent environment. Often the delineation of zones is a compromise between the planning issue at hand and the boundaries used in data sources such as the census.

INFORMATION CATEGORIES

The conventional categories used to organize planning information are physical, social and economic. It is important to consider both the source and the use of information. Traditional sources such as census and geographic information systems use standard physical, social and economic categories. Besides being readily available, such categories are also widely used by all kinds of agencies with which planners deal, and are readily understood by the general public — a not unimportant consideration. On the other hand, tailor-made categories organize information in ways that are specifically and immediately useful to planning analysis and evaluation. But the information may be too technical and the language too obscure for general use. A better approach is to have some commonsensical categories which are appropriate to land use planning needs and which can also accommodate information from traditional and easily accessible sources.

Chapin and Kaiser (1979: 113-114) suggest seven key information files for land use planning: economic, population, activity and space quality, land use, environment, transportation-utilities-communications, and guidance system. This is a meaningful way to organize planning information, and is adapted for use in this book.

The following approach is suggested for information organization. Land use planning deals essentially with matching users to appropriate land. There are three main categories of information: the user, the land, and the guidance mechanism for matching them. This approach can be used for city-wide planning schemes or site-specific development decisions.

1. The user can be an individual, group or corporation, public or private. These users perform various kinds of activities that have land use implications and needs. There are two kinds of user considerations: spatial and locational. These are generated by user characteristics (e.g., population size, socioeconomic attributes, perceptions and behaviour), and activities (e.g., living, working and recreation).

2. The land can be developed, developable, or protected from development. It has two essential attributes: locational suitability and site capacity. These are determined by its physical characteristics and user requirements. It has also a cost, in real money terms or terms of alternate development opportunities, both to the user and to the public, which affects its availability for particular uses.

3. Matching can be made through public regulation and investment as well as the marketplace. The choice is political as well as technical and is determined by the public interest to be served and resources and expertise available.

THE USER

Here, we are interested in how many users there are, who they are, what they do, what do they want, and what can they afford. We need general background information on demographics, and social and economic characteristics, as well as specific information on user activities, perceptions, needs and financial capability. Background information should be obtained for the overall planning area as well as the component analysis zones, and should cover past, current and projected situations. The following topics (and their combinations) are usually included:

> (i) population size by age, sex, occupation, income, and ethnic or language composition;

> (ii) households by size, income, age and sex of household head(s), stage in life cycle and selected ethnic or language groups;

> (iii) labour participation rates, female employment, and types of jobs;

> (iv) employment for selected sectors of industry, commerce and other economic activities, and their intensity grouping and spatial distribution;

> (v) retail sales for selected convenience and consumer goods.

Population
Information on population size and household characteristics is vital for land use planning. While city-wide figures are usually readily available from the Census of Population, suitable information for smaller areas is more difficult to obtain. The Census Tract (covering in the U.S. approximately 2500 to 8000 people) is the unit area most often used by planners. It is at this level that census reporting is the most comprehensive and detailed, although Tract boundaries are not necessarily related to any political jurisdiction or functional division. The census provides a wide range of information. In Canada, this includes demographics, language, social and cultural information, health and activity limitations, mobility, education, household activities (such as hours spent on housework and unpaid care of children), labour participation, housing and income. The U.S. Census covers even more items.

The smallest area in census reporting covers about 200 to 300 households (called an Enumeration Area in Canada, Enumeration District in the United Kingdom and Block Statistics in the United States). But the boundaries of this smallest area, or a cluster of them, may not coincide with those of the analysis zone. Also, these boundaries may change from one census count to the next, making comparison difficult. It is often unreliable to use small area census data for projections into the future. In particular, external pressures such as migrations, employment opportunities elsewhere, and regional housing shortages, can be very difficult to detect at this scale. Also, the planning proposals themselves will affect the future population size and make-up of the area.

Despite these problems, secondary sources of information are used widely by planning agencies for very compelling reasons. Not only are there savings in survey costs in most instances, but also there is the opportunity to relate local statistics to those for larger areas.

Two points should be noted when using census information. First, the Population Census is generally taken every ten years (although five-year censuses are often available), and the decennial census reports are the most comprehensive and reliable. There is a ten-year gap between actual census counts. Although there may be annual reports and estimates these are often "best guesses" only. Interim period information has to be generated by the planner. Second, not all population is counted nor every item enumerated every time a census is taken. Even for the all-important decennial census some questions (especially about income) are addressed only to a percentage (such as 20%) of the population. This means that some census figures are based on sample surveys with possible sampling errors. This is particularly worrisome with small area data where a small sampling error may have dramatic effect upon the figures produced. Combining data from surveys done at different years is risky. For example, population projection based on the population counts of one year and the mortality rates of another year can be unreliable. Specialized surveys, such as labour statistics and family expenditure surveys, cover specific items only and are not necessarily taken at comparable intervals to the population census.

Population estimates form the basis for most planning analyzes. Two questions are paramount: what is the current population; and what will be the population at a projected year.

Figure 4-1: Map Showing Some Census Tracts in a City

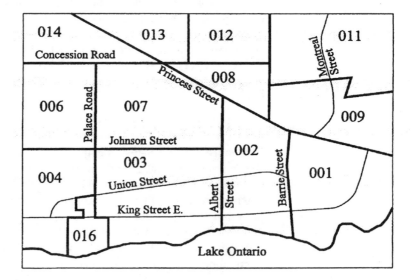

Figure 4-2: Map Showing One Census Tract (#003)

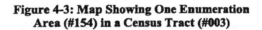

**Figure 4-3: Map Showing One Enumeration
Area (#154) in a Census Tract (#003)**

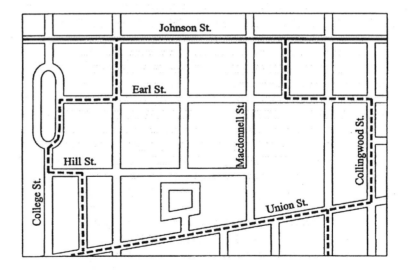

1. CURRENT ESTIMATES

Current estimates are sometimes needed for an interim year between censuses. Also, the population of a small area may have to be extracted from that of a larger area. A number of methods can be used: the component method, the ratio method and the symptomatic data method.

(1) Component Method. This is considered the best method. In this method, the last census count is adjusted to reflect changes due to births, deaths and migration. The following steps are used.

(i) Take population at last census count (note the official date of the census).

(ii) Compute the natural increase to date by summing up the yearly difference between births and deaths as reported by place of residence (data from health agencies). Adjust for less-than-one-calendar year figures, and correct for underregistration of births (as well as deaths in some cases).

(iii) One way to compute net migration is by referring to school enrolment changes from the last census date to the current date. First, assume the rate of net migration of the population is reflected precisely in the changing number of elementary school children. Second, estimate the number of elementary school-age children based on natural increase alone. Third, convert it to an "enrolment equivalent" by taking into consideration the fact that not all children of school age are in school. Fourth, obtain actual enrolment data. Fifth, find the difference between the actual enrolment and the "enrolment equivalent," and express this difference as a percentage of enrolment at the time of the last census. This difference is assumed to be equal to the net migration rate for the whole population. Finally, multiply the population at the last census by this rate to obtain net migration. Of course, this does not work when migration policies favour "family reunification" when more elderly immigrants will be expected.

(iv) Compute current population by adding up the population at the last census (Step i), natural increases (Step ii), and net migration (Step iii).

(2) Ratio Method. The "ratio" method for estimating current population starts with an estimate which is available for a larger area (usually a region) within which the locality is situated. This larger estimate is broken down directly or through successive stages by using predetermined formulae regarding the sharing of population among the localities within the larger area. This method assumes that population distribution among the localities is constant over time.

(3) Symptomatic Data Method. The "symptomatic data" method estimates the current population by adjusting the last census count by reference to some observed trends in data series such as vital statistics, school enrolment, listings in city directories, electric meter, water meter or telephone installations, dwelling unit counts, and registered voters. Usually a ratio method is employed, and different series may be used for estimating the size of different age segments of the population. It is important that the information of the data series is consistently assembled and accurately and adequately reported, and that it bears a significant relation to population trends.

2. PROJECTION

Population projection does not have a good record of accuracy. Too much reliance is placed on past trends and existing conditions which have a habit of not repeating themselves for the future. It is not wise to be too elaborate technically, giving an illusion of scientific exactitude that does not exist. Understandably, large area and short-time projections are more accurate, simply because there are fewer opportunities to make errors and greater latitude to bury them. However, the vulnerability of population projections to all sorts of errors does not obviate their necessity, but they must be used with caution. It is perhaps wise to make a range of estimates based on clearly described assumptions and then continually review and adjust them within the planning process. It is also possible to select different estimates for different planning analyzes. For example, a high estimate is used for evaluating the provision of public services to assure an adequate supply, and a low estimate is used for calculating tax revenues in order to be on the safe side. A number of projection methods are available: the cohort-survival method, the deduction and extrapolation methods, holding capacity methods, and a variety of analytic methods.

(1) Cohort-Survival Method. This is the most often used method, especially in larger cities (today there are ready-made computer programmes). Future estimates are based on an analysis of the major components of population change, that is, births, deaths and migration. It is the only method with an age-sex breakdown. The following is a brief description of a five-year cohort scheme.

> (i) The base year population is divided into males and females and grouped according to age at five-year intervals. Each age-sex group is called a cohort.

> (ii) Death rates for different cohorts are used to compute the number of survivors from each age group to be carried forward to the next five-year period.

> (iii) Net in-or-out-migrations during a five-year period are estimated for each age group.

> (iv) The sum of survivors and net in- or out-migrants of any age group becomes the estimate for the next higher age group at the beginning of the next five-year period.

> (v) The new 0-4 age group (that is, children born within the five-year period) is obtained by applying the fertility rate to the number of females of child-bearing age (15-44) at the beginning of the period.

> (vi) Repeat the above procedures for the next five-year period, and carry on for the entire projection time required.

Figure 4-4: Cohort-survival Method of Population Pojection
A Typical Age-Sex "Pyramid"

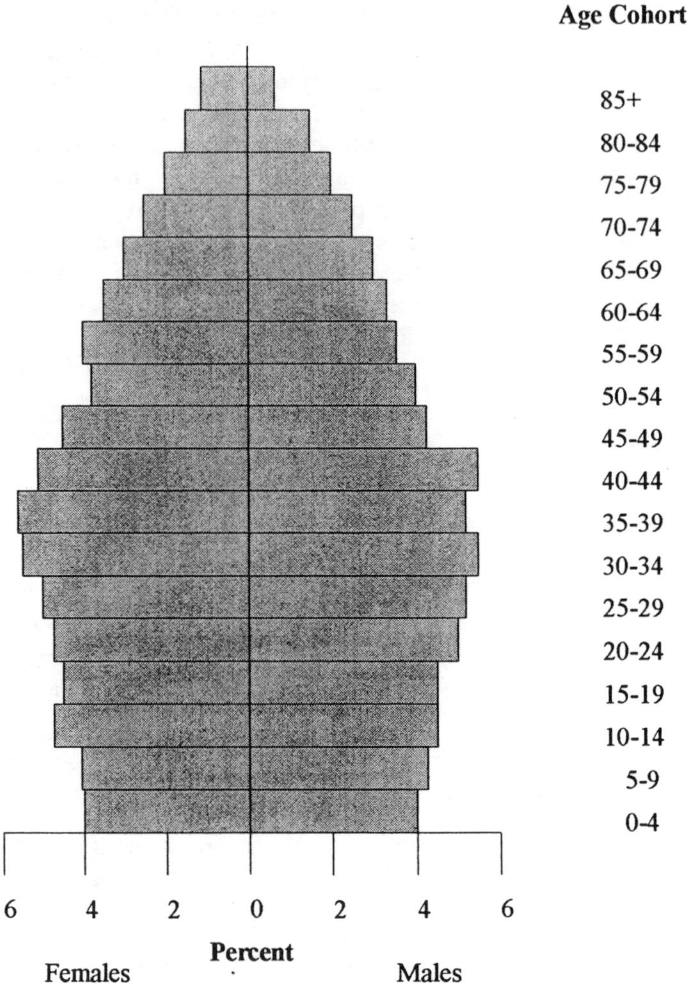

Age Cohort

85+	
80-84	
75-79	
70-74	
65-69	
60-64	
55-59	
50-54	
45-49	
40-44	
35-39	
30-34	
25-29	
20-24	
15-19	
10-14	
5-9	
0-4	

6   4   2   0   2   4   6

Percent

Females   Males

Birth rates (fertility rates), given as the number of children per one thousand females of child-bearing age (15-44), are based on long-range trends in local birth rates or special studies. Death rates (or mortality rates) are determined from standard life tables. In practice, where local birth and death rates are not available, as is often the case for a small locality, the rates for the larger area within which the locality is situated are used. Net migration rates are based on past trends in migration or future employment prospects. One way to determine past migration rates is through ex post comparison, that is, comparison between the actual population figures of a number of years and estimates obtained for the same years through applying natural increases and decreases. The difference between these two sets of figures represents net migration, but no distinction can be made between in-migration and out-migration. Migration estimates are usually very tricky, especially for a small area.

(2) Deduction and Extrapolation Methods. When the population forecast of a larger area (nation or region) is available a "ratio" method can be used to determine the share of population for a smaller local area. This method can be used to obtain projections at the city district or even neighbourhood level. It may involve a simple ratio between the larger and smaller area, or a series of interlinking ratios through a system of intermediate areas. Often the ratio is obtained from past trends. The population of the smaller area can be expressed as a percentage of the population of the larger area, and then various percentages over the past are plotted and then extrapolated into the future. The danger is, of course, in assuming that past population trends are still valid in the future. To counteract this, building construction trends and the amount and capacity of land suitable and available for development are introduced to add some realism.

Sometimes mathematical and graphic projections are used. All of them are based on extrapolation of past trends. It can be a straight-line arithmetic projection assuming the same numerical change for similar periods of time, or a geometric curve assuming same rates of change for similar periods of time.

A simple regression method can be used by fitting a straight line to a series of points representing past populations and then extending it into the future. A multiple-regression method uses past births, deaths and migration as independent variables and regresses these against past populations to obtain a straight-line projection for the future.

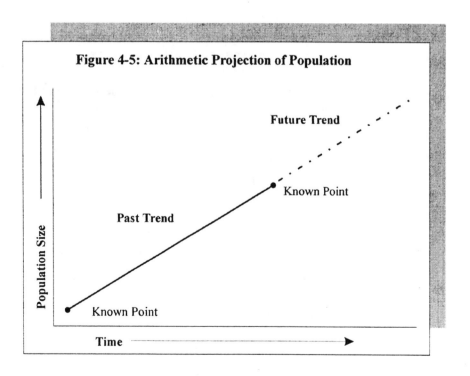

Figure 4-5: Arithmetic Projection of Population

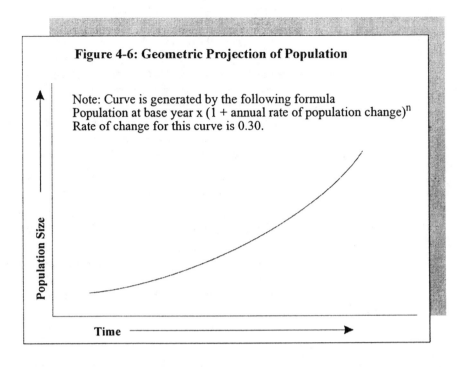

Figure 4-6: Geometric Projection of Population

Note: Curve is generated by the following formula
Population at base year x $(1 + \text{annual rate of population change})^n$
Rate of change for this curve is 0.30.

(Y-axis: Population Size)
(X-axis: Time)

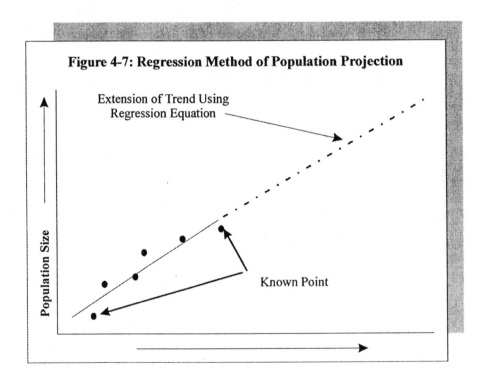

Figure 4-7: Regression Method of Population Projection

Extension of Trend Using Regression Equation

Known Point

(Y-axis: Population Size)

Projections can also be made by identifying some other cities which have, in the past, shown growth characteristics comparable to those presently experienced by the city in question, and then, using the recent growth trends of these other cities as a guide, project the population growth of the city in question.

Since there does not seem to be any mathematical law governing population growth these deduction and extrapolation methods are not "scientific" methods but are only expedient measures when there is a lack of information for more appropriate methods to be used, or in order to save costs. As a rule, these methods are less reliable than the cohort-survival method.

(3) Holding Capacity Methods. These methods rely on the holding capacity of land and the amount of resources within a bounded area to estimate the total population and activities that can be sustained. The scale can vary from a neighbourhood to a region. The idea is to determine the upper population threshold based on the amounts of land, infrastructure and environmental resources that are needed to support a certain level of human activities as well as the impacts of such activities on the land, infrastructure and environment. This approach permeates the book, and the reader should refer especially to the sections on Land Information, Transportation Information and Infrastructure Information in this chapter, Land Supply and Infrastructure in the Analysis chapter, and the Ecological Perspectives in the Synthesis chapter.

(4) Analytic Methods. The foregoing methods are by and large nonanalytic because they do not enquire into the "forces" of population changes, especially in the case of migration. A totally different approach uses employment as a key element in population forecast. Employment estimates are expanded into labour force estimates, which are in turn expanded to population equivalents. This approach does not only give a justification for population changes, especially in the case of migration, it also yields information about the economic health of the city. From a land use planning point of view, what is even more significant about this approach is that, although it normally treats a city or a region as a whole, it may also be used to examine employment changes brought about by changes in one sector of the economy, or even by one large firm or plant.

A word of caution must be given about "economic" studies in land use planning. They are employed to provide information for land use decisions, in this case, information for population estimates. Land use planning is not economic planning, and we should not get carried away and forget the purpose for which these studies are done. A good test of their relevance is whether the information they yield helps directly and definitely in the land use decision.

The most common and logically defensible method is the "economic base" method. It is best used for small urban centres outside the big urban regions. This method conceives the urban economy as made up of "basic" activities that produce and distribute goods and services for export to the outside, and "non-basic" activities whose goods and services are consumed within the area (Bendavid, 1974). Expansion in basic activities leads to expansion in the non-basic activities, through two kinds of multiplier effects: income and employment. A base multiplier is defined as the ratio between total income (or employment) and the income (or employment) attributable to a basic activity. This allows the economic relations between basic and non-basic activities to be worked out. The higher the multiplier the more beneficial the activity is to the total economy. This can signify a number of traits: a high degree of linkages within the economy, good agglomeration of complementary economic activities, and few leakages of economic benefits to the outside of the area. If the overall base multiplier is known (the subject of much research) and if the increase in basic employment can be estimated, then the increase in employment, both in the non-basic sector and in the total economy can be found. A number of practical considerations are needed in the application of this method to make employment forecasts. First is the distinction between basic and non-basic activities. Traditionally manufacturing, extractive industry, wholesale, finance and banking, tourism, large institutions, and the like are considered basic; while local-serving stores, schools, banks, doctors, city government and other similar activities are considered non-basic (or service). But this is obviously not entirely true. An activity can be partly basic and partly non-basic, depending on how and where its product or service is consumed. For instance, if a doctor's service is used beyond the boundary of the local economy it is "exported" and should be considered as basic. Activities may be interdependent, for example, the output of a parts manufacturer may be entirely absorbed by a local exporting fabricating plant. It is difficult to classify activities exclusively either as basic or non-basic. This is not helped by the conventional way in which economic activities are reported, which does not make distinctions about items such as imports of exportable goods, or non-basic activities which serve to attract basic activities to locate in the area.

The second practical consideration is the delineation of the boundary of the "base" area. This is usually done by a compromise between political jurisdiction and local trade areas. Trade areas are either taken from some other studies, or determined with reference to local newspapers' circulation, or as agreed by local credit, merchant or similar groups. Consumer surveys of where people go for household goods and services can be used to delineate retail trade areas but they are costly exercises. Reilly's (1931) "law of retail gravitation" suggests that the attraction of a city as a service centre to the consumer (that is, its trade area) is directly proportional to the size of the city's population and inversely proportional to the square of the distance between the city and the consumer. This helps to identify the breaking point in the spheres of influence between competing cities as service centres.

The third consideration is the determination of the proportions of employment engaged in basic and non-basic activities. We can do a sample survey of local firms about the proportions between local and non-local sales, customers, bank depositors and loans, and so on. The same proportions may be assumed as the share of basic and non-basic employment in the various sectors. Alternatively, we can use a "location quotient" technique. A location quotient of a particular industry is the ratio of employment in that industry to the total employment in the economy. The national quotient of an industry is used as an indicator of self-sufficiency. If the local quotient is greater than the national figure, then the industry is exporting (basic), and vice versa. In practice, although city-wide employment (unemployment) figures are reported regularly, smaller area figures are not. Also, there are troublesome problems about definition (unemployment, overemployment, underemployment), conversion (part-time and seasonal employment into equivalent full-time annual employment), and commutation (place of work versus place of residence). A variation of the location quotient technique is the "minimum requirement" technique where the location quotient of each industry in a number of similar cities is ranked and the lowest is taken as the benchmark to determine the proportions of basic and non-basic employment in that industry.

The "economic base" method has been criticized for two major weaknesses. First, it has an inherent bias towards "exporting" or basic activities. It is doubtful if an expanding basic sector is sufficient, or even necessary, for the economic well-being of an urban area. Second, the distinction between basic and non-basic activities is artificial and, at times, forced. Given the interdependent nature of modern economic structures, this method becomes less useful as the economy becomes more advanced and the distinction between basic and non-basic activities becomes more intractable. Therefore, this method is least suited for large metropolitan areas where the business and consumer services have now substituted the declining traditional export sector and have become the truly "basic" element of the metropolitan area economy.

In practice, the method is seldom used to examine the total economy or the total employment situation of a city. Most often it is used to estimate the employment impact of a new plant or firm. The "multiplier" is crucial because a small change in it can change the employment estimates significantly, sometimes enough to sway decisions about accepting or rejecting a new industry. When used in such a fashion there is no distinction between the basic and non-basic sector. Multipliers are often related to specific operations such as shopping malls, hotels, and not to an economic sector. They are obtained from planning literature, special studies of particular trades, and rules-of-thumb. There is ample opportunity for error.

Two other methods are also mentioned in planning literature although their actual application in land use planning has been extremely limited. Input-output analysis has been used to examine national, regional or large scale economies especially in tracing the employment consequence when a new production technology is introduced or when a certain economic sector is expanded. Shift-share analysis is used to make regional employment projections based on assumptions about changes in the region's industrial mix (shift) and in the region's share of the national employment in each industry (share). This method is most employed to examine changes in a region's "share" of the national employment as an indicator of the region's economic health.

In spite of their promise, the application of these economic analytic methods to estimate employment, and hence population changes, is not common in planning, with perhaps the exception of employment multipliers which are used to examine employment impacts of a new plant or firm. There does not seem to be the will or the resources to use them properly. The dependence of these methods on large data pools and sophisticated analytic skill, as well as the apparent volatility of the estimates, are important reasons why they are not widely used. These are really tools designed more for economic planning than for land use planning.

USER NEEDS

Essentially there are three generic types of land users: households, firms and institutions. Each of these has distinctive attributes, values, and needs. We should know about the frequency and amount of movements, interchanges, interactions and exchanges by and among persons, households, firms, and institutions. We also need to know their perceptions, attitudes and preference towards locational and space quality. In all of these, past, present and future trends must be taken into consideration.

Two reasons seem to lie behind a user's decision in choosing a particular structure or site for its activities: the opportunities offered by the location, and the quality of the accommodation. These reasons are strongly associated to what Chapin and Kaiser (1979: 201) have so convincingly argued as a combination of "preconditioning" and "predisposing" factors. Preconditioning factors are background characteristics of the user that influence (often constrain) a choice or preference. Predisposing factors are needs, attitudes, inclinations, or policies that influence the choice.

Admittedly, individual persons, households, firms, or institutions are all different in terms of their backgrounds, characteristics, needs, and attitudes. But in order to plan, we must assume that it is possible to identify some archetypical users. The following discussion focusses on how an archetypical land user is defined by its background characteristics; and what kinds of information are normally used to describe its activities, perceptions, and preferences.

1. Households

This group of users gets the most attention. The accepted unit for residential land use planning is the household, which includes single person households.

(1) Types

The following background characteristics are used most often to define archetypes: age, income and household size. In addition, sex, race, education, or other categories are also used.

Age data are important for defining life cycle stages which have implications on activity pattern, household moving behaviour, housing needs (currently much attention is focussed on the elderly), and community facility needs (especially schools and recreational facilities). The cohort-survival method automatically produces age groups. Population estimated by other methods has to be broken down by age, usually by referring to the proportion of various age groups in the total population in the past.

Household sizes are needed for residential land allocation and housing market analysis (especially for dealing with the question of appropriate and adequate housing). Again, past trends are used to estimate the relative proportion of households of different sizes in the population. Usually a range of estimates is prepared based on varying assumptions about economic trends, rate of household formation and birth rates.

Income and expenditure data are needed in housing market analysis, especially in dealing with the question of affordability, and in retail analysis to determine the siting of retail services. In Canada and the United States household income data are available from censuses, even for small areas, but not in Britain. Other sources include proxy measures such as socioeconomic groupings in the census, the Family and Expenditure Survey, and housing waiting lists. Specific surveys of income, expenditure or rents are not common because people are reluctant to answer such questions. Often, this information is obtained as part of a general housing survey.

Data on housing tenure are important for housing market analysis and can be obtained from the census (aggregate form) as well as from property assessment records (site-specific). Besides the censuses and other governmental sources, a planner can refer to secondary sources of information such as the local press, interviews with key persons in an area (school headmasters, priests, social workers), and even graffiti on the walls. By spending a lot of time in the area, a planner may develop a good sense about the housing situation.

Individual socioeconomic characteristics are often combined to form archetypes. For example, low-income single parent households are defined by combining data on income, marital status and household size. Much skill is called for in combining and reconciling data from different sources. The planner has to deal with data from different periods, with different spatial boundaries, and having different degrees of reliability. It is best to remember that the combined information is only as reliable as its weakest part.

The number of archetypes must be kept to the minimum. We should select only those which will likely produce very significant differences in activities and space preference. Conventional wisdom has it that income and stage in the life cycle of the householder (that is, size of household and age of household head) are the two most important background characteristics, followed by ethnicity.

(2) Activities, Perceptions and Preferences

The socioeconomic characteristics of the household members, especially those of the household head (the one most likely to make decisions about housing location and accommodation) are used as background information. The location of the dwelling is used to key the data to the different analysis zones of the planning area. The following is a list of the important information to be sought.

(i) What do people do? When and where do they do it? We need this information to analyze the proper location of residential land. Data can be obtained through a time-budget survey (or activity study). This is in essence a "diary" of a person's activities throughout the day: where they take place; how much time is spent on each; and how much time is spent in travelling between them. Although these activities can take place at the home and/or out of the home the focus should be on out-of-home activities. They normally include all forms of resting, working, learning, socializing, recreating and relaxing. The household members' perception about the relative importance of these activities and their satisfaction with them (especially with respect to the convenience and suitability of the location for these activities) should also be noted. A shorter version is to obtain, through interview, an activity listing of all out-of-home activities of the household. Supplementary data can be drawn from origin-and-destination surveys in transportation studies, if available. From these a picture can be constructed about the ebb and flow of people in a city during various times of the day. It is important that the survey covers a reasonable time period so that it will capture the "typical" day as well as the different activities during different periods of the year. Activities which happen more often or take up more time are naturally considered more important. The information should be screened and organized according to locational and spatial implications.

(ii) How do people like their residential environment, that is, their perception about the quality of space and environment? We need the information to analyze the amount and quality of residential land needed. Four kinds of space qualities are covered: the dwelling, the interior, the site and the neighbourhood. The most widely used technique to appraise these qualities is the "penalty scoring system" or one of its variations, first developed by the American Public Health Association. The following is a partial list of the items usually covered in the appraisal.

The dwelling: housing type (especially high-rise versus low-rise); maintenance level; and architectural and heritage merit.

The interior: number, size and layout of rooms; interior facilities such as the kitchen, bathroom (especially for the elderly), and storage space (especially its adequacy); interior services such as heating, ventilation, electrical and plumbing (especially for older dwellings); energy conservation (especially the adequacy of insulation and draught prevention); car parking adequacy and convenience.

The site: lot size, together with the siting and orientation of the dwelling unit for privacy and view; outdoor facilities and maintenance for convenience and looks; grading and drainage for access and maintenance.

The neighbourhood: socioeconomic characteristics of the neighbours; land use, housing type and density; availability and accessibility of facilities (measured in terms of distance and time) especially schools, convenience shopping and open space; availability of services, especially public transit, police, fire, garbage collection, and snow removal; street parking conditions; security from crime and traffic; and noise, privacy and visual amenities (especially vegetation).

We are also interested in the user's "perception" because it is upon such perception that the locational and accommodation choice will be made. At the same time, public decisions and investment on improving living conditions are based both on objective appraisal of the situation as well as on the subjective perception by the residents. Both are relevant information for planning analysis. However, attitudinal surveys often produce ambiguous findings. For instance, homeowners often express very high levels of satisfaction about their homes and neighbourhoods although they may register great dissatisfaction about specific items. Here, ownership pride is involved, and an owner would not acknowledge an inferior house and neighbourhood because he/she lives there. Such ambiguities may only reflect human nature generally. Attitudes are not always expressible in terms of yes, no, or even maybe. An answer can be yes and no simultaneously. The planner should not be distressed by ambiguous results (the positivistic approach of many social studies, which allows for only one answer to each question can be very unreliable too), but should be sensitive to the contingencies and complexity of human perceptions. There are well-written texts covering issues such as the range of items that should be included in a survey, the way that importance and satisfaction levels should be ranked, and so on (Babbie, 1973; Oppenheim, 1966; Selltiz, Wrightsman and Cook, 1976; the University of Michigan Survey Research Center, 1976; and Converse and Presser, 1986). Information can be obtained through standard-questionnaire sample surveys, qualitative surveys, or use of focus groups.

(iii) What do people prefer? Residential choice is based on a combination of activity opportunities offered by the location and the quality of the accommodation. Therefore, we need to find out people's locational preferences regarding desired distances (time) to various out-of-home activities and spatial preferences regarding dwelling, interior, site and neighbourhood qualities. For this purpose the same items as covered in (i) and (ii) should be used here. One very important point to note is that preference and behaviour can differ significantly. For instance, during the days of the energy "crisis" in the 1970s a large number of people expressed preference for smaller homes and cars but only a limited number actually did change to smaller homes and cars. An obvious explanation is that the change would have involved an immediate capital cost which would be quite out of proportion to the savings. This was a real constraint to actual behaviour in spite of expressed preference. Likewise, while most people today support recycling, many will not do it unless it is "hassle free". It is notoriously difficult to get residents in high-rise apartments to participate in recycling programmes. Stated preference could give a wrong lead about actual behaviour because there is no "cost" associated with an expression of preference, leading to exaggerated needs or unrealistic wishes. To counter this tendency, trade-off games may be used to elicit information by asking the respondent to select items according to some "real-world" constraints. For instance, a survey on environmental quality may include a question that asks the respondent to guess at the cost of his/her suggestion for environmental improvements and to identify funding sources to cover the cost.

Clues to household behaviour in the past may also be obtained by examining development records. But they have to be interpreted in some "macro" contexts such as economic cycles, regional migrations, and senior level government policies and programmes, all of which distort the nature and magnitude of household needs. A different approach is to focus on the developer who is the agent, who makes the initial speculative commitment to provide housing. The consumer (household) makes its locational choice from the supply of residential lots (with or without the dwelling) provided by the developer.

The developer's decision is therefore the first specific commitment to a location and a housing type. Residential development is largely a speculative commitment, not by the actual consumer but by the developer on the basis of forecasting consumer preferences. Therefore, developers' decisions are useful indicators of how the market responds to consumer demands (Kaiser, 1966). However, it should be noted that consumer demands are not necessarily perfect indicators of user needs. Also, developers are not a homogeneous group. They have different production, financing and marketing characteristics which make them respond differently to the market. Their land requirement is a function of their size of operation, whether they are local or national firms, their linkages with other developers, the level of integration of their operations, their specialization of housing types, and so on (Leung, 1987a). In most instances a planner deals much more directly with developers than with households and his/her perception about household needs is often "filtered" through developer activities.

2. Firms (commercial and industrial)

(1) Types

Unlike the case with households there is less flexibility with the classification of firms (commercial and industrial). In nearly all cases the Standard Industrial Classification scheme (SIC) or its variations is used. The following is a list of the single-digit categories. The classification scheme can become very detailed and specific by using multidigit numbers (as many as four digits).

One drawback about this classification scheme is that it is based on a firm's principal product or service rather than on the "process" of production or service delivery. Therefore, it is not easy to appreciate the locational and spatial implications of the use by simply looking at its classification. Data on use types can also be drawn from commercial directories and trade reports which give the number, type and address of different industrial and commercial establishments.

agriculture, forestry, and fishery	SIC	**0**
mining		**1**
processing industries		**2-3**
transportation		**4**
wholesale and retail		**5**
service (business and personal)		**6-7**
public service		**8**

Size of firm may be obtained from development control records which give type, location and size of proposed development, though not always the actual use. But there will be no record on firms which have existed for a long time and have not expanded or redeveloped. Property assessment records give clues to assessed property values which can be used as a proxy measure for size but the information is usually dated. Sales, purchase and employment figures are not public information, and special surveys have to be conducted. A common indicator of size is the number of employees. This gives a good basis for estimating space requirements. But we should try to obtain the average, annual and seasonal range of total employment, size of the largest shift at peak employment, and size of office staff (if there is an administrative office). Crude employment numbers can often be obtained from company reports of large firms, but not for small ones.

Detailed and site specific figures, as are often required for planning purposes, will have to be surveyed. The combination of product/service and size (employment) is the conventional way to define firm archetypes.

In planning practice there are some conventional "use" categories that relate activities to land use. Retail and commercial centres are often also centres of cultural, entertainment and civic activities. They often have a high degree of mixed land uses, including residential. The central business district (CBD) is usually compact, with small city blocks and continuous retail frontage. There are other types of centres: older business centres are found in the central city or older suburbs; shopping centres can serve a neighbourhood, community, or region; mixed-use developments are super-blocks that contains retail, offices, hotel, entertainment, and public/civic and residential uses; and highway commercial developments can serve the travelling public or special purposes such as automobile sales or "big-box" retail. Each of these categories has some established standards as to the amount of sales/office floor area needed for each employee and parking space needed for every thousand square feet of sales/office floors. (See also Tables 5-13 and 5-14.)

There are also conventional industrial use categories, too. The older industrial manufacturing) districts usually consist of multi-storied buildings with high site coverage, and locate near ports and rail lines. Newer ones have more mixed uses, such as manufacturing, research and development, wholesaling and warehouses, and offices. Industrial parks (industrial estates, R&D parks, etc.) are usually planned to provide an optimal environment for the activities that take place there, such as street layout and designs, infrastructure provision, site coverage and setbacks, off-street parking, landscaping and signage, building materials and appearances. There are also performance standards for noise, smoke, other emissions, buffers, parking and loading, and outdoor storage. And, for the more prestigious R&D parks, there is additional emphasis on aesthetics and a campus-like setting. Some will even include hotels, restaurants, health centres and recreational facilities, for both workers and visitors. Industrial firms can also be classified into intensive, intermediate and extensive types, based on the number of employees per acre (or hectare) of land. Of course, this can only be possible if we have the number of employees and the acreage of the plant. However, some crude but useful standards have been developed, which relate this classification scheme to the SIC scheme, and to locational requirements (Chapin and Kaiser, 1979: 244-247). (See also Tables 5-10 and 5-11.)

(2) Activities, Perceptions and Preferences
Activity patterns and space needs of archetypical firms can be obtained from planning literature such as the Urban Land Institute's "Community Development Series" about office, residential and shopping mall development (Urban Land Institute, 1975, 1982a, 1982b, 1987 and 1988). Indeed, literature search is the most common approach in identifying space needs. But in some cases, a special survey is needed to obtain the relevant information for a specific sector, firm or site.

Information on off-site activities yields insight on locational and transportational needs. The inputs to a firm include processing, storage, supplies and servicing. The origin, frequency and mode of shipment or service calls for these inputs should be noted. Then, the goods and services of a firm may have to be shipped out or delivered to the consumer. The destinations, frequency and mode of shipment or service calls should be recorded. The information should be organized according to the analysis zones.

Information about space quality at and around the site includes the size, layout and condition of the space, as well as the user's perception of the relative importance of different kinds of space and its satisfaction with respect to the situation. The following items should be covered in a survey.

> **Structure**: adequacy of floor areas for different kinds of activities; appropriateness of construction types; adequacy of utilities (water, power, waste disposal), both for existing operations and future changes.

> **Site**: Adequacy of area for parking, loading, storage and circulation; landscaping and buffering; problems with drainage; and access to the transport route.

> **Environment**: satisfaction with the maintenance of building; problems with vandalism and vacancies; cleanliness of streets; access to transport routes (in the case of industry and wholesale), and to main street systems (in the case of retail-commercial); and adequacy of amenities in the area, especially landscaping and open space for employee use.

Information about preferences should include whether, and why, the firm is contemplating expansion or modernization; the relative importance it places on different locational opportunities and space qualities; and the likelihood of changes in production technology, marketing method and consumer behaviour, which would affect its satisfaction and preference. Firms, unlike households, often have clearer positions, policies and practices with regard to their locational and space decisions. Interviewing with key informants can yield good insights.

A survey of commercial and industrial establishments may also help to assess the buoyancy of an area, the relationship between firms, the economic pressures on them, and their future intentions. A survey of firms and sites may sometimes be undertaken, to assess the effects of firms on the surrounding area, the development potential of vacant commercial properties, and the needs of local firms to expand. However, although local surveys yield important information, many crucial economic factors affecting locational and space choice by firms may have origins external to the area and are difficult, but essential, to ascertain.

Finally, information about the policies and intentions of the local government and other government agencies have to be obtained as well. The local government may have decided that a certain level of public investment is to be directed to a particular area, or that a certain level of private sector investment is to be encouraged, or that a certain increase in the rate of revenue is generated. All these will affect the activities, perceptions and preferences of firms in the area.

3. Institutions

Institutional mandates and procedures are quite formally established. Basically there are two archetypes: human development (educational, recreational, religious and political), and public service (health, protective services, and public works), each having its distinct locational and space quality requirement. Again, the number of employees is a good indicator of space needs. The off-site activities and on-site space needs of most institutions are similar to those of the service industry or retail business. However, besides the material inputs (supplies, storage, servicing) there are the political inputs to institutional activities which may be in the form of meetings, attendance, memberships, and so on. It is important to know how frequently meetings are held, how many people are involved, and where are the people coming from. Outputs from institutions are mostly in the form of services which are consumed at the site (such as school and hospital), or off the site (such as police, fire and utilities). It is important to know about the catchment or service area of their clients and target population, and the volume and frequency of different kinds of services provided (from daily to yearly figures).

With respect to buildings, it is necessary to record the amount and arrangements (linkages) of floor areas for different activities, the building and structure type used for the different activities, and the level of maintenance. With respect to the site, information is needed regarding the total site area and area for each component building; the adequacy of parking, loading, waiting and circulation; the general landscaping; and topographic conditions regarding access and drainage. With respect to the environment, the important information includes surrounding uses, general condition of surrounding areas, road and sidewalk maintenance, and access to public transport and major street systems. Finally, it is important to note the prospect for future expansion, modification, and move; the policies, standards, and guidelines regarding preferred locations and space qualities; and estimates of future changes in the nature and volume of service in light of changing political, technological and social conditions. Although there are rules-of-thumb about the locational and space needs for different types of institutions, in most cases institution-specific and site-specific studies are needed to obtain the necessary information.

User Surveys

Information on household activities, and their perceptions and preferences about the locational and space qualities of their dwellings is not so easy to obtain. One way is to review literature which reports ideas, findings, and experience of other planners or agencies, and then adapt these to the local situation. This method is relatively inexpensive and is the most common method although it has the problems of "information transfer" (goodness of fit between different cities, time periods, situations, problems, and so on). Sometimes, user surveys are necessary.

There are basically two approaches to user surveys: observation and communication (Lynch, 1971). Observation is on-the-spot survey of visible behaviour, by taking notes, taking pictures and tape recordings. It can be done for a continuous period of time, or at selected times and for selected people. The most common example of direct observation is the survey of movement patterns, especially traffic circulation — checking the mode, volumes, patterns, routes, origins and destinations. Another example is the survey of people's behaviour at a locality: how do they act and how do they interact. This includes the examination of behaviour settings such as a ball game or at a meeting; behaviour circuits such as those involved in buying food, in a day's work, in an evening's entertainment; behaviours in dealing with difficulties such as being lost and trying to find one's way in an urban setting; and behaviours in which the users have adapted the environment such as the use of a "cow path" instead of a paved walkway. But there are some general problems about this approach. The observations could yield only descriptions of behaviour with masses of data and no underlying theory. Observed behaviour gives no indication of the users' internal experience or their perception about the choices available to them.

Direct communication with the users helps us to get at their perceptions, feelings, knowledge, as well as their description of their own behaviour. Included in this approach are telephone, mail-back, and face-to-face interviews, with structured and/or open-ended questions. The main problem with this approach is that the respondent has to externalize his/her internal feelings and experience, which is not always easy or reliable. We could use a structured questionnaire based on a predetermined set of relevant questions. But this has the effect of conditioning the respondent and limiting the scope of responses. To compensate for this, free and open-ended questions can be used which allow the respondent to express his/her views and opinions freely. The answers can be very rich and suggestive, but it is very difficult to compare and quantify such free-form answers, although systematic "content analysis" may somewhat remedy this problem. It should be noted that interviews need not be just verbal questions and answers, but can include photographs, graphics, drawings or even models.

The direct communication approach is used most often for problem-identification through studying direct expressions of problems or indirect indication of dissatisfaction of an environment. But there are some problems with this approach. There may be stereotyping by the respondent because such surveys are usually about topical subjects with a lot of media influence already existing, which will have set up stereotypical problems, questions, or answers in the mind of the respondent. On the other extreme, the respondent may be quite unaware or unconscious of the problem and his/her response will be highly hypothetical or misdirected. There is also the opportunity for cheating. For instance, the incomes of people could change depending on who is asking the question. When people want to show off they would cite a higher income, and when people want to protect themselves from higher taxes, they would cite a much lower income. Then finally, the respondent may try to second-guess what the interviewer wants and supply the answers accordingly.

Surveys are expensive, especially when they involve face-to-face interviews. The actual scope of a survey depends on the planning issues to be addressed and the resources available. When special surveys and face-to-face interviews have to be done they should be well designed so that they not only serve to assess physical, social and economic circumstances, but also involve and inform the population. Surveys are time-consuming and cannot be used for projections. The success of any survey will depend in part on a good relationship between the planner and the people he/she is planning for, and good rapport between them is necessary in order to avoid misunderstandings. When interviewing people, the planner has to interpret the answers and not always take them at face value; but at the same time, he/she must avoid letting personal prejudices interfere.

LAND INFORMATION

In order to match users to land we need information about the land — its environmental attributes and its development attributes.

Environmental Attributes

Land has two sets of environmental attributes: natural and man-made. The spatial unit of the data collection must fit the purpose of the analysis. For instance, we need watershed data for drainage design, and "corridor" and "patch" data for habitat protection. The time-line of the data collection must also fit the purpose of the analysis. For instance, we need base-line data for environmental quality control, and life-cycle data for infrastructure planning. Environment Canada publishes a set of indicators (National Environmental Indicator Series). They track nationally significant environmental issues using a stress-condition-response model. They are published in the format of indicator bulletins, with graphs and texts. These include Ecological Life-Support Systems (ozone depletion, climate change, toxic contaminants in the environment, acid rain, etc.), Human Health and Well-Being (urban air quality, municipal water use and waste water treatment, etc.), National Resources Sustainability (forests, marine resources, agricultural resources, etc.), and Pervasive Influencing Factors (passenger transportation, energy consumption, solid and hazardous waste generation, urbanization, etc.).

There are several common environmental data sets.

1. Land

(i) Soil and Geology. They determine the resource value (capability to support agriculture, forestry and plant life) and development value (bearing capacity, drainage and filtering capacity, and use as construction material) of land. They can also be hazard factors (susceptibility to erosion, slides and collapse, corrosivity, transportation and retention of pollutants, etc.) The U.S. Department of Agriculture's Soil Conservation Service produces General Soils Maps for each county. Canada has the Canada Land Inventory, with its seven categories: Class 1 and 2 are prime agricultural land and urban use is generally prohibited.

(ii)Topography and Slope. They determine surface drainage patterns, solar aspects, view sheds, and site formation requirements. The gradient of a slope is the ratio between the vertical rise and the horizontal distance, and is expressed as a percentage. For instance, a rise of five feet over a distance of 100 feet is a 5% gradient. Incidentally, a gradient of less than 5% is considered gentle, and is suitable for most land uses. Any gradient exceeding 25% is considered too steep for most uses. Maximum sustained gradient for roads is about 10%. (Refer also to Table 5-15 for optimal gradients.)

The top of a slope is the drainage divide, which forms the boundary of a drainage basin, and is an essential piece of planning information. Topography also affects the amount and duration of sunlight that a site can get at different times of the year, as well as the views (good and bad) that can be seen from the site.

Topographic maps can be based on aerial photographs as well as ground surveys. (Refer to the section on Maps.)

(iii) Cover and Vegetation . Plants hold soil, absorb water, modulate microclimate, and have aesthetic value. Plant cover can act as index of soil conditions (drainage, acidity and humus content) as well as weather conditions (temperature, sunlight, moisture and wind). Data on local flora are usually available from local sources, such as universities, colleges, horticultural societies, etc.

Often a municipality requires the development application for a large site to provide a detail inventory of vegetation (especially mature trees), as well as conservation or remedial measures. In general, local species and planting of mixed age are preferred. It is important to think of the site's ecology and future maintenance.

2. Water

(i) Surface Streams and Lakes. Surface streams and lakes (and underground aquifer) supply our fresh water, and receive our runoffs and wastewater (sometimes treated and sometimes not). The amount and quality of water are essential determinants of land use potential.

Streams and lakes also provide for our transportation and recreation. As well, they moderate climatic extremes and provide views and visual relief. They can be damaged by human activities such as dredging, shoreline modification, effluent discharge from point sources (e.g., wastewater treatment plants) and non-point sources (e.g., urban runoff), and eutrophication (through agricultural or septic runoff). But they are also responsible for flooding, soil erosion, and transport and retention of pollutants.

The Canadian federal government produces water quality guidelines for different water uses: drinking, agriculture, recreation and industry. Provincial governments set standards for quality of effluents from wastewater treatment plants. There are no quality standards for urban runoffs. In the U.S., the Environmental Protection Agency (EPA) is in charge of setting effluent standards.

(ii) Floodplains and Wetlands. Floodplain information is essential for the protection of life and property. Most communities have floodplain maps, usually based on a hypothetical one-in-a-hundred-years flood event. They are the basis for insurance coverage as well as zoning control. Floodplain maps usually make a distinction between flood channel (where absolutely no structure is permitted) and flood fringe (where some structures and uses may be allowed). In Canada (Ontario), local conservation authorities carry out floodplain mapping. In the U.S. the Federal Emergency Management Agency publishes flood hazard boundary maps and flood insurance rate maps.

Wetland loss has now been recognized as a major environmental problem. Wetlands provide for ground water recharge, wildlife habitats, urban runoff quality control, as well as recreational and educational opportunities. In most cases, planners have to develop their own local information base.

3. Air (climate)

Land use planning does not deal directly with big climatic issues such as acid rain, ozone depletion, global warming, etc., although the cumulative results of land use decisions may be significant (such as the relationship between suburban sprawl and auto-emission). However, some land use decisions require specific information. For instance, data on wind-direction and speed are needed for the siting of "smoke-stack" industries, sun-path data for passive solar energy use, and rainfall data for runoff and drainage design.

More important to land use planning is microclimate. There are six inter-related factors: temperature, humidity, precipitation, cloudiness, wind speed and direction, and sun path. Together, they affect people's comfort level. In North America, a combination of about 70-80 degrees Fahrenheit (21-27 degrees Celsius), 20%-50% relative humidity, and a wind speed of 50-100 feet (15-30 metres) per minute, would be considered very pleasant. Of course, much depends on the experience, cultural background and degree of activity of the inhabitants. Planners need meteorological information on all these factors.

Equally importantly is the information on topography, vegetation and built form because these affect the microclimate significantly. Topography affects the amount of sunlight and air movement. A south-facing slope will get more sun; air moves faster on a crest than on flat ground; cold air comes down to a valley at night; and afternoon breezes come up the slope from a water body. People generally prefer to live on a south or southeast slope, near water, and on the upper or middle slope. Ground cover can modify the microclimate by altering the surface, increasing the areas of radiation and transpiration, providing shades, acting as air breaks or air traps. Generally, vegetation makes a cooler, more humid and more stable microclimate. Buildings affect air movements (air tunnels, wind shafts, etc), radiation, sunlight, and shades. But the relationship between urban buildings and microclimate is very complex and there are no general rules.

4. Habitats

Habitats (for both plants and animals) provide food and other renewable resources. They are an important component of natural processes such as the water cycle, nitrogen cycle, and carbon cycle. They moderate and mitigate natural hazards, and often have aesthetic and heritage values. On the other hand, they can pose health hazards (poisonous or disease-carrying species etc.) and injury and damages (falling trees, forest fires, etc.).

Land use decisions affect the welfare of "endangered" or "threatened" species. The landscape can be viewed as a mosaic of habitats ("corridors", "patches", or "islands"). Different species require habitats of different minimum sizes and optimal shapes. But habitats usually coincide with streams and wetlands.

Development Attributes

Since land use planning is concerned with the provision of appropriate and adequate land for different users, we need information about the suitability of land for different activities, and the amount, ownership, and development pressure on it. The following is a development-driven land use coding system commonly used by planners. There are nine one-digit categories.

Code	Categories
1	residential
2	manufacturing
3	manufacturing
4	transportation, communication, utilities
5	trade
6	services
7	cultural, entertainment and recreational
8	resource, production and extraction
9	undeveloped land and water areas

Source: Koppelman and DeChiara, 1975: Section 4-5. The categories can be made more detailed by adding on a second, third, or even fourth digit. For instance, 1.1 is household units, 1.2 is group quarters, and 1.3 is residential hotels.

1. Environmentally Sensitive Land

In a market economy, the most vulnerable land is environmentally sensitive land, which is readily lost to development pressure for short-term gains. In order to manage our land resources wisely we need to know the location and size of such land so that we can decide whether or not certain land ought to be protected from development or whether certain kinds of development can occur on the land. Environmentally sensitive land is usually identified for two purposes: enhancement of the environment, and protection of the environment, life and property. Information about recreational capability, plant species, animal habitats, and so on, would indicate the need to enhance an environmentally sensitive area. Information about lake capacity, water supply capacity, septic capacity, and so on, would indicate how much development should be allowed in certain areas. Information on flooding, erosion, subsidence, and so on, would indicate whether or not development should be allowed at all. We also need information on the direct and derived impact of urban development so that we can analyze how a development is taking advantage of, or is being detrimental to, an environmentally sensitive area. Of course, the determination of the appropriate indicators to measure environmental sensitivity is a political as well as a technical matter. However, our society is becoming more "sensitive" as it learns more about the intricate and delicate balance of the ecological systems and the devastating impact of man's recent activities on the natural environment.

2. Vacant Land

A second conventional land use category is vacant land that can be considered for development. There is a development-oriented bias. The assumption is that all vacant land can be considered for development. Therefore, in our inventory of the location and amount of vacant land we must discount areas which are environmentally sensitive. At the least, we should have information about the environmental suitability and effects of development in such areas. Generally, vacant land is classified according to its physiographic features, man-made improvements, accessibility and the existence of utilities.

(i) Geology. Soil type and depth, bearing capacity and suitability as plant medium, the necessity to fill, and the tendency to slide or subside are all important indicators of the developability of any land, as well as the cost of developing the land.

(ii) Topography. Contours, slopes, landform, and so on, are important for the analysis of site formation, drainage problems, slope for buildings, circulation and visibility.

(iii) Climatic conditions. Sun angles and wind direction and force are standard information. However, in most land use decisions, microclimates are just as important. These include warm and cool slopes, local wind direction, local breeze, sound levels, smell and atmospheric quality.

(iv) Water. There are several considerations: (a) surface drainage pattern, that is, the amount to be drained, blockages, and undrained depressions; (b) water table, both for potential water supply as well as potential problems for building underground structures; and, (c) water supply, both the quantity and quality of it.

(v) Man-made structures.

(vi) Circulation and utilities. These include the location, capacity and condition of roads and other modes of transportation, and storm and sanitary sewers. Roads, water supply and sanitary sewers are the three most important variables upon which suitability of development will be decided. It is also important to have information about the intention of various levels of government about these services in the area.

3. Developed Land

Most of the land in a city is developed land with an existing land use pattern. Information about the existing land use is very important in order to determine the compatability of existing and proposed uses. This should be augmented by information about the building fabric, especially age and condition, utilities and the transport network, and community facilities such as schools, shops, health and social centres, entertainment places, and open spaces.

One important analytic use of the above information is the assessment of urban blight. Urban blight can manifest itself by physical indicators of the buildings and the environment, as well as economic indicators. A frequently used technique to appraise urban blight is the American Public Health Association (APHA) score technique, as shown here. It is dated but the concept (the evaluation criteria and the way they are organized) is still very valid. Penalty points are given for buildings and environment which deviate from acceptable standards. This technique is used to assess residential areas. Commercial areas can be appraised according to some economic indicators such as vacancy rates and rental rates, in addition to physical indicators such as the obsolescence and deterioration of the structure, conflicting land uses, overcrowding, street conditions, parking problems, loading problems, and nuisance.

TABLE 4-1
URBAN BLIGHT APPRAISAL (APHA Technique)
A. Dwelling Condition Survey: Standard Penalty Scores

Item	Maximum Penalty Score
Facilities	
Structure:	
1. Main access	6
2. Water supply (source)*	25
3. Sewer connection *	25
4. Daylight obstruction	20
5. Stairs and fire escapes	30
6. Public hall lighting	18
Unit:	
7. Location in structure	8
8. Kitchen facilities	24
9. Toilet (location, type, sharing) *	45
10. Bath (location, type, sharing) *	20
11. Water supply (location and type) *	15
12. Washing facilities	8
13. Dual egress *	30
14. Electric lighting *	15
15. Central heating	3
16. Rooms lacking installed heat *	20
17. Rooms lacking window *	30
18. Rooms lacking closet	8
19. Rooms of substandard area	10
20. Combined room facilities (Items 16-19) For analytic purpose only. No separate score.	

TABLE 4-1

Maintenance

21. Toilet condition index	12
22. Deterioration index (structure, unit) *	50
23. Infestation index (structure, unit)	15
24. Sanitary index (structure, unit)	30
25. Basement condition index	13

Occupancy

26. Room crowding: persons per room *	30
27. Room crowding: persons per sleeping room *	25
28. Area crowding: sleeping area per person *	30
29. Area crowding: nonsleeping area per person	25
30. Doubling of basic families	10

NOTES:

1. Facilities Score 360; Maintance Score 120; Occupancy Score 120; Maximum Total Score 600

2. * = Condition constituting a basic deficiency.

3. Scheme is now dated. With improvement of general housing conditions, some of the items do not apply any more. But the approach is still useful

Source: Adapted from American Public Health Association (1946)

TABLE 4-1
URBAN BLIGHT APPRAISAL (APHA Technique)
B. Environmental Survey: Standard Penalty Scores

Item	Maximum Penalty
a) Land crowding	
1. Coverage by structures - 70% or more of block area covered.	24
2 Residential building density - ratio of residential floor area to total = 4 or more.	20
3. Population density - gross residential floor area per person 150 sq. ft. or less.	10
4. Residential yard areas - less than 20 ft. wide and 625 sq. ft. in 70% of residences.	16
b) Nonresidential land areas	
5. Areal incidence of nonresidential land use - 50% or more nonresidential	13
6. Linear incidence of nonresidential land use -- 50% or more nonresidential.	13
7. Specific nonresidential nuisances and hazards - noise and vibration, objectionable odours, fire or explosion, vermin, rodents, insects, smoke or dust, night glare, dilapidated structure, insanitary lot.	30
8. Hazards to morals and the public peace - pool-rooms, gambling places, bars, prostitution, liquor stores, nightclubs.	10
9. Smoke incidence - industries, docks, railroad yards, soft-coal use.	6
c) Hazards and nuisances from transportation system	
10. Street traffic - type of traffic, dwelling set-back, width of streets.	20
11. Railroads or switchyards - amount of noise, vibration, smoke, trains.	24
Airports or airlines - location of dwelling with respect to Runways and approaches.	20
d) Hazards and nuisances from natural causes	
13. Surface flooding - rivers, streams, tide, groundwater, drainage annual or more.	20
14. Swamps or marches - within 1000 yd., malarial mosquitoes	24
15. Topography - pits, rock outcrops, steep slopes, slides.	16

TABLE 4-1

e) Inadequate utilities and sanitation

16.	Sanitary sewerage system - available (within 300 ft.), adequate.	24
17.	Public water supply - available, adequate pressure and quantity.	20
18.	Streets and walks - grade, pavement, curbs, grass, sidewalks.	10

f) Inadequate basic community facilities

19.	Elementary public schools - beyond 2/3 mile, 3 or more dangerous crossings.	10
20.	Public playgrounds - less than 0.75 acres/1000 persons.	8
21	Public playfields - less than 1.25 acres/1000 persons.	4
22.	Other public parks - less than 1.00 acre/1000 persons.	8
23.	Public transportation - beyond 2/3 mile, less than 2 buses/hr.	12
24.	Food stores - dairy, vegetable, meat, grocery, bread, More than 1/3 mile.	6

NOTE: Maximum total score is 368.

Source: Adapted from American Public Health Association (1950).

TABLE 4-1

URBAN BLIGHT APPRAISAL (APHA Technique)

C. Combined Dwelling and Environmental Quality Score

	A	B	C	D	E
	Good	Acceptable	Borderline	Substandard	Unfit
Dwelling Score	0-29	30-59	60-89	90-119	>120
Environmental Score	0-19	20-39	40-59	60-79	>80
Sum of Dwelling and Environmental Scores	0-49	50-99	100-149	150-199	>200

Source: Adapted from American Public Health Association (1950).

4. Brownfields

The concept of brownfields emerged in the United States in the 1980s in initiatives such as the Chicago Brownfields Forum. At that time a lot of manufacturing plants had already moved out of the urban core, leaving the sites they once occupied blighted, stigmatized, or even hazardous. Brownfield redevelopment is seen as a way to revitalize the city core. But before this can happen, there are a number of barriers to overcome. In the United States, brownfields are most commonly found in cities in the Northeast and Upper Midwest. The Urban Land Institute (ULI) esti-mated in 1995 that 132,000 to 176,000 acres could be classified as brownfield sites in the United States (Wright, 1997).

The U.S. EPA defines brownfields as "abandoned, idled, or under-used industrial and commercial facilities where expansion or redevelopment is complicated by real or perceived environmental contamination". They are usually located in established urban areas and along transportation corridors, where existing municipal services are readily available. They may include, but are not limited to, decommissioned refineries, railway yards, dilapidated warehouses, abandoned gas stations, former dry cleaners, and other commercial properties where toxic substances may have been stored or used (National Round Table on the Environment and the Economy, 1997).

The U.S. EPA specifies the following land-use information as the basis for decision on clean-up remedy (Bartsch and Collation, 1997).

- Current land use
- Zoning laws
- Zoning maps
- Comprehensive community master plans
- Population growth patterns and projections
- Accessibility of site to existing infrastructure
- Institutional controls currently in place
- Site location in relation to urban, residential, commercial, industrial, agricultural, and recreation areas
- Federal/state land-use designation (e.g. Department of Defence facilities)
- Historical or recent development patterns
- Cultural factors
- Natural resources information
- Potential vulnerability of groundwater to contaminants that might migrate from soil
- Environmental justice issues
- Location of on-site or nearby wetlands
- Proximity of site to a floodplain
- Proximity of site to critical habitats of endangered or threatened species
- Geographic and geologic formation
- Location of wellhead protection areas, recharge areas, and other areas identified in a state's comprehensive groundwater protection pro-gramme.

5. Other Development Attributes

Some general development-oriented data include location information (street address, tax assessment reference, property registration number, census reference, political jurisdiction, etc.), intensity information (ratio between the number of people or dwelling units and land area, ratio between the amount of total floor space and land area, etc.), structural information (health and safety conditions, maintenance and repair needs, etc.), aesthetic information (architectural and heritage designations, urban design quality indicators, etc.), and time-line information (urban development programmes, capital improvement programmes, etc.). The following deserve special attention.

(i) Land ownership has been identified by some researchers as the prime determinant of land development patterns. The identity of the owners, the shapes and sizes of the land, the suitability of the land for various kinds of development, and the kind of land assembly action within an area are all important data. Ownership can be public or private and it can range from fee simple to leasehold and from private covenant to cooperative ownership, each of which represents a different level of control over the use and development of the land. The source of data often is confidential. Information may be obtained from land registry or property tax assessment records. The research can be very time consuming because these records show one address at a time. There is also the problem of owner identities hidden behind numbered companies, and it is very difficult to obtain a clear picture of the overall ownership pattern. Planners often have to rely on local estate agents or real estate boards for information.

(ii) Data on land values are used to analyze development trends and are a particularly important input to public decisions about the purchase and assembly of land for various public purposes, such as open space and low-cost housing. The whole subject of land values is very complex, especially when the data are needed to make future projections. Nevertheless, real estate boards often publish area-wide averages of sales. Land in urban areas is computed on the basis of square footages or on a frontage basis adjusted for lot depth, corner influence, and so on. In the fringe areas land values are computed on the acreage basis. It should be noted that transaction prices are not necessarily reflective of the market values of the land involved, and they often do not distinguish between the value of the land and the value of the buildings on the land. Assessment records can be used but, again, they list one property at a time and it is very difficult to use them for area-wide planning purposes. To generate any reliable information on land values is a very arduous undertaking.

(iii) Cityscape has not been receiving proper attention in spite of the fact that it is what many ordinary people consider to be an essential function of city planning. This is partly due to the persistent myth that visual perceptions are subjective and therefore entirely arbitrary, although it is interesting to note that equally subjective "satisfaction" measures of various kinds are given much weight in planning. More importantly, perhaps, is that visual studies are not a strong suit in the "social science" approach to planning. Although there are many studies of environmental images, especially by geographers, these tend to relate to large areas such as a whole country or a region or to fundamental cognitive constructs which are not directly useful for urban land use decisions. Kevin Lynch's (1960) "imageability" scheme is perhaps the most useful tool for analyzing visual perceptions at an urban scale. He argues that people organize the urban landscape into five elements: path, edge, node, district, and landmark (PENDL). This visual typology can be combined with Bacon's idea (1974) of "movement systems" to produce reliable data on "collective" perceptions. Bacon argues that the significance of a view is measured by the number of people who see it and the intensity of feeling that people have towards it. This, he suggests, depends on the movement systems in the city — the routes and modes of travel used by different groups of commuters and pedestrians. I found this combined approach very useful in a study of the collective perceptions between tourists and residents about the central area of a small tourist town (Leung, 1987b).

TRANSPORTATION INFORMATION

Although transportation planning is a very specialized discipline, a land use planner must deal with the movement systems in a city. These include not only land-based transports such as pedestrians, bicycles, automobiles, taxis, buses, rail and trucks but also waterborne movements and, in some case, air movements such as heliports. We need information about the volume of use, the routes and the capacity of the systems. This book deals with vehicular, bicycle and pedestrian traffic as well as public transit.

Vehicular Traffic

The road system deserves particular attention because that is what planners work with most of the time. Roads are classified according to their primary functions, amount of daily traffic, design speed, average traffic speed, vehicle types served, and connections to other roads. Classifications by the American Association of State Highway and Transportation Officials (AASHTO) and the Transportation Association of Canada (TAC) are very similar. (Speeds in brackets are Canadian standards.)

LOCAL ROADS

The primary function is access to land. Movement of traffic is a secondary consideration. They usually handle fewer than 3,000 vehicles daily. Design speeds are between 20-30 mph (30-50 km/h), with average running speeds of between 12-25 mph (approximately 20-40 km/h).

URBAN COLLECTORS

They are designed to maximize both traffic movement and land access. Traffic volumes range anywhere from 1,000 to 12,000 vehicles per day. Design speeds are between 30-50 mph (50-80 km/h), with average speeds of between 20-45 mph (30-70 km/h). They carry all types of vehicles and connect local roads to arterial roads. As a rule, developers avoid building collector roads because they do not add saleable road frontages to building lots.

URBAN ARTERIALS

Their primary function is traffic movement, with land access a secondary concern. They are designed to handle daily traffic volumes ranging between 5,000 to 20,000 vehicles, at design speeds of between 40-55 mph (60-90 km/h). Average speeds range between 25-45 mph (40-70 km/h). They carry all types of vehicles, although as many as 20% are trucks. They connect with urban collectors, freeways and other arterial roads.

URBAN FREEWAYS (EXPRESSWAYS)

Their function is optimum mobility. Therefore, they provide no land access. Traffic volumes generally exceed 20,000 vehicles per day, with design speed of between 50-75 mph (80-120 km/h). Average running speeds range between 45-60 mph (70-100 km/h). They are designed to support all vehicles types, including truck traffic of up to 20% of daily volume. They connect to other freeways and urban arterials.

Rural roads are similarly classified. In the U.S. Low Volume Roads have an average daily traffic volume of fewer than 200 vehicles. They may include special purpose roads such as isolated rural roads and recreational roads. In Canada, Resource Development Roads are used in forestry, mining and energy development. They are typically designed for heavy truck use only.

Three kinds of data should be collected: traffic, land use, and system capacity.

1. Traffic. Traffic information is usually obtained through vehicle counts at specific times. Data include the proportion between through and local traffic and the kind of vehicles (e.g., private cars and trucks). Congestion or bottlenecks and the negative effects of delays and difficulty in crossing should be noted. Data on accidents, dangerous junctions and points of conflicts are also important. In such matters, special attention should be paid to sensitive areas such as the vicinity of shopping malls or schools.

2. Land Use. Different land uses generate different types and volume of traffic. The Institute of Transportation Engineers (U.S.) publishes Trip Generation which gives information on trips generated by different land uses. The data are based on vehicular traffic counts entering and leaving a site. As such, these are about vehicle trips and not person trips. Sample sizes are usually small, and daily and seasonal variation are not normally included. Table 4-2 is a listing of the trip generation figures for more common land use types.

Also, certain land use types are particularly sensitive to the impact of traffic, or require exceptional parking space. For example, residential areas are sensitive to noise, dirt and fume pollution, visual intrusion and vibration, and danger of vehicular traffic to small children. Many existing shopping streets are, for historic reasons, also major thoroughfares, thus creating conflicts between different road users: vehicles making deliveries to shops, car-owning shoppers arriving or leaving the place, the pedestrian shoppers and shoppers who use public transit, and through traffic and traffic generated by other local uses such as residential.

TABLE 4-2

TRIP GENERATION BY LAND USE TYPES

Land Use Type	Average/day	Peak/hr
General light industry (<500 employees)	6.97/1000 sq. ft. GFA	1.08/1000 sq.ft. GFA
Heavy industry	1.50/1000 sq. ft. GFA	-
Industrial park	6.97/1000 sq. ft. GFA	0.86 sq.ft. GFA
Single-family detached	9.55/unit	1.01/unit
Townhouse	5.86/unit	0.54/unit
Low-rise apartment (1-2 storeys)	6.59/unit	0.62/unit
High-rise apartment (>10 storeys)	4.20/unit	0.40/unit
Hotel	8.70/occupied room	0.76/occupied room
Motel	10.19/occupied room	0.76/occupied room
Elementary school	1.09/student	0.28/student
High school	1.38/student	0.30/student
Daycare	79.26/1000 sq.ft. GFA	16.28/1000 sq.ft. GFA
Hospital	16.78/1000 sq.ft. GFA	1.42/1000 sq.ft. GFA
Office building *10,000 to 800,000 sq. ft.	24.60-8.46/1000 sq.ft. GLA	3.40-1.08/1000 sq.ft. GLA
Business park	14.37/1000 sq.ft. GLA	1.62/1000 sq.ft.GLA
Shopping centre * 10,000 sq. ft. to 1,600,000 sq. ft. (Saturday)	215.39-32.61/1000 sq.ft. GLA	20.63-3.24/1000 sq.ft. GLA
Supermarket (Saturday)	177.59/1000 sq.ft. GFA	15.33/1000 sq.ft. GFA
24-hr. convenience store (Saturday)	863.10/1000 sq.ft. GFA	64.05/1000 sq.ft. GFA

GFA = Gross Floor Area

GLA = Gross Leaseable Area

* The smaller the gross leaseable area, the more the trips.

Source: Adapted from the Institute of Transportation Engineers (1991).

3. Capacity. Road capacity is the maximum number of vehicles that can be expected to travel over a given section of roadway (or laneway). It is determined by two conditions. Prevailing roadway conditions include vertical and horizontal alignments, lane width, number of lanes, road surface, and type and number of intersections. Prevailing traffic conditions include traffic type, speed, volume, direction, control and driver skills; turning movements; bus lines and bus stops; and conflicting pedestrian and bicycle movements. The effects of these conditions determine the "service level". The most significant impact on service level comes from traffic interruption at at-grade intersections.

Service levels are typically represented by average operating speed. In the U.S., Level A is the highest and Level F the lowest (Transportation Research Board, 1985). Applied to freeways, Level A service means "free flow, limited only by alignment and speed limit; minimal delay." Level F service means "forced flow or breakdown of operation; stop and go waves; back-ups through up-stream intersections; long delays through two or more cycles of traffic signals." Typical design goal is Level C service: "Stable flow but freedom to select speed affected; maneuvering requires vigilance; comfort and convenience decline; vehicular conflict at many intersections."

For safety and environmental reasons, restrictions (e.g., traffic lights, "no parking", "one-way", and "no entry") are sometimes imposed on traffic that tries to avoid congested main roads by cutting through narrow residential streets. This reduces the capacity of the road system. The relationships between roads and buildings should also be noted, including parking on and off the streets, vehicular access to service areas, pedestrian traffic generated by the buildings, and so on.

Transit The debate between public transit and the private automobile has been the dominant issue in urban transportation since the 1950s. Automobile advocates had the upper hand in the 1950s, when highway programmes were popular. Substantial dissent began to appear in the 1960s, with opposition to freeway construction within cities, which brought wholesale urban clearance. This aroused grass-root protests all over North America. Transit did well in the 1970s as governments put money into it while highway construction virtually stopped. Since the 1980s, with the energy crisis only a faded memory and a new "crises" in aging infrastructure, highway building has made a comeback. At the same time, transit ridership has remained stagnant. The emergence of New Urbanism, and Transit-Oriented Development in particular, has refocused planners' interest in transit. (Refer to the section on New Urbanism in the Synthesis chapter.) The following are several sets of standard user information for transit planning: characteristics of travel, characteristics of riders, and attitudes of travelers.

1. Characteristics of Travel

(i) Purpose of the Trip. Most transit trips are trips to work and school. Other trip purposes (shopping, personal business, and social/recreation) are less amenable to transit use. For instance, shopping trips are dispersed and often involve carrying packages home, therefore, transit use is inconvenient. However, this may change with improved transit design.

(ii) Time of Day. Transit use tends to be concentrated at peak periods of the work day, while automobile use is heavier during midday and evening hours. During these peak periods highways are more congested for automobile use, while transit runs are more frequent. Improve scheduling and services during other periods of the day may encourage more transit use beyond peak periods.

(iii) Time of Week. Transit use is usually lower on weekends. Most transit systems have fewer runs. The same period has heavier automobile use. Again, this is very much influenced by transit scheduling and level of service.

(iv) Time of Year. Transit use tends to be heaviest in winter, especially when the weather is bad. In the summer, people take vacations and schools are closed.

(v) Location and Direction. Transit trips are heaviest to and from the CBD. This is because most of the jobs are there, parking is difficult and expensive, and highways in and out of it are usually the most congested.

(vi) Trip Length, Speed, and Time . Rail trips are usually the longest; subway trips next; and bus trips the shortest. Work trips are also longer than trips for other purposes. Trips to the CBD are usually longer than trips to other locations. Suburban trains are the fastest, often comparable to driving on an expressway; subways are the second fastest; and buses the slowest. With respect to time, though, railroad trips are the longest because they tend to cover the longest distances. But all transit modes tend to take more time than automobile trips.

2. Characteristics of Riders

(i) Income. Transit use is usually inversely related to income. An exception is suburban railroad riders, who tend to have higher incomes.

(ii) Automobile Ownership. Transit riders are less likely to own a car. There are two exceptions: suburban railroad riders who normally own cars and drive to the station; and wealthy people living in exclusive inner-city enclaves, who own cars but find transit use convenient. Automobile ownership is highly correlated with income. But for people with similar incomes, those who use transit tend to have no cars; and for people with cars, those who use transit tend to have lower incomes.

(iii) Race and Ethnicity. Minorities are more like to use transit. But there are interesting differences. According to Black (1995:291), African-Americans are more likely to ride the bus, and Hispanics are more likely to ride the subway, reflecting perhaps the transit services available in the cities where they are concentrated.

(iv) Gender. More than half of subway and bus riders are women, and less than half in commuter rail. But women also represent more than half of automobile users. The proportion of women riders are lower in peak periods and higher in off-peak periods, reflecting perhaps traditional gender roles.

(v) Age. The elderly used to ride transits more, but this is no longer the case.

(vi) Occupation. Despite the working-class image, white-collar workers use transit more than blue-collar workers. Clerical and sales workers make up the largest group, reflecting the fact that these jobs are concentrated in the CBD. Many blue-collar workers do not use transit because the factories are now located in the suburbs with poor transit service.

3. Attitudes of Travellers (Wachs, 1976)

(i) Time is important. But the value of time is very complex. The time from origin to destination is not as dominant a factor as assumed in transportation planning.

(ii) Reliability is very important, especially commuters. Because of that, they often leave earlier, thus lengthening their total journey time.

(iii) Out-of-vehicle time is subjective and is often considered more important than in-vehicle time. This includes time spent in walking, waiting, and transferring. Walking time is particular significant.

(iv) Out-of-pocket costs are important, but hidden costs are not. This makes transit use unattractive, because most of its cost is the fare, which is very visible. Automobile costs are often hidden (e.g., depreciation, insurance, and maintenance), with the exception perhaps of parking and toll charges.

(v) Getting a seat on the vehicle and air-conditioning in hot and humid weather are the two most important comfort factors. Other luxuries do not attract more ridership.

(vi) Security from accident and crime is taken for granted. Therefore, bad publicity has very dramatic influence.

(vii) Attitudes are quite similar across socioeconomic classes, except richer people have greater emphasis on time-savings while poorer people put greater emphasis on cost-savings. Of course, information is also required for special-needs groups, such as the poor, the elderly and disabled, and women, especially with respect to accessibility and safety issues. (Refer also to the section on Feminist Perspective in the Synthesis chapter.)

Pedestrian and Bicycle Traffic

Pedestrian and bicycle traffic is also an important land-use planning consideration. The following are some basic data.

1. Pedestrian Traffic

(i) Speeds. Walking speeds vary. Average adult speed is three miles or 4.8 km. per hour (260 feet per minute), elderly speed is about 215 feet per minute. But when people are bunched together their walking speed is reduced considerably, as in the case of sidewalk areas at street intersection. Speed also varies according to purpose: catching a bus, window-shopping, returning home from work, strolling with someone, etc.

(ii) Sidewalk Capacity. The capacity of sidewalk is essentially a function of its width and level of service. Along a crowded sidewalk people tend to keep to the right, forming 21/2-foot (0.75 m) channels in each direction. This also allows people to overtake each other. A recommended "lane" width is three feet. Recreational and scenic walks should be wider in order to enhance the walking experience. The level of service relates to pedestrian comfort and freedom from interruption. At an optimal walking speed of three miles per hour, with a clear forward space of 15 feet (4.5 m) per person to allow for a clear view of the ground ahead for comfortable walking, a "lane" has the capacity of 1,000 pedestrians per hour. In a square or other open space, ten square feet per person is optimal, and less than five square feet per person is unacceptable.

(iii) Walking Distance. Walking distance is not static. It is influenced by separation from cars, improved transit, weather protection, shortcuts, attractive shop windows, planting, street furniture, visual stimulation, etc. In North America, the norm is that about 75% of the people will walk 500 feet (150 m), 40% will walk 1000 feet (300 m), and only 10% will walk half a mile (about 2500 ft., 800 m, or 10 minutes) (Untermann, 1984:25). The U.S. Bureau of Public Roads uses 800 feet, (approx. 250 m) as an average commuter walking distance from car to work.

2. Bicycle Traffic

(i) Road Terms (Velo, 1992:14-15). * A bikeway is a right-of-way, with appropriate signage, intended to be used by bicycle traffic only, or to be shared by bicycles and other modes of transportation. A bikeway network is a group of linked bikeways in a given region or municipality. * A bicycle path is a path reserved for bicycle traffic only, independent of other traffic lanes or set apart from them by a physical barrier. * A bicycle lane is a portion of the roadway, usually situated at the side of the traveled way, reserved for cyclists only, and delineated by pavement markings or by a continuous physical barrier. * A bicycle-pedestrian lane is a portion of the roadway reserved for cyclists and pedestrians only. * A bicycle trail is often a wilderness trail, usually accessible by all-terrain bicycles. * A bicycle route is a route suitable for bicycle travel, linking two or more locations. This type of layout is primarily intended to offer maximum cycling safety and features the necessary facilities. The route may be marked by road signs, and a map may be available. A bicycle facility is any installation which facilitates bicycle travel: bikeways, parking areas, signage and related facilities (e.g., lighting, service areas, and rest areas).

(ii) Speeds and Road Dimensions. To ride comfortably and avoid fixed objects (sidewalk, borders, shrubs, potholes, etc.), a moving cyclist needs a corridor of at least five feet (1.5 m) wide. A space of ten feet is needed for two cyclists to pass each other. In an open area (e.g., without automobile parking on the side), cyclists require somewhat less space. However, if the corridor is next to moving motor traffic then there is a risk factor of the cyclist's balance being affected by the air displacement caused by heavy vehicles. This gets worse when strong winds are present. On flat terrain and in windless conditions, a cruising speed of between 12 and 20 mph (approximately 20 and 30 km/hr) is the norm. In descents, with a tailwind, the cruising speed can reach 30 mph (approximately 50 km/hr). A speed of 20 mph (approximately 30 km/hr) is normally assumed when designing grades, super-elevations, curves, and stopping sight distances. Older bikes (with fewer gears) still gives the rider difficulty to climb a sustained grade (i.e., more than 165 ft. or 50 m) of 10% or greater. But the newer all-terrain or touring bikes can easily climb a 15% grade.

(iii) Cyclist characteristics (Fegan, 1992). The following are based on the 1990, U.S. Census, the Nationwide Personal Transportation Survey (NPTS). More than three-quarters of cyclists are under 30 years of age, with the largest cohort between 20-29. Male to female ratio is 3 to 1. Families with older children (age 16 and older) make significantly more trips than other types of families. Most of the bicycle trips take place in central city areas. But cycling only accounts for 0.3% of home-to-work trips. While walking trips occur most frequently in urbanized areas of over one million people, bicycle trips occur most frequently in areas with less than one million people. A Toronto study (Mars and Kyriakides, 1986:13) shows that while the percentage of cyclists in the inner city and the metropolitan area are quite comparable (about 20% of the total population), a much higher proportion of inner-city cyclists ride to work, school and shop (41% compared to 29% for the metropolitan area).

INFRASTRUCTURE INFORMATION

Information on infrastructure is very important, especially that about water supply and trunk sewers, because these are very expensive investments and they determine whether new development should occur in a particular area. These systems have threshold capacities beyond which their performance will deteriorate rapidly or the systems will simply break down. It is, therefore, exceedingly important to coordinate the demand generated by the land users with the provision of infrastructure. For this, we need information on the location, type, quality, use and capacity of water supply and treatment facilities, and sewage treatment facilities. Other utilities such as power and gas are less crucial, but their provision may be important enough to determine whether development will occur or not. The following are some basic information needs for water supply, wastewater management, and storm water management.

Water Supply

Most municipal water supply does not make the distinction between potable (for drinking) and non-potable water (for agricultural and industrial use). A potable water supply system consists of acquisition, treatment and delivery. Water sources can be surface water or underground aquifer. (About two million of Canada's urban population rely exclusively on groundwater.) The treatment plant purifies the water through physical (e.g., filtration and sedimentation) and chemical means (e.g., chlorinating and fluoridation). It is then pumped to storage (underground or elevated reservoirs or tanks which help to level out peak and normal demands, and maintain a constant pressure or "head"). Water can be delivered through either a branch or loop system of pipes. The loop system provides constant pressure in the pipes and allows for continuous circulation of the water, but is more expensive.

The planning challenge is to match the demand on the supply system to its capacity. Different land uses generate different demands (especially peak demands). These affect withdrawal from the source, treatment plant size, storage and pumping needs, and distribution pipe sizes and locations. Therefore, we need accurate information on the supply system's yield (how much can be safely withdrawn from the source), storage capacity, location of mains, and service area boundaries. We also need information on current and projected demands, consumer preference, and policies and regulations regarding water quality.

Wastewater

The municipal sanitary sewage system consists of two components: collection and treatment. In Canada, in 1994, about 75% of the population was serviced by municipal systems.

Municipal sewage (domestic and industrial) is collected through a network of underground pipes, which is laid out to facilitate gravity flows as much as possible (pumping is expensive, and power and mechanical failures can cause severe problems). The amount of sewage produced is normally related to the amount of water supplied. A typical design norm is 115 gal. (520 litres) per day per person for domestic wastewater. This norm is going down as the general population becomes more environmentally conscientious and as more water-savings plumbing fixtures are used. Commercial and industrial wastewater volumes vary widely.

At the treatment plant solid and organic materials are removed. Primary treatment uses physical means (screening, sedimentation, etc.), secondary treatment uses biological means (bacterial action to digest the waste), and tertiary treatment uses bio-chemical means to remove phosphorus, nitrogen, etc. The effluent is discharged into a water body, injected into a deep aquifer, or reuse for irrigation or non-drinking purposes. Solid residue (sludge) from the treatment is sent to landfills or used as agricultural soil conditioner. In Canada, in 1994, for the population that was serviced by municipal systems, 39% received only primary treatment, 31% secondary, and 39% tertiary. The rest was served by systems that were not connected to treatment facilities, but discharged untreated into receiving water bodies.

The land use planning challenge is to match demand to collection and treatment capacity. Different land uses generate different demands on the system (especially peak hour demand). These have significant implication on pipe sizes and treatment capacity. In particular, because the system is essentially gravity-fed, and because it uses the same trenches as other underground infrastructure, there is very little flexibility once a system has been put in place. Therefore, we need information on location, size, age (as a measure of conditions) of the collection and treatment components; current demand and remaining capacity; characteristics of the waste stream; and policy and regulations regarding effluent and sludge disposal.

Storm Water   When rain falls and snow melts the water is held temporarily on the ground, then some finds its way into underground aquifers, some is absorbed by plants or ingested by animals, some evaporates, and the rest runs off toward receiving waters such as streams, lakes or the sea. Urban development increases the amount of impervious surfaces (roofs, paved roads and parking lots, etc.). This reduces the seepage into the ground and increases the volume and speed of the runoff, causing floods and soil erosion, as well as degrading the quality of the receiving waters. The last is particularly worrisome because urban runoffs can be highly polluted (especially at spring thaw or first storm) and is a non-point source of pollution - generated everywhere and enters into the receiving waters anywhere, dictated only by gravity.

A storm water system consists of surfaces and channels. Surface water drains towards a point where it is collected by a surface channel or underground conduit. The network of surface channels and underground conduits eventually drains into the receiving water. Along the way, ponds may be constructed to hold the water temporary or permanently. In some older cities or city parts, urban runoff shares the same underground conduits as the wastewater (combined sewers) and ends up at the wastewater treatment plant, creating severe stress on the treatment capacity. In fact, during wet seasons the combined storm water and wastewater is often diverted away from the treatment plant and discharged directly into the receiving waters, untreated.

The quality of urban runoff has become a major public health and environmental health concern in recent years. The composition of the runoff may include organic matters, nitrogen, phosphorus, chlorides, metals, suspended solids, oil and grease, dust, bacteria, etc., which come from traffic emission, industrial spills, household wastes, faulty septic systems, litters, street dirt, road deterioration, road deicers, etc. Poor quality runoff can contaminate the water supply, pollute recreational areas, increase sedimentation of rivers and lakes, and degrade aquatic habitats. In Ontario, urban runoffs are regularly sampled for a variety of substances and materials that may settle to form objectionable deposits;

float as debris, scum or oil; produce adverse physiological or behavioural responses in human, animals or plants; produce objectional colour, odour, taste or turbidity; and enhance undesirable aquatic life or nuisance species.

The planning challenge is to make land use decisions that minimize the disruption of natural seepage, minimize the production of pollution, and maximize the natural features that can detain or retain runoffs. Therefore, we need information for a watershed or catchment basin. It should include all conditions that affect runoff (soil, slope, ground cover, rainfall records, and land uses), flood record, types and levels of pollutants and their sources, and the natural systems that can be used to regulate the quantity and quality of runoffs.

GUIDANCE SYSTEMS

Land use planning is about matching users with land in order to produce an equitable and efficient land use pattern. Much of that match is handled through the marketplace, constrained or assisted by public regulations as well as public investment decisions. In fact, a plan adopted by a local government can be considered as a "local constitution" on land use, which has to be implemented through some regulatory, administrative, fiscal and financial devices. Chapters 7 and 8 of this book deal specifically with both the control-oriented and action-oriented measures used to implement the land use plan. We will, therefore, only mention briefly the general information needs about these guidance systems of planning.

Regulations can be in the form of maps (schedules) and texts. Information is needed about where and how regulations apply, as stipulated by law and in actual practice. The distinction is important because there can be great discrepancies between the law and the administration of the law. For example, illegal conversion of existing residences into multiple-unit apartments is tolerated because there is great housing shortage or because there is not enough manpower to police and enforce the law. Some part of the public guidance system may depend on voluntary compliance or may be advisory only. Typical regulations include development control measures (e.g., zoning by-laws, subdivision control); building construction, operation and maintenance codes; fire, sanitary and other safety codes; and environmental and development guidelines. Operation policies of different public service providers can affect land use, especially those about fire, police, health, library, water supply, and sewage and waste disposal. Public investment policies are also important, especially those on the overlay technique to organize land use information urban renewal, conservation, housing, transportation, and environmental protection. Of special significance to land use planning is the local government's investment and fiscal intentions, such as the level of public involvement and investment to be directed to a particular area, the expected increase in tax revenues, and the balance between public revenue and costs with respect to new private developments. Finally, information is needed on policies originating from higher levels of government, such as those on industrial location, office development, housing, and transportation.

Most of the matching between users and land is done through the marketplace. It is important to know how the market functions in the planning area. Quantitative and qualitative information is needed on the nature and scale of the development and redevelopment activities; the spatial and temporal trends; and the characteristics of, and the relations between, the actors involved in the market place.

MAPS AND GEOGRAPHIC INFORMATION SYSTEMS

Maps   Maps are needed to collect, record and analyze data. Usually, a planning office has a variety of engineering, topographic and property maps. Much of mapping data comes from aerial photographs. They are used to produce line-drawn cartographic base maps which show boundaries of towns and cities, rivers, railroads and highways, and land uses and structure, as well as photographic-image orthophoto base maps which show the actual images of the ground features. From these base maps topographic maps can be developed by adding contour lines and spot elevations. Map scales vary from 1 inch = 100 feet to 1 inch = 1mile (1:1,000 to 1:10,000 in Canada). Engineering maps that are used for site planning purposes have scales that vary from 1 inch = 50 feet to 1 inch = 100 feet (1:500 to 1:1,000 in Canada).

Cadastral maps show land parcels by ownership. In addition to the usual boundaries of government jurisdictions, roads, rivers and other features that help locate land parcels, each piece of land also has a parcel identification number (PIN) and is described by the owner's name, parcel boundaries and size (as computed from the boundaries, as registered in the deed, and as assessed for tax purposes). There are other kinds of maps, such as insurance, highway, census, historical, assessment, and real estate sales maps. In particular, some commercial maps produced by insurance companies can be very useful because they show the uses and layout of both the ground floor and the upper floors of the buildings.

General and specific planning maps may be produced from the above base maps, and may be used for land use surveys, subdivision reviews, zoning reviews and site planning purposes. Depending on the use, such maps may include streets and names of streets, planning area boundaries, railroads, major public buildings, lakes and rivers, and so on. These maps can be wall-size, table-size and letter-size. The very basic ones show roads and streets, railroads, waterways and area boundaries. The more detailed maps have property and easement lines, and the still more detailed ones include structures as well.

Figure 4-8: Land Use Field Survey

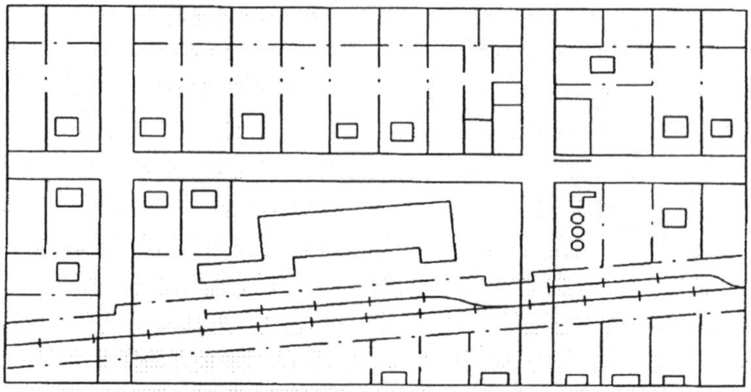

Typical Field Survey Base Map (part only)

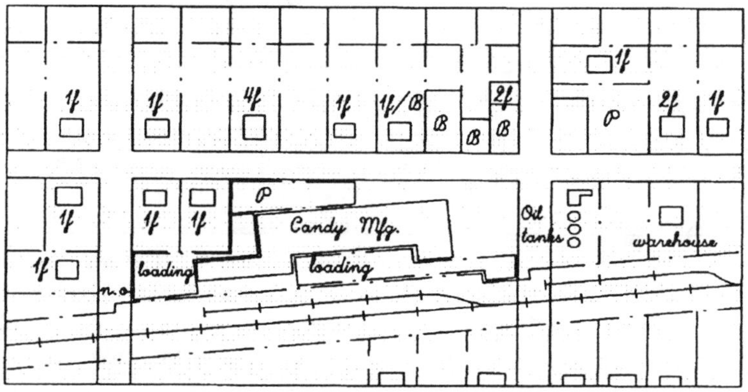

Typical Field Survey Notations

Legend:
1f = One Family
2f = Two Families
B = Business
P = Parking
N.O. = Not Open

Source: Adapted from Chapin and Kaiser (1979: 255)

Sometimes a survey is needed to obtain specific information. A survey is always demand-driven: to identify sites for development, to locate problem areas such as urban blight, or to evaluate the adequacy of certain facilities and services. It is, therefore, very important to have clear purposes so that the right kind of maps can be used. The most important consideration in devising standard maps for surveys is the appropriateness of the scale, coverage, and notations, and whether the maps are being regularly kept up-to-date. Once a base map is chosen, a manual of standard field procedures has to be developed to ensure that all field workers will follow the same procedure and record the same information. Before the survey actually takes place, the survey instruments should be pre-tested to ensure that they will produce the information needed.

Figure 4-9: The Overlay Technique to Organize Land Use Information

Map 1: Agricultural Land Capacity

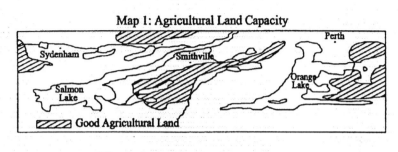

Map 2: Area under Development Pressure

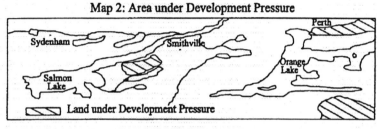

Map 3: Township Jurisdictions

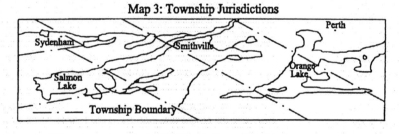

Map 4: (Overlay of Maps 1, 2 and 3)
Agricultural Land under Development Pressure in Different Townships

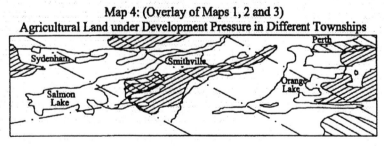

In the actual survey we can use either one of the following field recording techniques. Information can be written down directly on the base map. This map-notation system is the simplest technique, and is suitable for small cities. Alternatively, a field-listing technique can be used, where the field worker records the relevant information against an address or a location, and the information is later coded for machine manipulation. This technique is more complicated but more information can be recorded, and is suitable for larger cities. In central areas where a lot of information has to be recorded, especially when the different floors of the buildings have different uses or characteristics, the survey should be done on foot. In fringe areas where only the basic land use information is needed, a windshield (car) survey is probably sufficient.

The field information gathered can be organized in a number of ways. Point locations can be used to indicate where the information applies, particularly in the case of environmental surveys. Regular grids (usually rectangular) can also be used. The problem with points and grids is that they do not really relate to the boundaries of any sociopolitical divisions or to the natural boundaries of an environmental phenomenon. A third way is to use irregular polygons which coincide with sociopolitical divisions, functional boundaries, or environmental phenomenon, but data organized in this way are not easy to manipulate analytically.

The overlay technique is most often used to process land data (McHarg, 1969). The central question in land analysis is the suitability of particular pieces of land for different uses. "Single-indicator" maps can be produced on transparencies. For instance, we can have one map showing the distribution of population densities, another map showing the gradients of the natural terrains, and another showing the pattern of land values. By overlaying these maps, we can identify land parcels that are particularly suitable or problematic for the different uses, such as residential, commercial, industrial, open space, and institutional. The size of each parcel can be measured off the maps. They can be aggregated and presented in a tabular form, indicating the acreages and percentages of total land suitable for different uses. The data can also be processed to produce spatial clusterings such as suitable residential acreages in the various analysis zones, in the central areas, and at the fringe areas. However, the fact that a piece of land is suitable for a particular use does not mean that other uses are excluded. Land which is suitable for industrial uses can also accommodate institutional uses. Therefore it is important to rank the suitability of the land for the various uses, especially the acreages and percentages of undeveloped land, in varying degrees of suitability, for different uses within an analysis zone. All of the above graphic and numerical processing can be handled readily by the computer.

Geographic Information Systems

We now have sophisticated computerized geographic information systems. They use integrated spatial (geographic) and textural (attribute) databases to help monitor, analyze and model planning situations as well as make presentations (Star and Estes, 1990). In fact, some municipalities are using geographic information systems within their "corporate" function for a wide variety of tasks, such as tracking citizen complaints, monitoring expenditures, and assessing growth potentials.

A Geographic Information System (GIS) is one "in which data has some spatial or geographical referent, this data being ordered according to this referent, and displayed by software in such a form that some spatial analysis is possible" (Batty, 1993:52). It usually consists of the following components:

(i) Data input processing — the transformation of spatial and non-spatial information from both printed and digital files into a GIS database. A variety of methods may be used: digitizing, satellite images, scanning, keyboard entry, etc. The sources of the data may include maps, aerial photography, remote sensing, existing data sets and so on.

(ii) Data storage, retrieval and database management — the handling of data at different spatial scales and levels of resolution through the use of a database management system (DBMS).

(iii) Data manipulation and analysis — operations such as geometric calculations, topological operations, spatial comparison operations, multilayer spatial overlay and network analysis.

(iv) Display and product generation — statistical reports, maps or graphics.

(v) User interface — the interactions between the user and the GIS software.

Figure 4-10: Components of a Geographical Information System

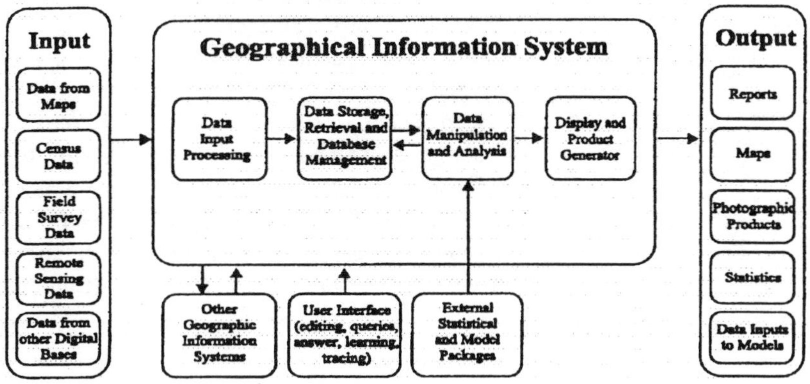

Source: Adapted from Fischer and Nijkamp (1993:5)

Besides being a data storage and analysis system its usefulness can be enhanced in a number of ways (Levine, 1996). (i) Land records can be modernized through GISs to become land information systems (LIS). (ii) There is now a thrust to develop statistical and GIS packages that can interface with one another, thus enhancing the capabilities of GISs to perform spatial analysis. (iii) GIS can interface with expert systems and spatial decisions systems to improve its decision making capabilities. (iv) There has also been a trend to specialize GISs into solvers of specific urban planning problems, such as land use zoning and transportation planning. However, only a few GISs can accommodate the extensive range of socio-economic, land-use, transportation, and other physical data that a typical land use planning exercise may require. More often, GIS is seen as a tool for visual communications than spatial analysis.

Successful use of geographic information systems has been the exception rather than the rule. Many planners have only vague notions about the systems, while some have unrealistic expectations. Few appreciate the need for appropriate laws, organizational arrangements, knowledge and practices that are needed to make them work. Often, different government agencies and departments have different software, data formats and standards. They also have their own management and access principles. All of these conspire against the successful implementation of GIS.

Thorpe (http://www.planweb.co.uk/tip/htm#top) suggests some useful tips for success. In selecting a system you need to develop your visions and focus only on the key priorities and their requirements; decide the overall shape of your GIS procurement at the outset; identify the first "showcase" project so as to ensure high visibility and maximum chance of successful implementation; obtain commitment from elected officials and senior managers; refine your requirements through supplier demonstrations and visits to other agencies that are active in GIS; structure the invitation-to-tender in such a way that you can make a meaningful comparison between suppliers; and assess suppliers to make sure that presentations, demonstrations and benchmarks are carried out to rules that you define. In implementing a GIS, you need to set "benefit targets" in advance; handpick the "project leader" based on skills in GIS, people management and troubleshooting; dedicate adequate resources, keep alive a detailed implementation plan and use it rigorously as the basis on which to monitor progress and take corrective actions; emphasize training; administer geographic data as a major corporate asset by putting in place procedures to ensure standardized definitions, responsible ownership and quality; maintain the support of the elected officials and senior managers; exploit opportunities for new ways of working which GIS can offer the local government; promote the successes and achievements; and keep reviewing the vision, strategy, implementation plan, benefits, and future direction.

CONCLUSION

Too often, too much information is gathered to serve no specific planning purpose. Information must be relevant to the intention for which it is gathered and it must facilitate the kinds of analysis and synthesis of which the planning agency is capable. Therefore, definitions and measurements of data must be meaningful to the planning problems or objectives at hand, and capable of spatial and locational analysis. For example, in analyzing the need for commercial and retail space, the number of employees may be a more relevant piece of information than the amount of sales.

There are four important considerations in designing an information system. First, the immediate utility of information has to be balanced against its future or on-going use. This means one should aim for a system which has a standardized format, is adaptable to machine use, and is capable of being updated. Of course, the benefit must be weighed against the cost of collecting, processing and retrieving the information.

Second, since information is to be gathered by many people and used by many different people again, it is necessary to ensure consistency and accuracy in the information collection phase. Surveys should be pre-tested, there should be adequate training for interviewers and field observers, and the field work has to be carefully monitored. The completeness of the information should be checked immediately so that remedial action can be taken before the survey is over. The coding should be consistent and carefully controlled.

Third, the way that information is classified and stored should be flexible enough to allow for new information to be added, for the information to be used for various kinds of analysis, and for new information technology to be incorporated, especially the use of new computer software and hardware. An equally important issue is the comparability between the information collected and the information that can be obtained from other sources, such as censuses. In this regard, compatible measurement units and definition of terms are essential, as well as the spatial units and the coverage of the survey.

Fourth, surveys should be conducted smoothly and economically. In this respect it is particularly relevant to consider carefully whether the survey should be done by information specialists or by the planning personnel. In-house information sources must be considered first, such as development application records and previous planning studies. It is better to have less information than the wrong information.

CHAPTER FIVE

ANALYSIS

L Land use analysis examines the match between user needs and land supply. This is true of a whole city as well as a specific site. The match can work in both directions: finding appropriate land for a use, or finding appropriate use for a piece of land.

Both user needs and land supply have two attributes — location (siting) and space (sizing). On the need side, locational needs are usually determined by referring to planning principles and standards, and space needs are established by a need-gap analysis. On the supply side, the suitability of the location of a piece of land is determined by referring to planning principles and standards similar to those used in establishing user needs, and the amount of space available for a particular use is established by a land capacity analysis.

In this chapter we will begin with some general observations about planning analysis and the use of planning standards. Then, we will discuss the matching of user needs and land supply for the following land use types: open space, residential, industrial, retail and commercial, community facilities, and transportation. Of course, the level of analysis must be appropriate to the task at hand and the resources available to do it. Generally the more significant the planning issue, the larger the number of people affected, and the greater the availability of time, money and expertise, the more rigorous and detailed the analysis. On the other hand, the size of the planning area (from a site to a city) and the type of plan (from a site plan to a general plan, and from a short-term action plan to a long-term master plan) do not dictate automatically the amount of analytic efforts.

ANALYTIC APPROACHES

There are a number of analytic approaches, and they overlap.

(i) Functional. This is perhaps the most common. Land provides space for different functions. The planning challenge is to match parcel characteristics (location, ownership, infrastructure, etc.) and environmental conditions (topography, soil capacity, microclimate, etc.) to the functional uses put to the land and the structures built to facilitate these uses.

(ii) Activity. This is a logical extension of the functional approach. Here, land use is seen as spatial manifestations of the activities of the users. Activities such as sleeping, eating, playing, talking, commuting and assembly take place in spaces as well as between spaces. The webs of activities in a society determine its land use pattern (types, locations and amounts). At the same time, the land use pattern constrains or liberates the activities through limiting or enhancing accesses, encounters, opportunities, etc. The planning challenge is to anticipate the dynamic relationship between land and use, which may sometimes produce unexpected consequences (e.g., urban renewal leading to suburban sprawl).

(iii) Development. Land, and its use, is seen as a commodity (real estate), the value of which is determined by its location, intensity and relative scarcity. This approach focuses on the "capacity" of land to be put to urban uses. It usually includes physical, economic (market and finance), legal and regulatory considerations. The planning challenge is to manage urban growth to avoid the extreme fluctuations of land supply and prices.

(iv) Moral-Aesthetic. In this approach, land, and its use, is seen as providing the necessary (though not sufficient) conditions for the fulfillment of the human spirit. The Parks Movement (Frederick Law Olmsted), City Beautify Movement (Daniel Burnham) and New Urbanism (Duany and Plater-Zyberk), etc., are all driven by some moral-aesthetic agendas which demand their own physical manifestations. The planning challenge is to make the physical manifestations legible (understandable) and imageable (having aesthetic meaning) to the inhabitants.

The greatest obstacle to meaningful user needs analysis is the "everything is related to everything else" syndrome (Friedmann, 1966: 195). The problem with this syndrome is vividly illustrated by Keeble as follows (1983: 96-97). In this view of planning, the city is seen as a kind of spider's web, but much more complex. Different physical, administrative, social, and economic systems overlap with one another. Any action will cause repercussions throughout the web, leading to all kinds of far-reaching effects, very difficult to predict. For instance, the development of a gas station at a particular location will cause changes in traffic patterns, perhaps extending miles beyond the site, changes in the relative attractiveness of housing in the vicinity, and changes, however small, in employment patterns. The practical difficulty is how all the consequences of allowing or refusing the development and operation of a gas station could be worked out and evaluated within the typically short time and small resources available for such decisions. In any city, dozens of such decisions would have to be made every month. Could this be done? Would the analysis be sufficiently complete and reliable? Given the usual limitations in theory and data, will the errors in this approach be at least as great as those resulting from the exercise of experienced professional common sense? It is certainly true that activities in an area would have linkages with other activities outside the area. But it is important to realize that in any situation, some things are always more related than others. This is why conventionally in a city-wide planning exercise we focus on employment, transportation, and open space, because these elements provide the basic spatial structure of the city. On the other hand, when we are dealing with smaller areas within a city, housing and shopping become the most important elements.

In planning we cannot avoid the notion of good and bad. There are positive aspects of an area and there are also its problems. The determination of these involve value judgements. The important point is to make these judgements explicit and relate them to the specific group that expresses them or to some established planning principles or standards. For example, if we identify an open space deficiency then we should point out whether this is in relation to some standards or to complaints expressed by the users. It is important that the peculiarity of the local situation is taken into account instead of relying solely on some general standards and assuming that they are universally applicable.

PLANNING STANDARDS

In land use planning much reliance is placed on the use of standards. This is unavoidable because professionals seldom have the time or inclination to return to basic analysis in their day-to-day functions. They rely on standards to assist them to make the right decisions. Today, the planning profession has accumulated a vast repertoire of such standards.

The standards we use are of two types. Traditional specification standards state requirements about location, such as access and convenience, and about space quality, such as density, size, and space separation. Performance standards are based on the use of tests to determine whether impacts by a particular land use at a particular location conform with standards of acceptability, especially with respect to environmental acceptability. The classic work on this subject is Lane Kendig's *Performance Zoning* (1980). The development and application of performance standards require higher levels of analytic skills, technical knowledge, more data, and special equipment. To date, the most successful application is Australia's Model Code for Residential Development (AMCORD). There are also some interesting U.S. cases, as in Bucks County, Pennsylvania, Fort Collins, Colorado, and Largo, Florida.

Land use standards are not absolutes but more in the nature of guides or criteria to be followed under "average" circumstances. Therefore, there may be a range of standards covering different circumstances or different locations. When standards are used in laws and regulations they are generally taken as minimum standards. But for the design of future land use, we may want to use standards of desirability. Most of the residential standards used in North America have come from the American Public Health Association standards of the 1960s; and many of the transportation standards (especially trip generation) have been based on observations made in the 1970s. At the same time, individual research efforts have produced vastly different standards for similar issues.

There are some problems about the use of standards, which should be very carefully noted. First, there is the question of paternalism, especially in the use of minimum standards. These standards are based on society's general consensus of what constitutes an acceptable use of land. This removal of choice from people who either do not want or cannot afford the standards can create resentment and apathy.

There is also the question of lack of rigorous research to justify the use of a particular standard. In the last 10 years there have been some efforts to re-evaluate conventional standards, especially in comparison to "New Urbanism" standards (e.g., Essiambre-Phillips-Desjardins Associates Ltd. et al., 1977). Typically, such research involves the comparative examinations of the effects of different standards on land consumption, energy conservation, and fiscal impact (Ontario Ministry of Municipal Affairs and Housing, 1983). Seldom does it explore the rationale and justifications for the use of specific standards, from width of streets to lot sizes, and from building heights to infrastructure requirements. Even important standards, such as the amount of parking space for different land uses, are very crude and many of them are confessedly tentative explorations of the subject. Much of the aura attached to certain standards is the result of thoughtless habits. These include standards on densities, road works, and privacy distances. They have been used for so long that they are now taken completely for granted.

Most standards were based on physical, social, economic and technological contexts of the past, which were different from the ones in which they are applied. Much more systematic study of the context-standards relationship is needed to gain insight into the process of standard formulation and develop a theoretically defensible framework to compare alternative standards as well as to formulate new ones. Only then will planners become more efficient in the use of land and more responsive to changing user needs, market conditions, and technological advances. In particular, the following contextual elements are crucial: environmental, climatic, and physical conditions, market pressures, consumer preferences, technological factors, institutional and administrative factors, the influence of tradition and convention, and the event that precipitated the establishment and/or change of the standards.

Finally, there is the question of conflicts and incompatibility among standards. For instance, density standards to ensure sufficient space and privacy may produce land use patterns that are spread out. On the other hand, service accessibility standards based on minimum distance and time may require development to be closer together. These two sets of standards conflict with each other, and trade-offs or priorities have to be set.

In our discussion we will often refer to standards, especially the more established ones. But we should realize that while standards are unavoidable, their use must be guided by caution and sensitivity. What follows is a systematic discussion of the analytic considerations in the siting and sizing of different land uses.

OPEN SPACE

Open space is the most important land use category in planning analysis because its siting and sizing requirements are the most varied of all uses. It gets the lowest priority in the market place, and any remedial measure later on is very expensive and difficult.

Siting   Open space has two functions: recreation and environmental enhancement or protection. In planning for open space it is important to determine at the outset the purpose of the open space. A natural environment can be vital to us for such concerns as water supply and flood control, or dangerous both to people and property, or sensitive to human intervention such as habitats, breeding grounds, and scenic or historic sites. The following are some principles for the siting of open space according to its purpose.

(i) If the purpose of an open space is the protection of investment and people from hazards, siting principles should include such considerations as setback from flood lines, prohibition of development in areas with fire hazards, or unstable shoreline or hillsides.

(ii) If the purpose is the protection and management of valuable and natural resources and environmental processes, then we will have to identify the ecosystem, and apply standards or guidelines to preserve and manage plant covers, infiltration and run-offs, erosion, sedimentation, etc. One such guideline can be the restriction of development on slopes greater than 25 percent. Environmentally sensitive areas may be designated and strict development control can be applied in or around such areas. As a rule, wildlife can be better supported by having a few large protected areas rather than a large number of small areas.

(iii) If the purpose is to protect and manage natural resources for economic reasons, which includes tourism, then the density of development should be controlled, especially in areas which have problems in underground water supply or areas with drainage problems. It is important to preserve the underground water supply against pollution by septic discharges or landfills.

(iv) If the purpose is to protect mineral aggregates, it is useful to think of development phasing so that the opportunity to extract these aggregates is not taken away by haphazard urban development on the land. In this regard, post-mining reclamation guidelines are important.

(v) If the purpose is to protect and enhance natural amenities, then priorities of these amenities have to be developed in terms of their rarity and the social values placed on them. Since such amenities are to be enjoyed there should be ample physical and visual access to them.

(vi) If the purpose is for outdoor recreation, education, and cultural purposes, user consideration is of primary importance. Accessibility should be geared to the pattern and frequency of use. For instance, tennis courts, golf courses, swimming pools, and picnic areas should be located very close to the users. The size of these areas can range from one acre to one hundred acres. Areas for hunting, fishing, camping, canoeing, and so on, are resource-based and their location should be determined by where such resources are available.

(vii) Open space can be used to shape the urban form. These spaces range from greenbelts and large buffer areas to setbacks and plazas. It is important to consider a visual hierarchy and to make use of vantage points and prominent locations.

(viii) Finally, open space can be considered as land reserve for future urban development, especially in the form of land banking. In this respect the kind of future urban development envisaged is an important determinant of the open space allocation.

The designation of large open spaces is usually preceded by very careful studies of their environmental and recreational aspects. It is the planning of small and local open spaces that is often neglected. These small open spaces have significant impact on the quality of life of city dwellers. William Whyte (1980) offers some very valuable insights. He observes that location rather than size is the more important criterion. The best and the most used sites are those located right in the city centre and are designed to accommodate a variety of activities, from sitting to eating or watching people go by. The dilemma is that such locations are also locations of high land values. This lends support to the argument that urban open space should be allocated first in any comprehensive planning exercise, and not as an afterthought.

In densely populated urban areas any kind of open space is scarce, from tot lots to the local park of a few acres. Variety of activities and forms is a key to success. Through the use of hedges and trees and changes in the ground levels, variety in form can be achieved. These can also act as a buffer to other uses and to traffic noise. Different kinds of activities can then take place at the same time without interfering with one another. Variety in ground textures can be achieved by using different ground covers, paving stones and flower beds, which can also serve to guide people's movements without having to resort to the obtrusive prohibition signs.

Paley Park in Manhattan, New York, is a successful example of a small urban open space. It is only about 40 by 100 feet and is wedged between tall buildings and a busy street. It is physically separated from the street by a few well-proportioned steps. But visually it is public and inviting, with a few trees, tables, and many seats and litter bins. The sidewalls are exposed brick, the ground is cobbled, and near the entry there is a sandwich stall. The main attraction is the backwall covered with a waterfall which cools the air during the summer and muffles the traffic noise, providing a haven from the hustle and bustle of the city. The treatment of the land reserved for the expansion of the Royal Opera House in Covent Garden, London, provides yet another successful example (Loew, 1979: 159-160). It is about 150 feet square but looks much larger, partly because it is surrounded by cleared space and the central market hall. Its layout has several levels with varied vegetation, a brick floor, sitting area, and a mock ruined temple.

It is a success story of citizen participation. The park was developed through the efforts of a group of local people who formed an open space committee. They used local manpower and resources to develop the park. As a result, they felt it was theirs and not a municipal imposition. Children were given a tree or shrub to plant and they were responsible for it. Vandalism was minimum because these children acted as vigilantes and would not let other kids destroy the trees they had planted. There is a substantial amount of unused public open space in any city, which may be put to very good use by handing it over to be managed by the local people.

It is probably a Victorian legacy that open space is synonymous with recreational uses. Planners have not been very innovative in creating space for indoor recreation, such as using an empty shop or building to provide play facilities, a workshop or rehearsal room. In any urban area there are vacant buildings awaiting either demolition, change of use, or simply a decision. With some flexibility and creativeness on the part of the planner, local skills and good will can be mobilized to turn an empty building into a community asset, and people's involvement in the project guarantees that it will be looked after and used. The neighbourhood schools offer great opportunities. They are well equipped for sports and cultural activities and are only used during part of the day and part of the year. Furthermore, reduction in enrolment has rendered many school buildings (or part of them) redundant. They can be put to good community recreational use. Churches have traditionally been involved in recreation. They too have a substantial amount of land and buildings which can be used more creatively as "breathing" space, especially in the inner city deprived areas.

Sizing

Sizing requirements of open space are less strict than those of other uses, and are often determined by whatever supply is available. The size of open spaces that serve the whole city can vary from a sports stadium to a country park or a nature reserve area. There are intermediate open spaces such as golf courses, race tracks, fairgrounds, and botanical gardens, which can be located at the edge of the urban area or at the end of public transit or major urban roads. Then there are neighbourhood open spaces which should be integrated with the other neighbourhood uses.

The sizing of open space involves three considerations: the number, the minimum size of each, and the minimum aggregate acreages. There are a number of approaches. The crudest one is to apply a standard to the total population, such as five acres per one thousand population. The U.S. National Recreation and Park Association recommends the following for every 1,000 population: 6.25-10.5 acres of close-to-home open space such as mini-parks, neighbourhood parks and playgrounds; and 15.2 acres of regional open space such as regional parks and park reserves. A more complex approach is to survey different population groups about their expected and preferred types of open space, and then work out the number and acreages of different types of open space based on the size of particular population groups and their preferences. The most frequently used approach is a combination of the above, that is, applying standards to population size and then involving the public in evaluating the appropriateness and adequacy of the existing or proposed open space scheme. Tables 5-1 and 5-2 show some standard recreation space requirements as well as standards for special recreation facilities.

TABLE 5-1
OPEN SPACE STANDARDS

Type	Use	Acres per 1,000 population	Service Area	Desirable Size
Minipark	For concentrated or limited population or specific group (tots or senior citizens)	0.25 to 0.5 (0.1 - 0.2 hectare)	Radius <1/4 mile	<1 acre or less (0.4 hectare)
Neighbourhood park / playground	For intense activities (e.g., field games, court games, skating, and picnicking) as well as general playground use.	1 to 2 (0.4 - 0.8 hectare)	- Radius between 1/4 to 1/2 mile (0.4- 0.8 km) - Population <5,000	>15 acres (10 hectares)
Community park	For diverse uses including intense recreational facilities, (e.g., athletic complexes and large swimming pools), natural outdoor recreation (e.g., viewing, sitting and picnicking) and any combination of the above.	5 to 8 (2 - 3.2 hectares)	- Radius 1-2 miles (1.6 - 3.2 km) - Several neighbourhoods	>25 acres (10 hectares)
Regional / metropolitan park	For natural or designed outdoor recreation (e.g., picnicking, boating, fishing, swimming, camping, and trails). May include play areas.	5 to 10 (2 - 4 hectares)	- 1 hour driving time - Several communities	>200 acres (80 hectares)
Regional park reserve	Generally with 80% area for conservation and resource management and 20% for nature-oriented outdoor recreation (e.g., viewing and studying nature, wildlife habitats, conservation, swimming, picnicking, hiking, fishing, boating, camping, and trails). May include active play areas.	Variable	- 1 hour driving time - Several communities	>1,000 acres (400 hecares), depending on resource preservation and management needs
Linear park	For recreational travel (e.g., hiking, biking snowmobiling, horseback riding, cross-country skiing, canoeing, and pleasure driving). May include active play areas.			

Source: Adapted from Kaiser, Godschalk and Chapin (1995:390-1, Table 15-3).

The need for open space is so much determined by geography, climate, and culture of the place and by the different characteristics of the people concerned that it would not be appropriate to use one single standard to determine the sizing requirements. Also, the need for recreational facilities can be affected by the supply. People do not necessarily express the desire for a facility such as a swimming pool until the facility is provided. Then their "need" for the facility will grow. Therefore, unlike the case with other uses, great sensitivity is required because the needs are very difficult to gauge.

TABLE 5-2
RECREATION FACILITIES SPACE STANDARDS

Facility	Standard Per Population Size
Baseball diamonds	1 per 6,000
Softball diamonds (and/or youth diamonds)	1 per 3,000
Tennis courts	1 per 2,000
Basketball courts	1 per 500
Swimming pools - 25 meter	1 per 10,000
Swimming pools - 50 meter	1 per 20,000
Skating rinks (artificial)	1 per 30,000
Neighbourhood centres	1 per 10,000
Community centres	1 per 25,000
Outdoor theatres (non commercial)	1 per 20,000
Shooting ranges	1 per 50,000
Golf courses (18-hole)	1 per 25,000

Source: Chapin and Kaiser (1979: 447), based on Buechner (1971:13).

There are some general guiding principles when considering the provision of open space.

> (i) The more accessible the site (that is, proximity to people and transport) the greater its suitability.

> (ii) The site which can offer a great variety of uses is a better site.

> (iii) Aesthetic qualities are very important when it comes to open space use.

> (iv) Costs are very important but they work both ways. The more accessible the site, the higher the cost, including actual as well as opportunity cost.

> (v) The greater the threat of loss of a site to urban development the higher the priority for its acquisition.

> (vi) If the proposed site is close to some existing recreation facilities, then we should take better use of the existing facilities first.

(vii) The ratio of existing supply to identified needs is an important criterion to establish priorities. An area with a lower ratio has a greater
urgency.

The above principles often conflict with one another. The community has to
determine what value it places on open spaces and what cost it is willing to pay for
this important but intangible aspect of the quality of urban life. A great part of the
planner's job is to identify the strength of these values and the community's
willingness to pay in their pursuit.

RESIDENTIAL USE

This section deals with the analysis of the siting and sizing of residential communities, focussing on housing but including elementary and high schools, and local
businesses and facilities.

Neighbourhood

A discussion about residential community is not possible without examining the
idea of neighbourhood. The expression "neighbourhood unit" was first introduced
by Clarence Perry in 1923. Since then, there has been much debate about this concept. What Perry meant by the term was, "that area which embraces all the public
facilities and conditions required for the average family for its comfort and proper
development within the vicinity of its dwellings."

According to Perry (1966: 94-109), six characteristics were necessary to
define a neighbourhood unit: its size (related to a primary school), its boundaries
which should be distinct, the open spaces needed for recreation, its centre
comprising of institutions such as school, church or library, its shopping districts
located at the periphery, and its internal road network.

The neighbourhood concept has been used very extensively in North
America and in Britain (especially in the development of the British new towns).
Residential areas are divided into units separated from each other, with open
spaces in between. Each area has its local centre and school. Through traffic is
excluded from the neighbourhoods, and they are linked with each other and with
the main city centre by radial and ring roads. The assumption is that social
interaction will occur within each neighbourhood and that people will have a sense
of belonging to the place.

A main difficulty with the neighbourhood concept is the idea of the "average
family." This implies homogeneity. Some argue that this homogeneity bias has
served to produce more rigid social stratification on the one hand, and vast areas of
look-alike subdivisions on the other. Others argue that social relations cannot be
contained in bounded spatial units. As a matter of fact, Hans Blumenfeld once

observed that the only common socializing aspect in a neighbourhood unit is the Parent Teacher Association. Today, with the large numbers of one- and two-person households, the idea of the "average family" is even more untenable.

Figure 5-1: Perry's Neighbouthood Unit

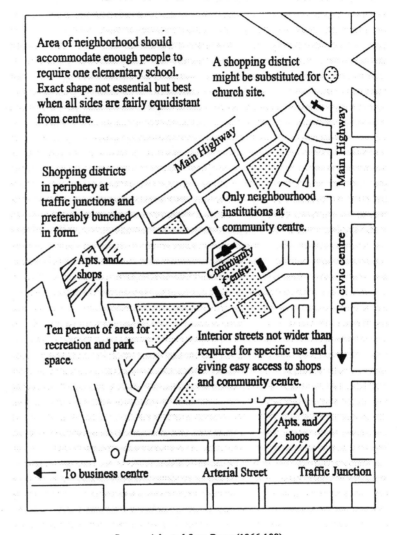

Source: Adapted from Perry (1966:108)

Also, the idea of "average family" conflicts with the planning ideal of the "balanced community." A balanced community implies the coexistence of different social classes, which is in direct contradiction to the inherent segregation of the neighbourhood concept. Of course, the ideal of a balanced community is also problematic. Many successful traditional communities did not show such a balance. There are other conflicts too, such as those between close neighbourly contacts and wider community involvement.

However, people seem to have a sense of "local" areas of a scale comparable to the traditional neighbourhood, that is, from a couple of thousand people to as large as ten thousand or more. People may have difficulties in describing the exact boundaries or precise characteristics of their neighbourhood but they have a strong sense of belonging to a locale because of some shared social values, culture, or institutions.

There are also entirely different conceptions of the neighbourhood. It may be a place of retreat from the total urban life, or a kind of known and secure refuge from the world. This feeling often increases with length of residence. Neighbourhoods may also emerge as the "neighbours" coalesce around an issue. But whatever the criticisms of the neighbourhood concept, and the transformations which the concept has undergone, it has remained firmly entrenched in the planner's mind. It has, in fact, attained a mythical status in people's psyche. G.K. Chesterton's classic, *The Napoleon of Notting Hill*, first published in 1904, is perhaps one of the most eloquent expressions. Andrew Greeley, the sociologist and priest, wrote a foreword to the 1978 edition of the book, which shows us that nothing has changed.

> G.K. Chesterton would have enjoyed the paradox thoroughly: In *The Napoleon of Notting Hill*, which he begins by explicitly excluding any exercise of prophecy, Chesterton lays down the most accurate of all the twentieth century utopian visions. H.G. Wells' scientific utopias have long since been discredited, and George Orwell's anti-utopia of 1984 seems less plausible now than it did even a few years ago.... Chesterton saw that eighty years after the publication of his book, London would be much the same as it was in his day, and the human love of "the neighborhood" would be as fierce and profound as it ever was....

> The neighborhood is in once again. Liberalism of the *fin de siecle* (twentieth-century style) is likely to be the liberalism of G.K. Chesterton and Auberon Quin, a liberalism of decentralization, localism, and the neighbourhood. And while Chesterton could not have anticipated the resurgence of interest in the neighborhood, it certainly would have delighted him.

> To understand *The Napoleon of Notting Hill* one must realize that the neighborhood (now, alas, the scene of frequent racial disturbances in London) was his neighborhood. He was born in the shadow of the waterworks, which figures so prominently in the story; and when Notting Hill's fiery Provost, Adam Wayne, takes arms to defend Notting Hill against those who built a road (should one read expressway?) through it, he was motivated by that same fierce pride in neighborhood that has led many Americans in more recent years to resist one way or another the bulldozers and devastation.

> No one who has ever lived in a neighborhood, a real neighborhood, and learned to love it can fail to be stirred by such a vision. The neighborhood is your turf, your little corner of the world, an extension of the family. Heaven helps he who dares to trespass on it to threaten it with destruction. It took more than seventy years before the notion that "small is beautiful" became popular, but the intellectual difference between E.F. Schumacher and G.K. Chesterton is almost nonexistent.

> All those rational city planners, all the PPBS accountants, all the geographers who erase neighborhood boundaries from their city maps, all the bureaucrats

who move local communities around like pieces on a checkerboard, all the politicians who lose touch with what goes on in the grass roots should read *The Napoleon of Notting Hill* and accept fair warning. There are a lot of people out in the neighborhoods who combine the comic of Auberon Quin and the serious commitment of Adam Wayne; they are willing to defend their turf come what may.

Of course, it is obvious that the elementary school is no longer the centre of activities for urban households. With increased social and physical mobility, people are less willing to be confined to a self-contained area with limited choices and a sense of isolation. Therefore, it seems futile to try to fit all services into the same unit size. As such, the neighbourhood unit is a planning fiction, but it has become a useful fiction. It contains some valuable ideas. These include the idea that local facilities should be distributed so as to be easily accessible to the residents, and that, when some facilities are associated in common centres, they have special convenience.

In terms of land use pattern, a layout very similar to the traditional neighbourhood layout will result when we organize land uses, roads, and services according to principles of good accessibility and safety, with adequate space for the various activities, efficient and safe traffic movement and the separation of incompatible uses. To make the catchment areas of various local services fall within the main road network (for reasons of enhanced safety and accessibility) we automatically create a series of fairly distinct physical units. To further improve on accessibility the housing is clustered around the services and the open spaces are placed outwards forming a physical boundary around the area.

However, the crucial point is the determination of the service catchment areas. Both demographic and public policy changes will affect them. For instance, if the birth rate falls, the population ages, or people migrate outside the area, the catchment area would have to be enlarged. On the other hand, education policies have changed very much over the years, especially with respect to the size of a school. Our past experience has shown that it is not possible to anticipate and keep pace with all of these demographic and policy changes. Therefore, it is wise not to have excessively hard edges, such as major roads, around all sides of a neighbourhood. This will create an inward-looking cell. Also, any change in the catchment areas of the various services beyond the boundaries would result in the following unsatisfactory situations. (i) Danger and delays will increase as more people need to cross a major road to get to local services. (ii) Fencing all the major roads will improve pedestrian safety but will reduce accessibility to local services. (iii) Pedestrian bridges and tunnels across the major roads or vertical separation of road intersections will improve safety and accessibility but greatly increase the cost.

In recent years, the concept of neo-traditional neighbourhood has been rigorously promoted by some planners (Krieger, 1992; Duany and Plater-Zyberk). Like Perry's neighbourhood it stresses walking and social interaction. But unlike Perry, it finds inspiration in 19th century American towns, with their gridiron streets and mixed land uses (Refer to New Urbanism in the Synthesis chapter).

Figure 5-2: Yield on Frontage

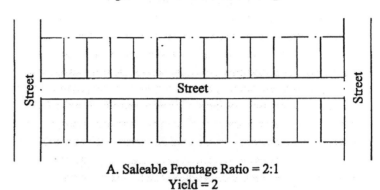

A. Saleable Frontage Ratio = 2:1
Yield = 2

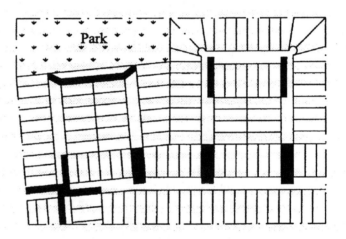

B. Saleable Frontage Ratio = 1.40
Yield = 1.40

Legend:

——— · ———   Boundary of Subdivision

▮▮▮▮▮▮   Unsaleable Frontage

Source: Ontario Ministry of Housing (1980: 35)

The following points can be kept in mind when considering a neighbourhood unit. It is a distinct geographical area with fairly clear boundaries and a certain degree of homogeneity in the buildings given by their size, style, state of repair, tenure, etc. Also, there may be a certain degree of social homogeneity given by the household size, age, class, and race. But this does not mean there cannot be a healthy mix of compatible and complementary uses. The actual size is not as important as a shared sense of belonging. There can be a single or a number of service centres. The important thing is to keep through traffic out of residential streets and to ensure that small children do not have to cross busy streets to get to their school. This means that there should be as much separation between pedestrian and vehicular traffic as possible. But this does not mean that major highways should surround the neighbourhood.

In practical terms, therefore, the neighbourhood unit concept means planning the land use in such a way that user needs can be satisfied locally. This means essential services and facilities can be reached with minimum effort and maximum safety. This requires a certain population size to support the services and a certain level of compactness. The precise form, the relative location of uses and the boundaries should be adjusted to reflect the particular situation on hand.

While planners should recognize the specific characteristics of a neighbourhood, reinforce them, and allow them to thrive instead of adopting a uniform pattern for all locations, developers want to maximize the saleable frontage of the roads created for a development. The following table shows the most common residential lot configuration in North America.

TABLE 5-3
RESIDENTIAL LOT SIZE

Housing Type	Conventional		New Urbanism	
	Frontage	Depth	Frontage	Depth
Single-detached	20-100 ft. (6-30m)	100 ft. (30m)	32-40 ft. (10-12m)	100 ft. (30m)
Semi-detached	-	-	26 ft. (8m)	100 ft. (30m)
Row houses	16-30 ft. (5-9m)	90-100 ft. (27-30m)	20 ft. (96m)	100 ft. (30m)
Apartments * (5-6 storeys)	100 ft. (30m)	*	*	100 ft. (30m)

* Note that in the conventional apartment lots the depths are more varied, whereas in the New Urbanism apartment lots the frontage widths are more varied.
Source: Koppelman and DeChiara (1975:149); and Essiambre-Phillips-Desjardins Associates Ltd., *et al.* (1997).

On a straight street with lots fronting on both sides, with the flanking street being provided by someone else, and with no requirement of any parkland, a developer can get a saleable frontage ratio of close to 2:1. (This is referred to as a yield of 2.) In a curvilinear layout, the typical ratio is about 1.6:1. This means that a balance has to be struck between variety and cost.

Lynch (1971: 230-232) suggests four tests for the layout of a residential neighbourhood development: (i) to move in imagination through its streets, checking its technical, social and aesthetic quality; (ii) to arrange a typical building on each lot to ensure that each lot has at least one good location for a building, which is satisfactory to the resident and the neighbours; (iii) to check the "buildability" of the lots to ensure that there will still be adequate light, air, access and privacy after compliance with all legal and planning restrictions; and (iv) to check the adequacy of land reserved for community facilities and future growths and changes.

Housing

The provision of adequate land for appropriate and affordable housing has always been a central focus in land use planning. "Bad" housing was traditionally defined on the basis of sanitary conditions, such as dampness, lack of bath, and overcrowding. Later on, nonphysical indicators have also been included, such as unemployment, low incomes, and a high proportion of elderly people. Lately, the converse of overcrowding (that is, underuse of housing) has also become a relevant consideration, especially in the case of "empty nesters" living in relatively large houses.

A central question is whether or not housing is a localized issue that can be dealt with in an area-by-area fashion. By assigning a spatial boundary to the housing problem, cases outside the area will tend to be overlooked. However, the improvement of some obviously bad living conditions in one area may be a significant achievement in itself especially when it can be done over a relatively short period of time, as in the case of most redevelopment or rehabilitation programmes.

Rigid standards on housing types and densities have contributed to the creation and continuation of the monotonous urban residential environments. For instance, rigid definitions of "single family" dwelling, which do not allow forms of shared living arrangements other than amongst members of one family, are obstacles to the formation of any but the very "standard" kind of community.

Different housing types present different planning opportunities and limitations. A single-family detached dwelling can range from a mobile home to a mansion, with a wide range of possible sizes, shapes and designs. In general, a single-family dwelling has the following advantages: air and light, space, direct access to street, privacy, individuality and noise control. On the other hand, it is difficult to design, consumes land at a higher rate than other housing types, contributes to urban sprawl, and is expensive to service with adequate infrastructure. Semi-detached dwellings have similar advantages, with less land consumption and greater design possibilities. However, people seem to prefer the detached house on account of unambiguous ownership and control. Row-housing economizes on land and infrastructure, and is energy-efficient because there are fewer external walls. But people dislike it for its lack of individuality, noise intrusion and difficulty in organizing the storage and service functions (bicycles, garbage and garden equipment). Low-rise walk-up apartments provide convenience and freedom of apartment living at low densities and with an intimate visual scale. There are great design possibilities with respect to clustering as well as the internal layouts. However, as density increases, the outdoor areas may be taken over by the automobile. High-rise apartments (with elevators) are "standard" solutions for high-density development. They offer the advantage of air, light, and view, and can support in-house services and social and recreational facilities not available to other housing types. Also, for those who like them, living in high-rise apartments offers anonymity and social freedom. But for those who do not like them, they are alienating and dangerous places. They are costly to construct, and special efforts are needed to provide privacy and ventilation and to deal with problems of winds, shadows, and glare. From an urban design point of view, the worst problem of the high-rise apartment is perhaps at the ground level where the continuity of the street is broken, creating a wasteland streetscape, which is both dead and dangerous.

It seems that medium density housing such as row housing and garden apartments, well designed, may offer the combined advantages of the detached house and high-rise with added bonuses of being energy efficient and providing a continuous street facade. In short, they are ideal--a planner's ideal. But what about the people who live in them? How do they feel? In a recent study comparing their attitudes with those people in single-family homes and high-rises, people in row houses and townhouses consistently give lower marks to their dwelling conditions, from storage space and home size to parking and sunlight (Leung, 1993).

Unlike the single-detached home, the row house's narrow lot and party walls create problems of congestion and interference in the home and on the street. And unlike the high-rise, the row house lacks the economic scale to provide underground parking or communal storage space, or the design flexibility to improve on sunlight and view. The mismatch between expectation and satisfaction gives rise to stress. People who live in single-detached homes expect peace and quiet, and the freedom to engage or withdraw, and the detached home delivers. The expectations of high-rise living are equally unambiguous: anonymity and mutual accommodation. You cannot change the interior layout, but you do not have to worry about the exterior maintenance, either. You can hear your neighbours and they can hear you, so you remember that when you have a party or an argument. What about the expectations of a row house? You can modify the interior, but you cannot have windows or doors on the sides. The flimsy party wall between you and your neighbour does not ensure noise privacy. You can change the roof tiles, paint the windows and mow the lawn, but unless your neighbours do the same it will make you look snooty or them look sloppy. In a single-family neighbourhood, neighbouring is optional; in a high-rise it is minimal; in a row-housing neighbourhood it is an unavoidable reality with unpredictable results.

Planners believe that one of the greatest assets of the row house is ground-level entry. There is no doubt that people like being close to the ground, and having direct access to the street and private outdoor space. But people like many other things, too, and ground-level entry is a low priority next to pressing needs for more sunlight, bigger rooms, better security and more convenient parking.

We could rework the row house by giving up ground-level entry and having low-rise condominium or apartment buildings (three or four storeys); but these would no longer be "houses" in most people's eyes. Alternatively, we could make the single-detached house more affordable by reducing minimum requirements on building and lot sizes, and dispensing with the archaic idea of one house per lot. Or we could revisit the high-rise solution. While no single housing type can satisfy the diverse needs of those wanting an affordable home, from society's viewpoint the row house is attractive for environmental and energy reasons. And given the high cost of land, it is probably the only affordable option for consumers who desire a "house" where their roof is not somebody else's floor, and where they own a piece of land that is not also owned by dozens of other people.

The problems with existing row-house design are its lack of privacy, ambiguous "neighbouring" and space restrictions. Some of these are unavoidable; but we could go some way toward meeting the expectations of a "house" through better-insulated party walls to increase audio privacy, preferably in masonry; more substantial and higher fences to define clearly territorial boundaries and neighbouring activities; and through-passages at ground level between front and back yards to improve access and use of space, perhaps incorporating a carport or driveway to relieve parking problems. It is not a panacea, but, with sensitivity to consumer needs and flexibility in development control, the row house may yet turn out to be the form of housing that will deliver the best balance between affordability and livability to the largest number of first-home buyers.

We will now turn to some principles and practices of housing analysis that help planners determine locational and space requirements, and the quality and amount of the land supply to meet such needs.

Siting   The appropriateness of a location for residential use depends on the needs of the household. On a theoretical level there are needs pertaining to shelter, security, childbearing, symbolic identification, social interaction, leisure, and accessibility to activity opportunities required to maintain a household in our society (Chapin and Kaiser, 1979: 397-398). When translated into practical terms, these mean convenience, safety, economy and choice; proximity to work and leisure by means of public transit and road network; proximity to community facilities and local open space by means of walking; protection from traffic and incompatible uses; economy, energy efficiency and attractiveness of the development; and sufficient choice of housing type, and density. The most commonly held criterion in the siting of residential use is "convenience standards."

TABLE 5-4
DISTANCE STANDARDS (A)

Destination	Maximum Distance	
	Mile	Km.
Walking		
Grade school	1.0	(1.6)
Local shopping	0.75	(1.2)
Vehicular		
High school	1.5	(2.4)
Recreation and church	3.5	(5.6)
Major shopping	4.0	(6.4)
Employment	40 minutes	

Source: Urban Land Institute (1960:29)

These are maximum time and/or distance standards. Ideally they should be based on assumptions about local terrains, prevailing residential densities, local transportation systems, school and recreation policies, and so on. But in practice, universal standards, such as the following, are used. It should be noted that our expectations have gone up over time, as shown in the two different tables (4 and 5) about standards used in the 1960s and at present.

Privacy and noise considerations are especially important in residential location. Visual and audio privacy can be achieved through separation distances (horizontal and vertical) and buffers (hedges, trees and walls). Noise intrusion by traffic and other uses can be dealt with through increasing the distance between the noise source and receiver; introducing buffers between them; masking the noise with other more pleasant sounds, such as running water and rustling leaves; or abandoning the outdoor space. Table 6 shows the noise levels associated with different activities.

TABLE 5-5
DISTANCE STANDARDS (B)

Destination	Maximum Distance		
	Mile	**(Km)**	**Minutes**
Walking			
Grade school	0.5	(0.8)	
High school, junior	1.0	(1.6)	
High school, senior	1.0 - 1.5	(1.6 - 2.4)	20 - 30
Local shopping	0.5	(0.8)	10
Playground & local parks	0.5	(0.8)	
Public transit	1000 ft.	(300 m)	
Vehicular			
Major shopping (CBD)			30 - 45
Employment			20 - 30

Source: Chapin and Kaiser (1979:350); and Lynch and Hack (1984:467).

For locating residential use within a developed area one should examine if there is adequate protection from incompatible uses, traffic intrusion, floods and other natural hazards; and if the land falls within the boundaries of acceptable catchment areas for different essential facilities and services. The locational choice should be sensitive to the existing social order, especially ethnic grouping, lifestyle, stage of family cycle and economic constraints.

Locating residential use in a new (undeveloped) area is more complicated. There are the usual environmental considerations that the land should be above flood level, away from fragile ecosystems, and that the development would involve minimum disruption of the existing terrain and vegetation. Premature development means development on land that is inadequately serviced. This includes "hard" services such as water supply and sewage disposal and "soft" services, particularly schools. In deciding the location for residential development in a generally undeveloped area, it is important to consider its proximity to essential facilities and services and the surplus capacity of these to take on the new development.

The density of development is especially crucial, in terms of its implication both on the demand for services and the impact on the environment. Two points should be borne in mind. (1) Initial development in an undeveloped area is usually low density. It is often not profitable for a developer to provide higher density development from the beginning. Also, the first residents are likely to resist fiercely the newcomers for fear that they would destroy the rural ambience of the place, for which these first residents came. Low-density urban sprawl would result. (2) At the initial stage when agricultural land is being replaced by urban development, there is usually not much resistance from the farmers because their land values would go up and the impact of the development would be limited. Then, as more urban development occurs, the new residents would find the farming operation a nuisance and would force the farmers to move out. At the beginning, the amount of agricultural land lost is not too high, but the aggregate loss over a period of time can be very significant. Besides, there is always the symbolic stand taken to protect agriculture, which could never be justified by a restrictive economic cost and benefit calculation.

TABLE 5-6
NOISE LEVELS

Activities	Decibels
Threshold of hearing	0
Quiet rustle of leaves	10
Soft whisper	20-30
Ambient noise, house kitchen or noisy office (speech interference begins)	50
Light car traffic or normal conversation	60
Highway traffic at 50 ft. (15 m)	70-80
Subway, freight train, heavy truck at 50 ft. (15 m)	90-100
Automobile horn, pneumatic hammer	110-120
Military jet	130
Preferred outdoor (conversation possible)	max. 55
Preferred indoor (background)	max. 40
Preferred sleeping or study	max. 35

Source: Lynch and Hack (1984:465)

The density of development affects energy consumption. It should be sufficiently high to allow for energy-saving transport, with respect to both the internal roads system and commuting distance and use of public transit and bicycle. Often times, slope gradients are used to set density limits. Less than five percent slope may support high-density development, and more than ten percent slope would indicate lower density development.

Figure 5-3: Achieving Privacy Through Grades

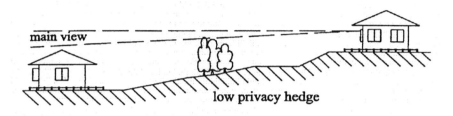

Source: Ontario Ministry of Housing (1980:33)

Figure 5-4: Using Land Relief and Contours to Protect Against Intrusion of Noise, Fumes and Chemicals

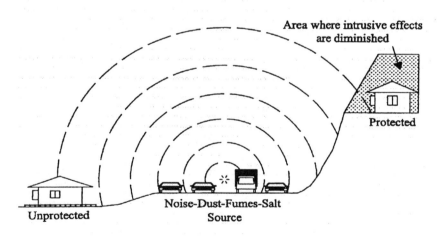

Source: Ontario Ministry of Housing (1980: 33)

Figure 5-5: Using Earth Barriers for Noise, Dust and Visual Protection

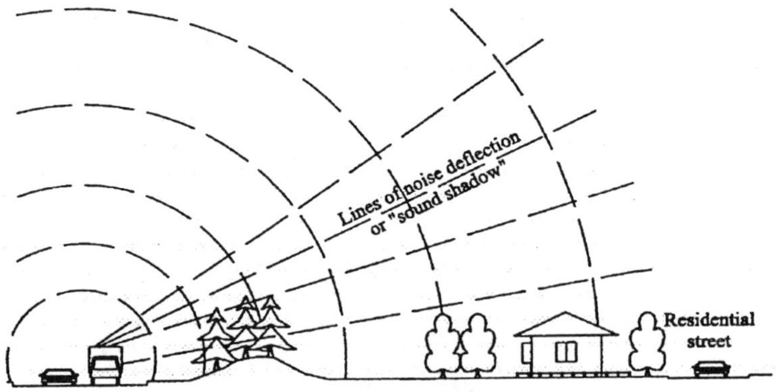

Source: Ontario Ministry of Housing (1980:34)

Notes: 1. The height of a berm should be calculated to give adequate protection to the dwellings and is site-specific.
2. Trees planted on the berm will help filter dust and fumes but may deflect soundwaves downward, reducing the quality of sound protection. Coniferous tress reflect sound waves less and are effective year round.
3. All planted material should be climate-hardy and able to resist salt-spray if necessary.

Sizing   The question is how much land is required to accommodate the housing needs. This depends on how much, and what type, of housing is needed. The key measure is the number and type of households to be accommodated. A typical analysis involves the following logical steps. First, the size of the population to be housed is estimated. From that the number of families or households of various sizes, and the stage in their family cycle, are established. These numbers form the basis to estimate the number of dwelling units of various sizes and types needed. Dwelling sizes are usually measured by the number of bedrooms per dwelling unit; and dwelling types include the whole range from the single-family house to high-rise apartment. Building density thresholds for each dwelling type are then used to convert the number of dwelling units into acreages of land needed for that type of housing. The final figures would show the acreages required for single-detached housing, for semi-detached housing, for row housing, and so on. The same logic can be used for a site-specific analysis, except that the steps are reversed. The question is no longer how much land is required, but how many units of a particular housing type, or combination of types, can be accommodated on a parcel of land of a given size; or what housing type, or combination of types, should be provided in order to accommodate a particular number of dwelling units on a parcel of land. The following describes how the analysis is actually carried out.

The sizing exercise is essentially a need-gap analysis. It involves first the establishment of future needs in terms of the number of dwellings of different sizes and types, and then the comparison of the future needs to the existing housing stock. The difference between the two is the need-gap. This determines how much more land is needed for each housing type, or conversely, how much land is "wasted" by having inappropriate housing on it.

The first step is to establish the housing needs for some future period. We start by estimating the net population change, which, as described earlier, is a function of births, deaths, and migration. The prevailing living patterns, as well as the likely shifts in these patterns, especially in terms of household type and size, are studied. From the above findings the number of households of different sizes for the population are determined. Then the number of housing units of different types and sizes are also determined, usually by referring to some occupancy standards (number of people per habitable room). Wherever possible, this should be done according to analysis zones rather than the city as a whole.

The second step is to examine the existing housing stock in terms of housing type and number. At this point the amount of existing residential land should be noted and the prevailing residential densities by analysis zones should be identified. These serve as the basis for density standards for the future. It is useful to distinguish between those zones in the central area and those at the fringe. Housing stock data can often be obtained from planning and other municipal records, but densities may have to be surveyed.

The third step is to compare the findings of the previous two steps (housing needs and housing stock). This will give us estimates of different types of new dwellings needed, but the amount of land has yet to be determined. However, before this is done we have to adjust the estimates of new dwellings for units that would be lost during the interim period. There can be several kinds of losses. (1) Some units may be lost to public works programmes such as highway construction or property standards code enforcement. (2) Units may be removed from the stock through urban renewal or redevelopment actions. We should consider both past rates of loss and anticipated renewal rates. (3) Some units may be lost on account of invasion by other uses, especially in the central area where residential units may be converted to commercial uses. (4) Loss may be due to fires and other catastrophes. It is useful to examine past rates, but adjustment should be made for improvement in fire fighting and other effective renewal, building and maintenance codes. (5) Dwelling units may be abandoned. For this loss, assumptions have to be made about code enforcements, rent control policies, and so on.

Having accounted for housing losses, an allowance for vacancies has to be added. The conventional practice is to assume a five-percent vacancy rate but this is now considered too high. In an upswing market, even a one-percent vacancy rate is very significant. On choosing a vacancy rate, it is important to bear in mind seasonal fluctuations, especially in places like university towns or tourist resorts.

Having adjusted the estimates for losses and vacancies, we need to decide on the proportion of the housing gap that will be met by conversion and rehabilitation of the existing stock and the proportion met by new construction, by housing type and size. Only in the case of new construction is additional land supply required.

For this, recent construction trends should be studied. Data can be obtained from building permit records.

The following is a summary of the steps used to determine the future housing needs in a city by means of a need-gap analysis.

(i) a Estimate future population and its demographic profile.

b Translate population into the number of households by household size and type.

c Translate (using criteria of appropriate and adequate housing) the number of households into number of dwelling units by dwelling size and housing type.

(ii) Find out the number of existing dwelling units, by size and type.

(iii) a Calculate the basic need-gap: (i) c - (ii).

b Calculate the reasonable need-gap: basic need-gap plus obsolescence, demolition, abandonment, renewal, invasion by other uses, loss due to fire and other catastrophes, and allowance for vacancies.

(iv) Calculate the need for new housing construction: need-gap minus housing units created by conversion and rehabilitation.

Once the amount of new housing construction is established, it has to be matched to the land supply. There are two ways to go about this. The number of new housing units can be converted into land requirements in acreages by applying different land use density standards to the various housing types. The crucial element is therefore the density standards we use.

Alternatively, we can hold the supply of residential land as fixed (the amount being determined in the land supply analysis), and then work out the number of new housing units that can be accommodated for given density and design standards. Or, we can assume that all the new housing needs are to be met by a fixed supply of residential land and then work out the implied densities. In examining the land supply capacity, both vacant land and renewal areas should be considered. Each analysis zone has a holding capacity for residential use. This is defined as the number of dwelling units which the vacant and renewal land in the zone can accommodate according to some pattern of residential densities. The holding capacity should not include areas which are unavailable for development because of whims of the property owners, legal entanglements, unbuildable land, and so on. The central issue in this approach is the desired pattern of residential densities.

Residential Density

Density standards can be given as the number of dwellings per acre or hectare. These are appropriate indicators of land use and appearance. Density standards can also be given as the number of population, or households per acre or hectare.

These are appropriate indicators of potential markets and social needs. Both measures should be used to provide a complete picture. In addition, the ratio between the total floor space of the building and the area of land can also be used (referred to as Floor Area Ratio (FAR), Floor Space Index (FSI), or Plot Ratio (PR).

The density figures found in zoning by-laws or planning regulations are usually net densities (also known as parcel densities, lot densities, and net site densities). Two net density measures are typically used: "units per acre (hectare)" which is used to define the densities on individual lots, and "Floor Area Ratio" which is used in situations where the impacts of large buildings is a concern. These measures are based on land areas that have excluded roads, public open spaces, and community facilities. They are appropriate for estimating land needs in the developed or partially developed areas in a city. Gross densities, which include internal roads and some proportion of boundary roads, are more appropriate for newly developed areas. Neighbourhood densities, which include roads, public open spaces, local shopping areas and schools, are more meaningful for large undeveloped areas, and renewal or clearance areas. Extending beyond the residential areas, the gross density for the whole municipality (also known as community density or population density) is a ratio between its total population or dwelling units and the total land area of the municipality, including non-residential lands, undeveloped lands and undevelopable lands. This suggests that a municipality with a large share of industrial or other nonresidential uses might have a low municipal gross density even though many of its neighbourhoods might have very high neighbourhood densities.

TABLE 5-7
RESIDENTIAL DENSITY STANDARDS (A)
in units per acre (units per hectare)

Dwelling Type	Net Density		Neighbourhood Density	
Single-detached	Up to 8	(20)	Up to 5	(12)
Zero-lot-line detached	8 - 10	(20 - 25)	6	(15)
Semi-detached	10 - 12	(25 - 30)	7	(18)
Row houses	16 - 24	(40 - 60)	12	(30)
Stacked townhouses	25 - 40	(60 - 100)	18	(45)
Three-storey walkup apartments	40 - 50	(100 - 125)	20	(50)
Six-storey elevator apartments	65 - 75	(160 - 190)	30	(75)
Thirteen-storey elevator apartment	85 - 95	(215 - 240)	40	(100)

Source: Lynch and Hack (1984: 466)

Density standards should be related to local conditions. Even for the same housing type in the same city, different density standards may be used for the central area and the fringe area. After all, a single-detached house could be a one-bedroom bungalow or a mansion. Lynch and Hack (1984) suggest the following net densities as being "reasonable" under normal practice and according to accepted standards for circulation, open space, and community facilities (Table 5-7). Of course, by abandoning parking or play space one can increase the net density markedly. Chapin and Kaiser's (1979) standards are based on the recommendations of the American Public Health Association (Table 5-8).

TABLE 5-8
RESIDENTIAL DENSITY STANDARDS (B)
in units per acre (units per hectare)

Dwelling Type	Net Density			
	Desirable		Maximum	
Single-detached	5	(12)	7	(18)
Semi-detached	10	(25)	12	(30)
Row houses	16	(40)	19	(48)
Multi-family: 2 storey	25	(60)	30	(75)
3 storey	40	(100)	45	(115)
6 storey	65	(160)	75	(190)
9 storey	75	(190)	85	(215)
13 storey	85	(215)	95	(240)

Source: Chapin and Kaiser (1979: 455)

The range of net densities might perhaps be set between one and 120 dwellings (households) per acre (approx. between 2.5 and 300 dwellings per hectare). A density lower than one dwelling per acre produces expensive and scattered development. The living environment may be pleasant in itself but it leads to excessive sprawl, a costly transport system, and less accessible community facilities. On the other hand, areas with a density higher than 120 households per acre can be built only with the loss of open space and substandard living conditions. This limit may change, however, as technologies in transportation and utilities progress and as living habits change, or as we become more able to incorporate open spaces into the building at above-ground levels. It must also be emphasized that this range of densities relates to North America only, and is based on the idea of "privacy through distance," such as window-to-window distance and set-backs from the street and property line. It is obvious that these prescribed distances can only be very crude generalizations, and innovative design can provide as much privacy as that achieved through separation distance. However, it appears that separation distance is still required when dealing with sound and smell intrusion.

According to Lynch (1971: 317), the character of development may change according to some density thresholds. At a density of about 12 households to an acre (30 per hectare), problems of noise control and privacy begin to emerge. On the other hand, a density less than that would mean more difficulty in providing common maintenance of grounds or group facilities such as nurseries or laundries within very close range of the dwelling. Above 20 households per acre (50 per hectare) and we may find it increasingly difficult to provide outdoor space and direct access from all the units to the ground, and surface parking may become more difficult. At 45 households per acre (110 per hectare), we begin to lose "human scale." At 80 households per acre (200 per hectare), we will feel shortage of space for parking, landscaping and recreation. But at the same time, certain urban characteristics may emerge such as a greater variety of accessible activities and facilities. At above 100 households per acre (250 per hectare), we are likely to find problems about unit size and circulation congestion. These are very general clues to the quality of the residential environment associated with different kinds of housing types and densities, and they are dependent on culture, lifestyle, and expectations. It should also be noted that these standards are based on the number of dwellings or households per acre. Much reliance is placed on finding an acceptable definition of the elusive "average household." For this reason, the population per acre is often used as a supplementary density standard.

Hitchcock (1994:16-24) suggests a set of rules-of-thumb to gauge the impacts of increasing residential density on a neighbourhood.

(i) For the same housing type, the net density or parcel density (net of roads, open spaces, etc.) will be higher than the neighbourhood density (inclusive of roads, open spaces, local shops, schools, etc.) which will in turn be higher than the community density (inclusive of roads, open spaces, etc., as well as all non-residential lands, undeveloped lands, and undevelopable lands, etc.)

(ii) Density and housing types are related. Three housing design features are critical: width of the dwelling unit, width of side yards, and provision of parking. Considering minimum dimensions for living spaces, internal circulation, and privacy, the very upper limit of single-detached housing, with one garage, is 12 units per acre (30 units per hectare). The resultant lot dimension is 36 ft. (11m) by 100 ft. (30m), accommodating a two-storey house with a width of 14.5 ft. (4.5m), two side yards of 5 ft. (1.5m) each, and a garage of 11.5 ft. (3.5m) width. Similarly, the upper limit of semi-detached housing (with only one side yard) is 16 units per acre (40 units per hectare), with a lot frontage of 31 ft. (9.5m). The upper limit of row housing (with no side yards) is 24 units per acre (60 units per hectare) with a lot frontage of 26 ft. (8m).

(iii) The upper threshold for the Floor Area Ratio (FAR) of a "low density residential area" is 1.0 (Toronto's norm). A typical low density residential area is defined as a mixture of single-detached and semi-detached houses with a smattering of two-three-storey apartments.

(iv) Considering a residential area as a total unit, increasing neighbourhood density increases the economy of scale for the provision of urban services and amenities, such as retail facilities, public transit, and school within walking distance. But open space provision will be constrained. Neighbourhood density is a good index.

(v) Considering residential built-forms, especially their relationship to one another and to the ground, increasing density leads to less choice in site layout. But this is not necessarily undesirable. The higher density provides economies of scale in construction to permit more attractive (and expensive) building materials and landscaping, but there will be greater design challenges in providing privacy, recreation space and visual amenities. Net density (parcel density) is a good index.

(vi) Insider's view and outsider's views may conflict. Take the high-rise, the residents (insiders) get more light, air and view, while the neighbours (outsiders) get less view, more shadows, and a building they may not like.

(vii) A certain density level for a neighbourhood does not mean that all the houses in that neighbourhood correspond to that density. The larger the neighbourhood, the greater the possible difference between the overall average density and the housing type(s) in any particular part or parcel.

Allocating Residential Land

So far we have matched new housing construction needs to residential land requirements in a general way. Admittedly, many locations have similar qualities for residential use. Where will people actually go? In a market economy it is not possible to "assign" population to land. Our land use guidance systems work through development control and public investment. It is therefore essential that planners appreciate the dynamics of urban development and the logic of population distribution. There are some land development modelling techniques which try to simulate and predict residential allocation. The use of sophisticated models is rare, but we will introduce one which has an appealing logic and has also been the most used. The Lowry Model (Lowry, 1964) begins with an economic base submodel (discussed under Population Projection in the Information chapter) which generates population size from employment figures. Lowry uses the terms basic and non-basic sectors of the economy in a very practical sense. He suggests that the basic sector comprises industries which choose their location by considering, primarily, the appropriateness of the site for their own operation. On the other hand, the locational choice of the non-basic, or retail, sector is much more a function of the residential population which it serves. In the Lowry Model the basic sector is generally the "heavy" industries and the non-basic sector the whole range of commerce, services and institutions, from the neighbourhood level to the metropolitan level.

The model is designed to generate land use for a bounded region. Assumptions or actual data regarding the geographic distribution of basic employment serve as input to the model. Usually, basic employment is distributed by cells of a regular grid superimposed on the whole city region. Then, the land available for residential use in each cell is calculated. The computer distributes around each cluster of workplaces a residential population (households), which is needed to work in the industry. The logic of distributions of the residential population is based on minimum distances between places of residence and places of work, constrained by income. If the residential land in the cell is not sufficient for the working population, the overflow is reassigned to other cells. This spatially distributed residential population then serves as a basis for the location of the non-basic activities, from elementary school to department store. Then, the employees of these retail and service activities represent new population (households) which has to be accommodated and located. This population also creates additional demand for still more retail and services. Thus, iterations proceed in this manner until a stable co-distribution of all employment and all residences is achieved within the constraints of available land, efficient scales of operation for enterprises, and density ceilings for residential population. The logic of the model depends very much on the reliability of the economic base theory, and the operation of the model requires numerous assumptions and data. For instance, we will need to know the amount of available land in each cell; the behaviour about work trips and shopping trips; market potentials for various retails and services, and so on. In practice, the planner assigns residential land by examining the recent demand trends in order to guess at the amount of land needed, and by looking at the pattern of urban development and redevelopment in order to figure out the likelihood of development, at the different locations. Sophisticated land use models exist but are seldom used.

Other Land Uses in a Residential Community

Three additional elements, apart from housing, are essential in designing a total residential environment: open spaces, schools, and shops. Dispersal of these services or facilities will enable more people to live conveniently close to them. But, on the other hand, dispersal would mean a reduced level of service which may not be sufficient or varied enough to satisfy user needs. Thus, we should be thinking of hierarchies of such facilities and services. Ordinarily, a location which is suitable for one of these facilities is usually suitable for all others. Through careful choice of locations and layouts, it should be possible to combine the catchment areas of schools and shops. Then, a hierarchy of open spaces can be integrated with the school/shop centres to produce a satisfying residential environment. (For open space, refer to the previous section in this chapter.)

TABLE 5-9a
SCHOOL SITING AND SIZING STANDARDS

Type of School	Population Served			Students * per 1,000 pop. (or 275-300 households)	Size of Student Body		
	Min.	Max.	Average		Min.	Max.	Average
Nursery	1,000	2,000	1,500	60	60	120	90
Elementary	1,500	7,000	5,000	175	250	1,200	800
Junior High	10,000	20,000	16,000	75	800	1,600	1,200
High	14,000	34,000	24,000	75	1,000	2,600	1,800

* Assumptions and population characteristics should reflect local education policy.

Source: Adapted from Kaiser, Godschalk and Chapin (1995:386, Table 15-2)

TABLE 5-9b
SCHOOL SITING AND SIZING STANDARDS

Type of School	General Location	Radius of Catchment area		Land Requirement		
		Desirable	Max.	Min.	Max.	Average
Nursery	Near an elementary school or community centre	1- 2 blocks	1/3 mile (1/2 km)	4,000 sq. ft. (1200 sm)	8,000 sq. ft. (2400 sm)	6,000 sq. ft. (1800 sm)
Elementary	- Near centre of residential area - Near or adjacent to community facilities	1/4 mile (0.4 km)	1/2 mile (0.8 km)	7-8 acre (2.8 - 3.2 hectares)	16-18 acres (6.4 - 7.2 hectares)	12-14 acres (4.8 - 5.6 hectares)
Junior High	- Near centre of residential area - Away from major roads	1/2 mile (0.8 km)	3/4 mile (1.2 km)	18-20 acres (7.2 - 8 hectares)	30-32 acres (12 - 12.8 hectares)	24-26 acres (9.6 - 10.4 hectares)
High	- Central location - Proximity to community facilities - Adjacent to parks	3/4 mile (1.2 km)	1 mile (1.6 km)	32-34 acres (12.8 - 13.6 hectares)	48-50 acres (19.2 - 20 hectares)	40-42 acres (16 - 16.8 hectares)

Source: Adapted from Kaiser, Godschalk and Chapin (1995:386, Table 15-2).

1. Schools. The siting of a school is a function of the size of the school and the catchment area to be served by the school. Distance standards are normally used. The amount of land to be allocated for a publicly funded school is determined by government policies. A planner may agree to disagree with these policies, but can do little to change them. Yet, at the same time a planner has to recognize that these policies will affect the numbers, kinds, and sizes of schools needed for a given population. Usually, school standards are given as acreage of land per thousand population. It is very important to recognize that population size is not a reliable basis for estimating school size. School size should depend on the number of enrolment, which is a function of the number of population as well as family cycle, education policies, social expectations, and so on. The following is a table of some very crude standards used in North America.

2. Local Businesses and Facilities. The main siting criterion of local business is that it should be within convenient walking distance of the resident population, or driving distance when it is a very low-density neighbourhood. If the business is serving a larger area than the immediate neighbourhood, such as a shopping centre, then it should be located with transit access and adjacent to major thoroughfares or at the intersection of these. For this reason, shopping centres are usually situated toward the in-town edge of tributary trade area.

The sizing of land for local business is commonly done by using standards, such as the number of acres per thousand population. These standards vary with different residential densities and local conditions. A very important determinant of land requirements is parking ratio, that is, the area of parking to the area of retail floor space. (Refer to a later section on Retail and Commercial Use.)

The space needs for local facilities, whether they are community-oriented or neighbourhood-oriented, are established based on local trends and projected population size and composition. They are also commonly stated in acreages per thousand population or square footages per person.

To conclude, in the siting of residential use, the central question is the congruence between user needs and the locational qualities of the land. The solution to this question may differ, depending on whether the land is located in an established or a new area. In an established area, the emphasis is the protection from other uses, traffic and natural hazards. In a new area, the emphasis is the protection from natural hazards and the impact of the proposed use on the environment. It is important to examine both the suitability of the land to the proposed use and the impact of the use on the land and the neighbours. For this reason, a residential development may be considered inappropriate not only when the traffic congestion around the site affects its proper use, but also when it creates traffic conditions that are detrimental to the neighbouring uses. Conversely, a development may be considered inappropriate on account of its shadow effect on its neighbours as well as the shadow effects of the neighbours on the land where the development is to be situated. Then there is the question of availability and accessibility of facilities and services, and expectations in this respect are much higher in the case of an established area than that of a new area. Finally, in an established area, sensitivity towards existing visual orders and other human activities and concerns is more important. In a new area, sensitivity towards ecosystems, topography, microclimate, and so on, is more important.

In the sizing of residential land, the focus is on the match between the needs of new housing construction and the holding capacity of the land. The determining criteria are density thresholds of various housing types. The main issue is whether there is sufficient suitable land to accommodate the new housing needs. If not, then the housing needs have to be adjusted, or the density standards have to be revised, or the land supply and/or capacity have to be increased. However, the present trend is towards conservation, rehabilitation and adaptive reuse of existing buildings. This opens up new opportunities for innovative thinking about the "supply" or housing and land in built-up areas.

INDUSTRIAL USE

Siting   Our conception of industrial land use is very much outdated. Most planners (as manifested in planning regulations) are still thinking of industries as noisy, dirty and unsightly operations. In reality, many industrial operations and workers demand a cleaner, healthier and more pleasant environment than some residential and community uses. Planners should be ready to consider mixed uses in the siting of nonpolluting or small scale industries.

For industries which are not oriented to local consumers and where the site selection is relatively unconstrained by access to local markets, the following general principles can still be used (Chapin and Kaiser, 1979: 388-389; and Kaiser, Godschalk and Chapin, 1995: 324-326).

(1) The site should preferably be level or less than five percent slope. If not, the terrain and soil conditions must be such that they should be gradable at low cost. The site should also be outside the flood plains and environmental sensitive areas.

(2) For extensive manufacturing, large open sites (more than five acres) are needed, which should also provide sufficient room for storage, access and parking. For intensive manufacturing where a single- or multi-storey building may be used, the lot area can be less than five acres.

(3) There should be direct access to commercial transport. If the site is located at a fringe area, access to railroad and major trucking routes is important. Only airport-related manufacturing needs to be located near airports. A prime site would have its front on a major highway and its back to a railroad with the depth of the site greater than 1000 feet (2000 feet is even better). For industries which require water haulage, closeness to water channels and port facilities is important.

(4) The site should be located within easy commuting tie with the residential labour force. This means that it should be close to public transport routes or thoroughfares to housing areas.

(5) Utilities should be available at, or at least near, the site. Large industrial plants often supply their own utilities but the smaller ones do not.

(6) The use should be compatible with the surrounding uses. Consideration should be given to prevailing winds, greenbelts as buffers, and amenity factors both within and adjoining the site.

(7) A preferred location is a prominent site on a major highway. This gives good advertising opportunity and is also good for employee access. But highway sites should have a minimum depth of 600 to 800 feet because space is needed for frontage and service road access.

(8) The environ should be attractive and not blighted, otherwise such a site is not marketable.

Hok-Lin Leung

(9) If the industry involves wastes, then adequate space for on-site pre-treatment is necessary.

(10) The size of individual lots may vary. For an individual plant it could be between two and ten acres. Industrial parks range from 50 to 500 acres or more.

(11) Location for nuisance-type industries, such as junkyards and fuel storage deserve more consideration about hazards and appearance. They should be close to highways so as to minimize travel through residential areas.

(12) Compatibility with surrounding areas is more important for industrial processes that produce off-site noise, glare, odour, smoke, traffic, danger-ous emissions and waste-storage. In particular, truck and automobile traf-fic generated on site should not intrude into residential areas.

Sizing　Land required by manufacturing industry is often considered as a function of the number of workers. But with increasing automation fewer workers are needed for a given volume of production. However, the overall land requirement may not have diminished because the new manufacturing process and storage of raw mate-rial often take up more space. It is also becoming apparent that offices which do not need to have much contact with the general public are better sited in industrial areas than in city centres. The space standards used for office workers are much lower than those used for industrial workers. The net result is that there is a mix-ture of industrial and office workers at the urban fringe, and the actual amount of land needed for the mixed uses is not significantly different from that required under the traditional industrial space standards. The following is a brief description of the logic used in estimating aggregate land requirements for industries.

The most important analysis is existing densities. The overall density of a particular industry is a ratio between the total floor space and/or acreage of land used by that industry and the number of employees in that industry. There are two common units of measurement: floor space per worker, and the number of workers per acre or hectare. The latter is used more frequently. Often, densities at different locations are obtained, such as central areas versus the outlying areas. In this way, densities for different industry types can be established for different locations. There are two ways to classify an industry: the first is according to its product, such as food, tobacco, and textile; the second is according to the intensity in its use of land, such as intensive, intermediate, and extensive, as measured by the number of workers for a given floor area. The first approach is better suited for data collection, the second for land use analysis and design. Maybe it is best to gather data by using the first approach and reorganize the data according to the land use intensities. It should be remembered that data on existing densities are usually net densities based on the actual number of workers, floor area, and site area. When planning for land requirements gross densities are required, which take into consideration streets, railroads, and other service facilities. Based on the existing densities, standards for the future can be formulated. These standards recognize the shortages and excesses of the existing densities, in particular, the adequacy of both floor areas and ground areas for industrial operation, recent trends in industrial space design and usage, and adequacy of parking and circulation space.

TABLE 5-10
INDUSTRIAL SITE PLANNING STANDARDS

Size	
Range	100-500 acres (40-200 ha.)
Average	300 acres (120 ha.)
Minimum size	35 acres (14 ha.)
Block size	400-1000 ft. x 1000-2000 ft.
	(120 - 300 m x 300 - 600 m.)
Floor area ratio (F.A.R.)	0.1 - 0.3
Parking	0.8-1.0/employee
Employee density (overall)	10 - 30 per acre (25 - 75 per hectare)
Intensive industry	30 per net acre (75 per hectare)
Intermediate industry	14 per net acre (35 per hectare)
Extensive industry	8 per net acre (20 per hectare)

Source: Lynch and Hack (1984:306-311 and 468); and Urban Land Institute (1975:167-168)

It is not useful to have too many density standards. For a small city, say with less than 100,000 population, a single density standard may be used. In North America the range is from 10 to 25 workers per net acre for new industries. Even for large metropolitan areas, two or three classes of densities are quite sufficient, such as intensive (electrical equipment and instruments, textile and apparel, printing and publishing, etc.), intermediate (lumber and wood, furniture and fixture, primary metals, rubber and plastics, etc.), and extensive (petroleum and coal, leather, glass, tobacco, wholesale, etc.). Tables 5-10 and 5-11 show some conventional standards. However,·standards should really be established locally, based on local conditions about industrial mix, technological changes and land supply. Furthermore, different standards should be used for addition or conversion at existing sites as opposed to construction at new sites.

Based on the density and land requirement standards, space (land) needs for the future can be estimated. For a small city this can be done by applying the local standard to the projected employment to obtain the total amount of industrial land needed. The difference between this estimate and the existing industrial land is the amount of land needs for the future. This should be adjusted by a safety factor for the possible lowering of densities in the future, as is apparent in the recent trend. Then land "reserves" for future expansion should be added. It is standard practice to allocate more land to industrial use than is needed immediately because of all the uncertainties associated with changing employment patterns and manufacturing techniques. Also, there should be space for retail and other recreational open space in large industrial areas. For a larger city, the logic of allocation is the same, except that the determination of the density standards is more elaborate and detailed. Distinctions are made between central areas and outlying areas, and different density standards are applied to different types of industrial operations (based on their labour intensities).

TABLE 5-11
INDUSTRIAL LAND REQUIREMENT STANDARDS (AREA-WIDE)

% workforce of total population	35-40%
% industrial workers to total workforce	30-35%
% heavy industry workers to total industrial workers	60-70%
% light industry workers to total industrial workers	30-40%
Gross land required for industry	12 acres/1000 population
Land required for light industry	2 acres/1000 population
Land required for heavy industry	10 acres/1000 population
Land required for reserve	50 years growth

Source: Koppelman and DeChiara (1975:459).

The following is a summary of the steps used to determine the need for industrial land for a city (or a sub-area).

(i) Identify existing density (intensity of use) by location (e.g., centre area and outlying area) and/or density category (e.g., intensive, intermediate and extensive). Densities are expressed as number of workers per acre or hectare of land, or amount of floor space per worker.

(ii) Based on the deficiencies or excesses of the existing densities, determine the appropriate density standards that should be used in the future (for growth as well as restructuring).

(iii) Estimate employment growth/decline.

(iv) Estimate land needs (by areas and categories if necessary).

Basic needs = density standard x employment growth or decline

Reasonable needs = basic needs modified by safety factor (for possible lowering of densities), and reserves for expansion.

More often, the planning question is not to estimate the total needs but to analyze the land use implications of changing industrial structure and production technologies. Two issues are involved: how to provide suitable land for the new industrial needs, and what to do with existing industrial land which is no longer suited to the industrial user requirements. To answer these questions a survey may be conducted to examine the detailed space needs of a certain industry. In such a survey information on user activities, as well as on the land requirements, is gathered. Data on floor space and its usage are more useful than those on land areas alone, and actual shift employment figures are more useful than total employment figures.

Detailed studies may also be needed for the development of planned industrial districts, or industrial parks. There are good manuals on the planning, organization, finance and development of industrial parks (Urban Land Institute, 1975 and 1988). Independent surveys have found that the average size of an industrial park is about 300 acres, but it is better to have a larger number of smaller parks than a few very large ones. Finally, in planning for industrial parks, it is particularly important to consider phasing and reserves because industrial land requirements, especially location and minimum lot size, are more stringent than commercial and residential uses.

RETAIL AND COMMERCIAL USES

Retail uses cover the range of uses from the neighbourhood corner store to shopping street, shopping district, suburban mall, and to the so-called "new-format" retail (essentially the big-box).

The neighbourhood corner stores, easily accessible to most local residents, staying open at odd hours, and offering a personal service, including some form of credit, have mostly disappeared. The independent retailers in shopping districts and main streets have also suffered much decline, and are being replaced by the chain supermarkets and department stores. The small independent shops will continue to lose out as people who manage these shops are retiring and are not being replaced. The premises are getting older and not easily modernized. Delivery services are becoming more tailored to large operations and not small shops. Rents and taxes keep rising in many central areas where these shops have traditionally been located. At the same time, as the population is redistributed from the inner city to the outer suburbs (although the trend has reversed somewhat in recent years with the gentrification of inner city areas), inner city small shops have been losing customers. Those customers they have retained usually have lower incomes and less mobility. The automobile-dependent and bulk-purchasing suburbanite finds the old main street, with its lack of parking, narrow sidewalks, personal but often slow service, and often higher prices, an unattractive place to do his/her regular shopping. The planner and the developer have also contributed to the decline of small shops by encouraging the concentration of shops in centres, thereby eliminating smaller, weaker groups in the surrounding areas, and by allowing very little space for small shops or charging very high rents in redevelopment schemes.

However, the small shops, especially in the form of the corner store, have transcended their role of being just a business enterprise, and are playing a valuable social role for certain segments of the population. They offer a point of contact, and a meeting place, for the less mobile, such as the elderly and children. The disappearance of the well-known, independent shops in inner city declining areas is seen as almost a personal loss by those to whom they were familiar. Even in the suburbs the absence of small local stores has been noted as one of the possible causes for the lack of community feeling. However, a clear distinction should be made between a general shop and a neighbourhood shop. If we are to encourage or sustain local neighbourhood shops, we should have more flexible policies to allow these shops to expand when they need to and encourage the provision of housing above the shops or the conversion of a ground floor of a house into a shop. Table 5-12 shows some land requirement standards for combined community-neighbourhood shopping.

TABLE 5-12

LAND REQUIREMENT STANDARDS FOR COMBINED COMMUNITY-NEIGHBOURHOOD SHOPPING

(in acres per 1000 population)

Selected neighbourhood population size, in communities of 30,000 - 50,000 population	1:1*	2:1*	3:1*
5,000	0.5 acre	0.7 acre	0.9 acre
2,500	0.6 acre	0.8 acre	1.01 acre
1,000	0.9 acre	1.1 acres	1.5 acres

* Parking space to retail floor space ratio

Source: Adapted from Kaiser, Godschalk and Chapin (1995:362, Table 14.9).

Much planning effort has been devoted to the modernizing of old shopping streets in order to make them economically viable. The key to success is to be selective. The boundary of the area for improvement should be drawn up carefully (political considerations notwithstanding) possibly at the expense of other adjoining areas. A combination of tactics is often used, including pedestrianizing the street or introducing some restrictions upon the automobile, the closure of some shops, a certain amount of redevelopment, the beautification of building facades, the introduction of rear access and parking facilities, the improvement of housing accommodation above and around the shops, and possibly the inclusion of community facilities such as a library, a clinic, or a public office. In most cases, though, streetscaping is the main emphasis, such as the planting of trees, the provision of benches, new pavement, and street signs.

For a new shopping centre, mixed uses such as housing and other employment uses should be considered. These will make the centre more lively and ensure that it will be used over a longer period of time during the course of a day. If a new centre is part of a new housing project or a new neighbourhood the phasing of shopping and residential development should be carefully coordinated to ensure that the residents' shopping needs and the financial considerations of the merchants are compatible. This includes the proper allocation of the type, size, number, and location of shops for each phase of residential growth. Flexibility should be incorporated to allow for changes even after the completion of the development.

Many shoppers have expressed a preference for the combination of modern retail facilities in more traditional settings. For this, a new shopping centre may provide some small units at low cost for small independent shops to be located there. This will allow the small operators to survive and will provide a more comfortable surrounding for many shoppers. Sometimes, even substandard or unconventional developments are encouraged, such as stalls or carts in a small centre and a street market in a larger centre, in order to give variety and vitality to a shopping centre.

If a centre has more than one level then movement between levels must be effortless and natural. Sometimes, levels are accessed by different modes of transportation, for instance, one level by car and the other level by pedestrian and public transit. Protection from the weather is desirable especially where the climate is harsh, but it is not always necessary to have a completely enclosed and air conditioned mall. An arcade can be cheaper and more pleasant.

The most significant retail development in the last ten years has been the "new format" retail which includes large discount stores, warehouse membership clubs (e.g., Price Club and Costco), category-dominant retailers (e.g., Winners and Home Depot), and factory outlets, etc. This trend began in the U.S. (first Price Club in San Diego in 1976) and has become a significant retail approach. Planning practice (especially in Canada) has been caught unprepared. As a result, large retailers have been able to locate on commercial or industrial land rather than on retail land, thus avoiding higher land costs and property taxes. Their main success is in their ability to attract consumers through competitively lower prices, "to the point where they would drive 20 kilometres to shop in such a complex; these same consumers were prepared to travel only three kilometres to shop in a grocery store" (Crowe and Siemonsen 1996:25-26). Besides low prices, they offer large selection, free parking and convenient shopping hours.

Supermarket chains in Canada brought a case to the Ontario Municipal Board (OMB) to prevent a zoning application by Costco, arguing that it was primarily a retail business and should be subject to zoning regulations on retail land use. The OMB rejected the appeal. But this brought out the real land use planning issue--Is this wholesale or retail? Of course, there are those "new format" retailers who are doing exclusively retail business, such as optical outlets, sporting goods, office equipment, and toys. Yet, they too seek to locate on non-retail sites.

Warehouse clubs or the like try to avoid the many land use regulations for commercial activity by calling themselves a warehouse or wholesaler. Some U.S. municipalities have adopted "high-volume retail" zones to accommodate uses generating significant traffic while others have established special site designations for these warehouse clubs (Faludi, 1992). Toderian (1996) finds a number of responses in Canada. Some municipalities rework their zoning regulations to have more permitted uses, and then develop design guidelines to control site planning (especially with respect to pedestrian connections). Some eliminate the requirement of the traditional anchor stores required in shopping centres, replacing them by the "new format" stores or by small tenants. Some introduce a "special purpose commercial" designation which allows large-scale new-format facilities that require large parcels of land. Some permit "new format" retail in the same designation as small retail, but encourage them to locate around existing regional shopping areas. Finally, some take an aggressive approach to attract them, and review impediments for their development, such as site requirements and land availability. The land use planning issues about "new format" retail should also include their effect on traditional shopping areas; flexibility in replacing the traditional anchors with numerous smaller operations; incorporation of community-related uses; and possibility of retrofitting or reuse in future markets.

Office uses can be divided into five types: (i) offices for professionals and institutions, such as headquarter offices, financial institutions, legal and accounting firms, etc.; (ii) general commercial offices; (iii) medical offices; (iv) quasi-industrial offices that are often mixed with warehouses, light manufacturing and distribution facilities; and (v) industrial offices for the own use of large industrial cooperations (O'Mara, 1982). There are three classes of "quality" measures. Class A buildings have excellent location and access, attract high quality tenants, and are managed professionally. Building materials are superior and rents are competitive with other new buildings. Class B buildings have good location, management and construction, and tenant standards are high. Buildings have very little functional obsolescence and deterioration. Class C buildings are typically 15 to 25 years old but are maintaining steady occupancy. The demand for office space is based, ultimately, on population and the economy, but for land use planning purposes employment forecasts are preferred because these can be more readily translated into space needs.

Siting   The estimation of the locational and space needs for retail and commercial uses follows similar logic as the other uses. For retail uses, locational needs depend on the kinds of retail. It is useful to consider general areas such as central business districts, suburban centres, and highway-oriented retail areas. The neighbourhood corner store is best treated as part of the residential environment.

The location and size of the different retail and commercial areas should be determined by the role that they are going to play in the overall pattern of land use and development, and the contribution they are going to make towards the general planning goals for the city as a whole. The central business district (CBD) is characterized by its high land values, the multiplicity of retail types, and the generally commercial character of the area. On the other side, the CBD often has traffic problems, parking problems, and the problem of decline owing to competition by outlying commercial and shopping centres which are developed with the automobile-owning consumers in mind. The suburban centres include the older satellite centres; the more modern regional shopping centres with all the combinations of civic, social, entertainment, and retail services; and the office employment centres for both consumer and business services. Many of these centres first began to develop as retailers and offices sought the lower land values at various outlying locations. But most of these centres are now well established. Highway-oriented commercial uses are usually less planned and less concentrated than the CBD and suburban centres, and they cater primarily to the highway users. These retailers often require a large amount of land and should not be located close to residential areas.

The CBD is usually located at, or close to, the peak flow of vehicular and pedestrian traffic. There should be sufficient accommodations for professional, financial and related services. There should be easy access to adequate parking, transit, and regional transportation services for shoppers and workers in the CBD.

Suburban centres should be located close to major transit routes and intersections of major roads, as well as to residential areas. There should be a complete line of shops and stores, eating and entertainment facilities, and other businesses and services sufficient to fill several hours of the shopper's time. The site should also be large enough to accommodate peak parking needs. As a general rule, the size of such a centre should be between 30 and 150 acres, so as to avoid too large a concentration of traffic and impervious ground cover.

Highway-oriented commercial uses should be located in outlying areas on major highway approaches to the urban area. The site should be adequate for drive-in services and parking, while taking into full consideration highway safety, roadside beauty, and the general amenity of the adjoining users.

Another approach to the siting of commercial uses is based on service radii and size of population served, such as neighbourhood, community, and regional shopping locations. Table 5-13 shows some common shopping centre standards.

TABLE 5-13
SHOPPING CENTRE STANDARDS

	Neighbourhood	Community	Regional
Forms	Strip	Mall or "U"	Cluster
Location	Intersection of collectors and secondary roads	Intersections of major roads and expressway	Intersection of express freeways
Service radius	1.5 mile	3 - 5 miles	> 8 miles
Catchment area	5 - 10 min. drive	10 - 20 min. drive	20 - 30 min. drive
Population served	4,000 - 10,000	35,000 - 150,000	over 150,000
Gross land area	2.5 - 10 acres	10 - 30 acres	10 - 60 acres
Av. gross floor area	30,000 - 75,000 sq.ft.	100,000 - 250,000 sq.ft.	300,000 - 1,000,000 sq.ft.
Typical gross floor area	50,000 sq.ft.	150,000 sq.ft.	400,000 sq.ft.
No. of stores	5 - 20	15 - 40	40 - 80
Parking Index #/1000 sq.ft. GLA	8	7	5 - 6

Max distance of all parking to building = 650 ft.

Max distance of normal day parking to building = 300 ft.

Source: Adapted from Urban Land Institute (1982b); Lynch and Hack (1984); and Kaiser, Godschalk and Chapin (1995).

At the project level, there has been a long history of retail location strategies. Usually, there are three steps (Thompson, 1986).

(i) Area Identification. Sales performance of a sample of stores is analyzed against a basket of demographic and socioeconomic data (e.g., household sizes and household incomes), by using a multiple regression analysis. Significant variables are identified, which are then used to generate the most favourable area to locate the project.

(ii) Sub-Area Identification. Market support for the project is calculated, that is, the number of additional square footage of the specific retail that can be supported in a sub-area. This calculation requires data on local residents, their per capita expenditure, their spending habits, and the locations and sizes of competitors, as well as an accurate population forecast. This is then followed by a tentative location strategy, taking into consideration of the road network, and psychological and physical barriers.

(iii) Site Selection. A number of potential sites are tested to identify the one with the highest potential sales. A number of methods can be used. (a) A multiple regression model, similar to the one used in step (i), can be employed to locate the project within the sub-area. But given the level of specificity and details required the model is difficult to calibrate. (b) A "normal formula" describes the way the market share of a store changes in relation to a number of variables. For instance, distance is one of the main variables. Through home interviews (e.g., respondents' weekly expenditure in different stores in the trade areas) data on the percentage of consumer expenditures in different stores are obtained. These expenditures are then plotted against the distances between consumers and stores to generate a "decay curve" showing how the market share decreases with distance. This information is then combined with the population densities of the different consumer groups to generate a "normal formula curve," which can then be used to identify the location with the highest potential sales. In theory, this normal curve can be applied under all circumstances; but in practice, there are difficulties in adjusting the curve to the realities on the ground. (c) An analog method uses historical records to forecast sales. Customer information (especially addresses) is collected at existing stores to delimit trade areas. Based on such data rules-of-thumb about primary trade areas have been developed for different retail categories. They are simple to use but lack sophistication. (d) A gravity model assumes that customer share of a store is directly proportional to the attractiveness of a store (size is used as a surrogate measure for selection and depth of merchandise) and inversely proportional to distance (usually straight-line distances). It provides a rapid estimation of sales at a proposed location under a variety of scenarios about size and type of operations, as well as an assessment of probable reaction of competitors. However, it has limited ability to include demographic patterns.

With respect to office location much depends on whether the office function is oriented toward consumer services or not. If it is, then it should be located in commercial centres in order to maximize client access. Offices for professionals and major institutions should be located in central areas and prime sites for visibility, prestige and convenience. General commercial offices need good access, and suburban sites near freeways (expressways) are suitable if there is adequate parking. Medical offices should be close to hospitals. Industrial offices are often located in industrial districts and parks.

Office use and retail use can be mixed or separate. Whether it is a single office building or an office park, location and access are key considerations. Adjacent uses should enhance, or have the potential to enhance, the site. The office use should have ready access by pedestrians, public transit, and private automobiles. Commuting time by workers should be kept within 30 minutes. Automobile access is still critical for suburban locations. Table 5-14 shows some common office space standards.

Sizing   For site-specific analysis there are usually two questions. First, is the operation too large for the site? The concern is about the adequacy of space for the activities to be carried out satisfactorily, such as internal circulation, parking and loading, and visual amenities. Second, is the operation too large for the general environ? Here the concerns are the activities and traffic generated by the retail and commercial use, its environmental impact, and compatibility with the surrounding uses.

TABLE 5-14
OFFICE SPACE STANDARDS

Ratio of class "A" space to "B" and "C" space

No growth situation	1:2	
Expanding market	1:4	

Office space/worker	**sq.ft.**	**sq.m.**
General worker	65 - 80	6 - 7
Supervisor	100 - 120	9 - 11
Administrative assistant	150	14
Executive assistant	200 - 250	18 - 23
Administrator	300	28
Executive	400 - 500	36 - 46

NOTE:

Class A buildings have excellent location and access, attract high quality tenants, and are managed professionally. Building materials are superior and rents are competitive with other new buildings.

Class B buildings have good location, management and construction, and tenant standards are high. Buildings should have very little functional obsolescence and deterioration.

Class C buildings are typically 15 - 25 years old but are maintaining steady occupancy.

Source: Urban Land Institute (1982a:18 and 19).

For a whole city or an analysis zone, there is usually more land allocated for commercial use than is really needed, especially in suburban areas and along highways. It is customary to designate long strips of land along a main road as commercial simply because such land has commercial "potential." This leads to spotty development which generates haphazard traffic patterns and excessive financial burden on municipalities to maintain the underutilized roads.

The aggregate space needs for retail should be a function of the population. An increase in population means an increase in consumer purchase power, and hence an increase in floor space (and land) needed for retail. The problem with this approach is that it assumes consumer behaviour to remain unchanged, and has therefore an inherent bias against new types of marketing techniques, such as electronic purchases. It also assumes a static relationship between people's income and their purchase power and shopping habit. Our present knowledge in these areas is limited and can allow us to work out only crude estimates of overall land requirements.

After an estimated increase in consumer spending is obtained it has to be allocated between CBD and the other centres. This is often based on judgement of trends in shopping behaviour, merchandising practice, transport opportunities, and standards about convenience and amenities, guided by goals and policies about the relative roles to be played by the CBD and the other centres, and their growth or consolidation strategies. Consumer spending is translated into the number of shoppers and number of employees in the various business areas.

The next step is to apply space standards on the number of shoppers or the number of employees to arrive at the amount of retail or office floor space. Comparing this with existing floor space will give the size of the need gap to be filled. These floor space estimates are then divided by the number of retail and office floors in buildings normally associated with such businesses to arrive at the amount of land required. To this, land needed for parking is added. Different parking area standards are used for different kinds of business areas. Very often planners require more extravagant off-street (on-site) parking for new retailers to make up for the deficiency in the existing parking situation. There is, however, a trade-off between on-site parking and the use of public transit. More on-site parking means that there is less reliance on public transit and, therefore, less support of transit use. The final estimate should also include land for landscaping, drainage retention, internal roads for the development, and so on. The calculation will become even more complex for multiple-use centres where civic and social functions and open space are to be integrated.

Much good reference material exists in both the siting and sizing of retail and commercial land uses. The most valuable are the Urban Land Institute manuals (1982a and 1982b) on commercial and office development. But planners should also consult studies about the travel and shopping behaviour of consumers, the location behaviour of commercial centre developers, and market behaviour of retailers and shopping centre operators. As well, planners can refer to family expenditure surveys, income surveys, and surveys of consumer habits.

In summary, the logic of estimating retail use land is as follows. Based on the number and type of households and assumptions about average incomes, the total disposable income of the population is obtained, which in turn yields the total gross retail expenditure of the population. From that, the gross retail sales at different business areas are determined, which are broken down further by store types. From the sales figures the number of shoppers and the number of retail employees are established. Floor space standards are then applied to obtain the floor areas for different store types at different locations. The floor areas are then aggregated and converted to land acreage requirements, taking into consideration parking ratios and loading area factors. Planners can refer to the literature for income, sales and space standards as well as for technical guidance if they want to do their own study.

COMMUNITY FACILITIES

The basic siting principle for community facilities is the adequacy of service delivery. Two considerations are paramount: convenience to the users, especially when it is a recreational facility, and economy of development.

Community facilities can be recreational, educational, or cultural. Each has its special needs but there are some general locational principles (Chapin and Kaiser, 1979:395-400).

(1) The site should be reasonably level because most facilities include buildings and parking and some facilities also have active recreational uses. Normally the slope should not be greater than five percent. However, where a large open space is associated with the facility, the ground form can be varied and slope limits are less important.

(2) Major parks, golf courses, and so on, are usually located at the urban fringe. But institutions such as community colleges and medical centres should be located on level or gentle gradient, and be sufficiently protected from traffic and incompatible uses.

(3) Direct access to major thoroughfares or public transit is very important.

(4) The size of the site should be adequate for the activities, the grounds should be pleasant, and the approach should be visible from a distance.

(5) Cultural facilities, places of worship, and spectator sports are usually located more centrally although at the same time they are not located on sites with high land values.

(6) Many community facilities need fairly large sites and most of them are not very intensively built up, therefore they can be considered as part of the open space system contributing to the city's visual texture.

(7) The siting of smaller community facilities such as fire halls, police stations, libraries, and post offices, are often guided by national service standards. For instance, the distance of a fire station to business and industrial areas should not be greater than three-quarters of a mile for a pumper

company or one mile for a ladder company. For a police station the speed and efficiency of moving personnel and equipment are the most important considerations and there is also the difference between the beat system and a patrol cruiser system. For libraries, too, there are national standards, such as the local service radius which should not be greater than a mile. Post offices are best located near business centres.

(8) Branch municipal government offices should be located near focal points of several residential neighbourhoods, near or adjacent to a shopping centre, and where possible, consolidated with fire, police, clinic, branch libraries, etc.

Special studies are usually needed to determine the appropriate site size. It should be pointed out that many such studies involve interviews with administrators and officials, such as those from a hospital board or a school board, who are the clients but are not always the users. Patience and sensitivity are required if one is to get relevant answers. For example, in a hospital study one could interview the administrators, doctors, nurses, and even the patients. However, the people who use the site the most are not those working or staying in the hospital, but visitors who are often left out by the study. In general, sizing depends on the amount of facilities to be accommodated and how intensively the site is to be used, for example, the number of storeys of the buildings and the site coverage by buildings. Land values and design objectives are often the deciding factors.

The principles used in siting community facilities are not much different from those for industrial and commercial uses. Catchment area or service area, compatibility of the use with other adjoining uses, and traffic in and around the site, are the most important considerations. The sizing question is often less crucial; usually the site area is a trade-off between the number of facilities or the level of services to be provided and the desirable intensity of development at the location.

MIXED USES

One of the main criticisms of modern planning is the segregation of uses. In the past 20 years, the thrust of sustainable development, whether it is driven by environmentalism or New Urbanism, is the mixing of different land uses. (Refer to the New Urbanism and Ecological Perspectives discussions in the Synthesis chapter.) It is also argued that mixing land uses can improve the use of infrastructure, exploit economies of scale, and enhance a site's development potential. In particular, mixed development in inner city areas can generate attention and activities, thus helping to revitalize the area, increase transit ridership and strengthen the local tax base. Mixed-use projects can also act as an attractive transition between different land uses or districts. No wonder many municipalities have tried to encourage mixed uses through mixed-use zoning, multi-use planned unit development (PUD), and the creation of special-purpose districts. The following are some standard planning criteria, at the scale of individual projects.

A mixed-use development usually has three or more revenue-producing uses, which are functionally and physically integrated within a coherent plan. Sometimes office space is the dominant use; sometimes retail, residential or hotel spaces are the dominant uses; and sometimes there are no clear dominant uses.

Mixed-use development is an intensive land use. This means that low-density, spread-out developments do not have significant physical and functional integration to qualify as "mixed-use." Project sizes often exceed 500,000 square feet, excluding parking. It can be a single mega-structure, a number of structures around a central plaza, or a number of structures connected by a pedestrian network. A 1987 study by the Urban Land Institute puts the average site area at 15 acres, and average Floor Area Ratio (FAR) at 1 or more in the suburbs and 3 or more in city centres. However, New Urbanism projects built in the last fifteen years are much larger.

Compatibility of mix and scale of uses are extremely important considerations, e.g., a first class hotel should be matched by up-scale office space. The following are some important attributes (Urban Land Institute, 1987:52).

- Proximity to adjacent activity centres and neighbouring uses.
- Access to, and visibility from highways, transit systems and pedestrians.
- Site characteristics such as size, shape, topography and soils.
- Availability of utilities, roads, and public facilities and services.
- Land use control regime such as zoning, subdivision regulations, building codes and local government attitudes.
- Potential use, including the type and quality of use and the timing and size of the market for it.
- Land cost, in relation to the above attributes.

Some people have criticize mixed-use developments for disorienting their visitors, destroying the existing urban fabric, creating enclaves and fortresses, and replicating suburbia in downtown areas. Therefore, the physical layout of a project and its relationship to the urban environ are critical. The key is the public open spaces. They should be well proportioned, and provided with good access, natural lighting, landscaping, sittable spaces, signage, entertainment, commercial services and food, as well as quiet areas. In particular, the residential component should be designed for security, privacy and views.

LAND SUPPLY

So far we have focussed on the siting and sizing needs of various kinds of land uses. These have to be matched to the supply. A most crucial exercise in planning analysis is to look at the capability of the existing vacant and renewal land to identify its potential for, and limitations to, development. The physiographic features and the presence or absence of such man-made improvements to the land as roads and drainage facilities, accessibility to the transportation network, and the existence of utilities, especially water supply and sanitary drainage near the site must be taken into account. The purpose is to evaluate the vacant (greenfield and infill) or renewal (brownfield) land to determine whether it is prime or marginal for various kinds of development. This approach has a development bias.

Vacant Land

Vacant land ("greenfields") analysis uses the following logic. Marginal lands are identified first: land that is too low; land that is marshy or subject to flooding; derelict land such as abandoned quarries; or land that is too steep to be used for building. The standard optimal gradients for various activities are shown in Table 5-15. Individual parcels which are too small or too irregular are also not good for urban development. For city-wide planning consideration, individual lots with less than five acres are usually considered marginal. Land which has a slope over five percent is still acceptable for residential uses but would not be good for industrial uses. Obvious marginal lands are excluded from the supply first.

TABLE 5-15
OPTIMUM GRADIENTS

Activity Type	Gradient
General purpose	max. 4%
Informal	max. 10%
Planted area	min. 1%
Grass banks	max. 25%
Unmown planted banks	max. 50-60%
Paved area	min. 1%
Roads	0.5-8%
Drainage swales and ditches	2-10%

Source: Lynch and Hack (1984: 40 and 235); and Koppelman and DeChiara (1975: 162).

The second step is to use a topographic map to identify the larger pieces of vacant land. Further subclasses can be introduced to indicate the development capability of land. Land which satisfies the physiographic requirements, as well as having all the necessary improvements, will be considered the best. Additional information required includes whether the owners are willing to release the land for urban development, whether there is a clear title to the land, and whether there is any restriction to the future use of the land by covenants. Tables can be drawn up to show the acreage of different classes of developable land in the various analysis zones, and maps can be used to show the location and configuration of the parcels of land. The outputs of this analysis include tables, maps and texts describing land parcels which are available for urban use: where they are, how suitable they are, and how many there are. This same approach can be used for the analysis of a specific site.

The next question is whether the land parcel should be developed, and what kind of development should take place on it. A balance is needed between urban development and environmental protection and enhancement. For instance, any development will reduce the natural seepage of the land, causing floods or requiring artificial drainage. (Refer to the section on Infrastructure for some typical urban runoff coefficients.)

Such environmental degradation, or threats to property and life, have to be mitigated, sometimes at great costs. However, development should not be allowed simply because the landform is acceptable and services and facilities are available. This is not to say that environmental protection and enhancement are necessarily in conflict with urban development. Environmental protection and enhancement are often for the benefit of urban development and for the protection of property and life. But before committing land to development, its environmental vulnerability has to be determined. There are a number of approaches. Vulnerability can be based on a single environmental characteristic, such as soil. Soil properties can be translated into engineering factors such as erodability, permeability, shrink/swell potential, and compressibility. On that basis, we can evaluate the vulnerability of the land for such things as septic tanks and building foundations, which can then be used to serve as clues for the appropriate land use, such as low density residential or high density residential. Similarly, agricultural quality of land can be used to determine the vulnerability of the land to various urban uses.

Sometimes a number of environmental characteristics are combined to encompass logical ecosystem units, important natural processes, biotic communities, and so on. In land use planning various combinations of the following environmental characteristics are usually used: geology, minerals, elevation, slope, soil, streams and drainage basins, flood plains, groundwater, and woodlands. The analytic task is to interpret the appropriateness of these characteristics at various locations for human activities and the impacts of various types of human activities on them. It is crucial to make explicit the rules and procedures used in analysis. Through analyzing the potential environmental impacts by urban uses we can identify areas which are particularly vulnerable to certain or all urban uses, or which constitute a significant hazard to life or property. The general structure of any environmental impact analysis may have the following components.

- Present conditions (including base-line conditions).
- Short-term and long-term, negative and positive, impacts of the proposal.
- Testing of possible alternatives (engineering, design, location, etc.) by repeating the above steps.

- Recommendations, including mitigation methods of unavoidable negative impacts.

A number of analytic techniques can be used.

(i) Descriptive Checklist. The scope of a checklist may vary with the type and size of projects, but it normally covers impacts on air quality (public health and land use), water quality (surface and sub-surface), ecology (plants and animals), soil erosion, noise, and hazards (natural and man-made). A checklist allows for systematic thinking and concise presentation, but it cannot deal with interactions among impacts.

(ii) Trade-off Matrix. It relates the costs and benefits of impacts to the groups affected. The relationship can be qualitative, physical or monetary. The relative importance of the different relationships is not weighted, and is left to be determined through the political process. With this technique the planner scrupulously avoids judgment, but opts for an explicit political resolution of differences. However, such a matrix can involve many relationships (cells) which are difficult to judge and summarize. And, by focusing on costs and benefits to groups it may obscure the factual data of the environmental impacts.

(iii) Spreadsheet Modeling. This is used to calculate linked impacts (where the outcome of one relationship is the input to another relationship) and/or evaluate different scenarios (different base-lines, proposals, or assumptions). The merit of this technique is that computer software is usually very user-friendly, and the analysis transparent. The disadvantage is that it requires a high level of analytic skills in order to develop the necessary formulae and transform all data to similar units.

(iv) Composite Mapping. This provides an aggregate picture of the impacts of all the relevant factors, considered together. The best known is McHarg's composite mapping (1969) or its variations (e.g. the U.S. EPA's DRASTIC model [Allen et al., 1987]). Essentially this involves an overlay of maps, each representing an analysis of a particular environmental factor. Various factors can be combined. One problem is that not all the factors are equally significant or important. Therefore, the relative significance or importance should be recognized explicitly when making a composite map. Another problem is about the boundaries of the environmental factors. They are not easy to define, and they do not coincide necessarily with boundaries of political jurisdictions or planning analysis zones. This technique can accommodate the combined impacts in a complex system without obscuring individual impacts. The visual power of a composite map can be very convincing. But data requirements can be huge, and it often relies too much on expert judgment about factor weighting.

All of these techniques are geared to individual projects. But over time, land use decisions, individually or in aggregate, produce overwhelming cumulative impacts. In order to track and analyze cumulative and aggregate impacts we need a good inventory, good base-lines, and regular monitoring of key environmental indicators. This is particularly important when making long-term city-wide or region-wide plans. No single technique can answer all these questions because the natural systems are complex and interrelated. Cumulative impacts can result from both similar and dissimilar actions taken over a long period of time, and across a large area. Changes in the natural systems are both incremental and synergistic and can be immediate and delayed (Constant and Wiggins, 1990). Planners can only try their best, within cost and time constraints.

Infill development is receiving wide attention. Many see it as an antidote to urban renewal and redevelopment. From a city government viewpoint, infill development can help protect and enhance older neighbourhoods, preserve land while accommodating growth, and reduce infrastructure cost by using existing roads and services. Some developers, too, like it because they are encountering difficulties in finding land at the urban fringe and obtaining the necessary permits to develop it (Brett, 1982). Infill development is particularly suitable when there is a rapidly growing population; strong CBD and local employment nodes; extensive investment in neighbourhood preservation and upgrading; dispersed land parcels that can serve a variety of income groups; growth controls on the urban fringe; high costs for urban fringe development; and a shallow land price gradient from the urban fringe to the inner city.

Unlike greenfields, infill development is more often considered on a site-by-site basis. Individual parcels have different location and size characteristics. Sizes can range from less than 1/4 acre to over 20 acres. Suburban sites are usually larger. Many infill parcels are also located adjacent to vacant land, which allows for land assembly to enhance development and market potentials. But there can be many challenges to infill development. Infrastructure may have to be upgraded. Sites may be too small and too expensive, and ownership too fragmented. Existing residents and businesses may want to preserve potential sites as open space and may be concerned about the compatibility of building scale and style. Of course, many of the concerns can be dealt with through appropriate regulations (e.g., higher allowable density to offset higher land costs) and good design guidelines (e.g., emphasis on design compatibility).

A good inventory should be developed, which should include the following information for each parcel: zoning, planned use, utility service, road access, physical limitations, parcel size, owner name/address (including public owner), assessed value, tax delinquency, tax-exempt sites, and recent sale information. Governments can promote infill development by a number of techniques. (i) Stimulate developers' interest through a publicity campaign and parcel information. (ii) Remove obstacles by modifying zoning, reducing the time for project review, and removing inappropriate urban design standards. (iii) Foster neighbourhood support by requiring neighbourhood plans to include strategies for dealing with vacant lots. (iv) Provide incentives such as special financial terms and demonstration projects. (v) Reduce land cost through density bonuses, tax abatement and leasing of publicly owned land. (Real Estate Research Corporation, 1982)

Brownfields   Brownfield sites present challenges. Because of their prime location and well-serviced characteristics, many are considered a good location for redevelopment. Governments also encourage the redevelopment of brownfields for three kinds of reasons: cost efficiency, urban renewal, and revenue generation.

> (i) It is generally more cost-effective to redevelop lands that already have municipal services such as transportation, sewer and water, and utilities, and much of which are under-used because of deindustrialization. Less money has to be spent on extending the same services to develop "greenfields" beyond the urban boundaries.

> (ii) The redevelopment of large tracts of land in inner cities can kick-start other urban renewal and development projects, while residential intensification on brownfields can slow down inefficient urban sprawl. Also, cleaning up these sites will improve the condition of the land and public health, and reduce under-utilized properties that provide safe haven for criminal activities. The improved appearance of city centres will attract more domestic and foreign investment. And, populating inner cities can bring vitality and safety to otherwise derelict areas, as well as support existing commercial enterprises.

> (iii) Redevelopment will eliminate the "orphan site" situation, and ensure that property taxes are paid. The redevelopment itself also produces property tax revenues and development charges.

The land development approval processes of brownfields are complex. Generally it is driven by five principles: pollution pays; beneficiary pays; fairness; openness, accessibility and participation; and sustainable development (Delcan Corporation, et al. 1997a). The process involves the identification and the remediation of contamination, the determination of liability, risk communication and public participation. However, these requirements can create uncertainty and add extra cost and time to the development proponent. The financial and insurance institutions also have rigorous protocol when dealing with brownfield sites.

In the United States, the Comprehensive Environmental Response, Compensation, and Liability Act (CERCLA, or Superfund) specifies a complex cleanup process, with the following basic stages: site identification; preliminary assessment; site inspection; National Priorities Listing (NPL); remedial investigation and feasibility study; record of decision; remedial design; remedial action; construction completion; delisting from NPL (Hird 1994). Canada has a four-step process: phase I Environmental Site Assessment (non-intrusive assessment); phase II Environmental Site Assessment (intrusive characterization); remediation, design and implementation; and verification and compliance monitoring (Delcan Corporation, et al., 1997b).

There are four general options to deal with contamination: (i) Soil excavation and landfill disposal. (ii) In-situ treatment, where contaminants are treated on-site without excavating soil. (iii) Ex-situ treatment, where soil is excavated and treated on-site by such means as landfarming, bio-pile, and soil vapour extraction. (iv) In-place management, where the contamination is deep and the cost of using conventional remediation is high. This includes isolation from receptors by barriers; partial clean-up; criteria-based zoning, that is, to continue site use with a less restrictive remediation criteria; and any combination of the above, often with different approaches for different areas of the site.

At the end of our land supply analysis we should have two sets of results: land capacity based on physiographic characteristics and the accessibility and availability of facilities and services; and land vulnerability (that is, limitations to urban development on the land) based on environmental qualities and hazards. But these do not constitute a land use design. First, some areas may be highly suited for a number of different uses which may or may not be compatible with each other. Where the uses are compatible they can be allowed, or even encouraged, to coexist. Where the uses are incompatible other non-environmental factors would have to be considered. Second, trade-offs have to be made between environmental vulnerability of a piece of land and its attractiveness to development. The physical and environmental characteristics of a piece of land are not the sole determinants of its most suitable use. Much depends on the relative scarcity of suitable sites to the demand for such sites, that is, the demand by different land uses for a particular site as well as the supply of alternative sites for a particular land use. However, the supply of urban sites is often influenced by transportation and infrastructure planning, as illustrated in the following section.

TRANSPORTATION

Transportation planning has traditionally focussed on highway systems without much coordination with the planning of other modes of transportation, and still much less with the planning of land use. In this section we will examine both the relationship between land use and transportation and the efficiency of traffic movements.

The relationship between land use and transportation can be examined in a number of ways. First, transportation can be seen as a service which enables people, firms, and institutions to carry out activities in separate locations. The emphasis is on coordination of activity patterns, activity centres, and movement systems. Second, land use can be seen as an important determinant of demand for travel. The type and location of land use and intensity of activity can increase or reduce travel demand, or the use of public transit. Third, transportation can have an important impact on how land is used. Since transportation confers accessibility, it affects the development or redevelopment potential of land.

Typically, transportation planning at the site level involves the following steps: (i) determination of land uses at the site; (ii) estimation of trips generated, based on the type and intensity of the uses; (iii) distribution of the trips to major approach roads; (iv) assignment of vehicle volumes to the roadway network; and (v) analysis of the capacity of the roadways to handle the traffic (Greenberg and Hecimocvich, 1984).

At a regional scale, transportation planning is based on a network of nodes and links. A region is divided into traffic zones, which may be as small as a city block or as large as one square mile. Often, these zones coincide with the census tracts. It is assumed that all trips end (origins and destinations) in a zone occur at a point, or a node, referred to as zone centroid. Nodes are connected by links. Each link is described by its flow (number of trips that use the link) and friction (cost or penalty incurred by each trip, that is, time and cost to traverse the link).

Regional transportation analysis has four steps (Black, 1995:183-184). (1) Trip generation is the estimation of person-trip ends in each traffic zone. The important variables are land use, population and economic activity. For a residential land use, the key considerations are income, automobile ownership, and household size. For a nonresidential land use, the key considerations are employment, floor space, and land area. (2) Trip distribution is the estimation of the number of trips starting in each zone and ending in every other zone. Mathematical models are used. Growth-factor models apply a growth factor to some base-year data on trip distribution to obtain a forecast. Synthetic models estimate trip distribution by examining causal factors. A favourite is the gravity model which uses the "attraction" between zones (based on population sizes and levels of socioeconomic activities) and "repulsion" between zones (based on travel time and costs) to assign trip distribution. (3) Modal split is the division of person-trips into two modal groups: automobile or transit trips. (4) Traffic (or network) assignment is the estimation of the routes that the trips will take. For automobile trips these will form a network of expressways and arterial streets. For transit trips these will form a network of rail lines and bus routes. At an earlier time the assignment would have used a "minimum-path" approach. More recently, the assignment is done with an "equilibrium" approach (an equilibrium is reached when there is no more benefit to be gained by switching to another route). Assignments are made for a 24-hour period as well as peak periods. From the above analysis will emerge a listing of estimates of the number of vehicles using every link of the highway network and the number of passengers using every link of the transit network.

A typical larger scale land use and transportation planning analysis usually involves an iterative process with three components: modeling, demand forecasting, and testing (Stover and Koepke, 1988). First, a future spatial structure is modeled, based on population and employment forecasts, land use pattern assumptions and transportation network assumptions. Second, the future spatial structure generates travel demands, based on trip generation, trip distribution and model choice between transit and automobile. Third, the travel demands (transit and automobile) are tested against the capacity of the transportation systems and acceptable service levels, in order to determine the impacts on costs, accessibility (especially for specific population subgroups) and the community. If the impacts are acceptable, the plan is implemented; if not, the process is repeated.

Existing practice and conventional standards in traffic planning are a legacy from decades of reliance on the private automobile as the principal mode of transportation. While the general planning literature has been essentially anti-automobile, there are some dissenting opinions. Bruce-Briggs (1977) offers an interesting "psychological" perspective of an automobile apologist. He contends that the U.S. is a mass production society in which the common people can afford many of the same goods as the rich, such as a car and a suburban home. The upper class resents the erosion of its quality of life by the masses which, it thinks, are responsible for the congested highways and ugly suburbs. Opinion makers, such as intellectuals and media people, either belong to the upper and upper-middle classes or are affiliated with them. This elite, which Bruce-Briggs calls the "new class", has been spearheading the war against the automobile and the suburbs. In the meantime, the "silent majority" of people want to hang on to their private automobiles and suburban homes. In a democratic society, Bruce-Briggs contends, they have every right to do so.

The following subsections deal with roads and traffic, public transit, pedestrians and cyclists, and telecommuting and teleshopping.

Roads and Traffic

We will first examine the efficiency of roads and traffic. A road is a strip of land specially prepared and reserved for the passage of people and goods. Although it may include railways, tramways, canals, and so on, we will focus on motoring needs. A road system can be considered as a network of channels with terminals and interchanges. In general there are three design approaches. The gridiron pattern does not differentiate between intensities of use, disregards topographic constraints, does not discourage through traffic, and is visually monotonous. However, it allows for alternative routes between destinations, and the problems cited above can be dealt with through road designs that are more responsive to topographic conditions and traffic pattern, and through sensitive landscaping along the routes. A radial pattern (with a single centre or multiple centres) offers the most direct line of travel between destinations, but is resistive to interruptions at any point. A linear pattern consists of parallel lines joining different origins and destinations, but has the same advantages and problems of the radial pattern. Of course, in some situations, the road network may show no particular pattern, such as where the terrain is very difficult or where through traffic is to be discouraged (e.g., a residential subdivision). It is essential that the planner should look beyond the map and try to "see" things at ground level.

Although the terms may vary, in an urban setting we have a hierarchy of roads consisting of major, minor, collector, and local roads. A hierarchical system is cheaper and consumes less land than an all-purpose system where the speeds and widths of roads are not differentiated.

Major roads (arterials and freeways) are designed for large quantities of traffic moving at a relatively high speed. Speed and safety are the key, which means that there must be no frontal access for vehicles to such roads, that intersections and junctions with other roads are infrequent and are properly designed, and that the roadway is divided physically to minimize the chance of collision for vehicles travelling in opposite directions.

Minor roads (local roads) provide access. They are often used by pedestrians as well as vehicles, and are flanked by buildings from which people may emerge quite suddenly and dangerously. In a residential neighbourhood, these roads can be laid out in a grid pattern as well as in the form of a loop, crescent, or cul-de-sac. Vehicular speeds on minor roads are much reduced. This can be achieved by a number of means. (Generally known as traffic calming. Refer also to later discussion in this section as well as to the section on Pedestrians and Cyclists.)

First, the roadway is made as narrow as possible while not impeding free passage. This may mean more minor scrape collisions but fewer serious accidents. The actual widths may vary but it is useful to allow only just enough space for two vehicles to pass each other and for curb-side parking. Additional space may be needed in some places to store snow in winter. Second, junctions or right-angled bends are introduced as frequently as practicable. The 600 feet (180 m) long city block is a useful rule-of-thumb. This reduces the temptation to drivers to accelerate to dangerously high speeds. Third, physical constraints such as speed bumps can be used. They are usually more successful than speed limits and fines.

Figure 5-6: Road Patterns

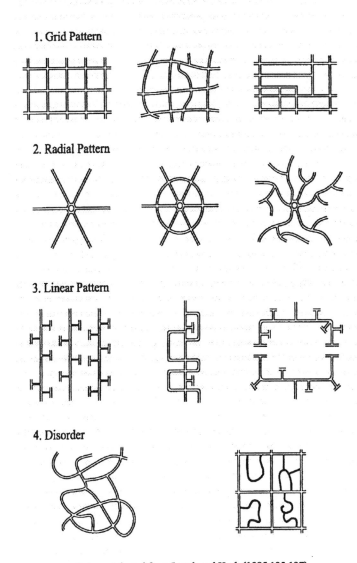

1. Grid Pattern

2. Radial Pattern

3. Linear Pattern

4. Disorder

Source: Adapted from Lynch and Hack (1985:195-197)

Collector roads are to collect traffic from the local roads and feed it into the major roads. They are more often used in residential areas. To function effectively they have to be kept free of frontage access. This means they provide no financial return from developable road frontage. Therefore, they should be as few and short as possible. But they are often needed to ensure a safe and practicable road system.

The capacity of a roadway depends on its width, surface, alignment, conditions at the edge and the characteristics of the traffic (e.g., vehicle type, speed, control, and driver skill). The theoretical capacity of a traffic lane is 1800 to 2000 cars per hour where this flow is completely steady, uninterrupted, and at optimum speed and spacing. In practice, a multilane restricted-access highway can carry up to 1500 cars per hour per lane, while a congested street with frequent friction on the side due to cars parking and entering may carry only 200 to 300 cars per hour on the outside lane. A typical local residential street will carry about 400 to 500 cars per hour per lane. Four lanes in each direction seem to be the maximum, even for a major highway, before driving on it becomes a harrowing experience. The volumes of traffic in suburban areas may be estimated by using some rules-of-thumb based on population, housing densities, and the number of vehicle trips at peak hours generated by each dwelling. (For trip generation data, refer to Transportation in the Information chapter.) Larger, denser, or more complex areas require more careful traffic assignment studies.

Road capacity is affected by traffic behaviour. The maximum number of vehicles which can pass a point in a given time is a function of the speed and the distance interval between vehicles. The greater the probable speeds along a road the wider it needs to be, and the greater likelihood that pedestrians have to be separated from vehicles, and vehicles travelling in opposite directions separated from each other. As speed increases the required distances between vehicles for reaction time increases more than proportionately. Therefore, the capacity of a road is determined by the optimum combination of speed and safe interval. In practice, 1,500 vehicles per hour per lane seems to be a reasonable maximum. Also, it seems any more than four lanes in one direction creates confusion to drivers, and produces frictional loss to road capacity on account of weaving of traffic between lanes. So, 6,000 vehicles an hour is about the practical maximum capacity for each direction for any road. Increasing the speed and reducing the intervals further may not increase the road capacity because there will be more minor bumper-to-bumper collisions which would reduce the overall road capacity to the above theoretical maximum.

Road capacity will be reduced by speed reduction at road junctions and crossings. In planning for a road intersection, the first principle is to maintain the traffic flow by avoiding conflicting traffic maneuvers or at least moderating their difficulty, and by separating maneuvers in time and space. These are achieved by traffic signals which stop some traffic while allowing others to go through, or by such channelization as a rotary, which converts crossing traffic into merging and diverging traffic. But there is a limit beyond which multilevel intersections are needed, depending on the volume of the traffic and the flow of the traffic in different directions. These are in turn affected by the types, sizes, and locations of land uses with strong traffic generating or attractive potentials, such as city centres and industrial parks. As a rule-of-thumb, vertical separation should be considered when there are more than 3,000 vehicles per hour passing along the major channel at the intersection. Vertical separation is costly, space-demanding, confusing to users and inflexible to change.

A general principle in designing a road system is to minimize "average" distances between destinations without increasing total road lengths beyond reasonable limits. In economic and social terms, time spent travelling is a dead loss, so journey time should be minimized. (There is suggestion that some people rather like commuting to work and consider that to be "enjoyable" time.) However, there is inherent conflict. Road users want to minimize their travel distances and road providers want to minimize the total length of roads. In addition, there are the considerations of topography, convenience, safety, and appearance. Therefore, there can be a number of answers for a given set of circumstances. Worse still, circumstances can change too, making the problem even more intractable. Peter Haggett (1977) mentions that there are 479,002,000 ways of connecting 13 cities in the western United States, only one of which is optimum in terms of average distance between the cities. Of course, there are many solutions which are very close to the optimum but even so, the design of road systems can be a very complex undertaking.

In determining the optimum spacing of main roads in an urban network it is important to ensure that the intervals are close enough to prevent the roads from being overloaded and yet are not too close as to increase significantly the total length of the road in the system. As a rule, the closer the road network the greater the total length of roads and therefore the construction costs, but the intersections will be less elaborate and expensive because there is less traffic in each intersection. Some balance has to be struck to optimize road lengths and the number of intersections.

Roads are costly to construct and maintain, so their total length should be as short as possible and individual lengths of roads should not be wider than necessary. In general, it is more cost-effective if there is continuous development on both sides of a road; and it is more economical to provide a system of roads each designed for its specific function than to have all general-purpose roads. Roads confer access and define properties. As such, they affect the development potential and the social status of a site as well as the socializing or privacy prospect of its users.

The public right-of-way is the total strip of land within which there is public control and common right of passage, and within which all vehicular lanes, sidewalks, utility lines are located. Depending on its functions and features it can be as narrow as 30 feet or as wide as 600 feet. Most right-of-ways for local and minor roads are between 50 feet to 100 feet wide. The actual road width for vehicular traffic is computed by summing up the number of traffic and parking lanes required. Curb-side parking is usually about eight feet wide. A traffic lane is nine to ten feet wide on a minor road and up to 12 feet on a major road. For a local road, an 18 feet pavement is needed for a single lane with curb-side parking, 20 feet for two-way traffic, and 28 feet for two-way traffic and curb-side parking on one side. The minimum vertical clearance is usually 14 feet to allow for the passage of trucks. A planting strip is often provided to separate the sidewalk from the vehicular roadway for convenience and safety, to make room for utilities and street fixtures both above and below ground, to provide space for storage of snow during winter, and to accommodate the planting of street trees and other vegetation. Table 5-16 shows some conventional road terms and dimensions and Table 5-17 shows some New Urbanism road dimensions.

TABLE 5-16

ROAD DIMENSIONS

Road Type	Right-of-Way in ft. (m)	Roadway Width (curb to curb) in ft. (m)	Min. Spacing of Inter-section or Max. length in ft. (m)
Major freeway	600 (180)		min. 3000-5000 (910-1520)
Major or collector road	60-100 (18-30)	34-72 (10-22)	min. 800 (240)
Secondary road	60-80 (18-24)	34-48 (10-14)	
Minor road	40-60 (12-18)	26-28 (8 - 8.5)	max. block length: 1600-2000 (480-600) max. loop: 1600 (480) min. separation for T-junction: 130 (40)
Minimum	30 (9)		
Average	50 (15)		
Single-family homes and cul-de-sacs		28 (8.5)	max. length: 400-500 (120-150)
Multi-family develop-ment	60 (18)	34-36 (10-11)	
cul-de-sacs		80-100 (24-30) diame-ter	max. dist. to dwg: 50-300 (15-90)
Sidewalk		min. 3 (1)	

Source: Adapted from Lynch and Hack (1984:212, 214, 458, and 460); Urban Land Institute (1960:106, 124-125, and 132); and Koppleman and DeChiara (1975:206-207).

Road intersections are important for traffic safety as well as for dividing up the land into lots for development. Intersections should be within 20 degrees of the perpendicular. Intersections of an acute angle are difficult to negotiate and limit the approach visibility, as well as creating odd-shaped lots which are difficult to develop. Cross junctions or junctions that are offset by at least 150 feet are preferable to slight offsets which frustrate the cross traffic and disturb the flow on the lane that is being crossed. Although there are standards about the maximum depth of a loop or cul-de-sac, or the maximum length of a city block, the general principle is that as the depth or length increases, circulation becomes more indirect, service deliveries longer, and emergency access more liable to misdirection.

TABLE 5-17
SOME NEW URBANISM ROAD DIMENSIONS

Road Type	Right-of-Way in ft. (m)		Roadway Width in ft. (m)	
Regional road	100-130	(30-40)	48	(14.5)
Major collector	85	(26)	48	(14.5)
Main street collector	65	(20)	38	(11.5)
Collector	65	(20)	38	(11.5)
Boulevard collector	65	(20)	33	(10)
Local street	58	(17.5)	26	(8)
Front lane	33	(10)	20	(6)
Rear lane	20	(6)	10	(3)

Source: Adapted from Essiambre-Phillips-Desjardins Associates Ltd., *et al.* (1997:16, Table 4).

Generally, leveled ground is preferred, but road surface should have at least a half percent gradient to allow for positive drainage. At the other extreme, the maximum gradient is a function of the designed traffic speed. Depending on winter conditions and prevailing terrains (which affect local driving habits) a maximum gradient of ten percent is the norm. Table 5-18 shows some road alignment standards.

If traffic volume is very high (the threshold is 3,000 vehicles per hour), grade separations may be necessary. The amount of land required for the grade separation is a function of the maximum ramp grade, the minimum ramp radii, and the minimum lengths of acceleration and deceleration lanes.

Parking is a thorny issue in land use planning. Characteristically, parking is needed most in locations where land values are the highest. At the same time, the availability of parking contributes to high land values. It seems, however, in North America even a short walking distance between the parking lot and the office or shop is not acceptable. Parking may be provided in various ways on the street, which is convenient but is disturbing to moving traffic; in small parking bays; in large parking lots, which are the cheapest, but may be inconvenient or unsightly; or in underground, ramp structures, or garages which are the most expensive ways.

The perpendicular or 90 degree parking layout is the most space-efficient, and the 30 degree angle-parking the least. Overall space requirement for off-street parking ranges from 250 square feet to 400 square feet per car, including internal circulation space (300 square feet per car is the norm). Table 5-19 shows the common parking standards used.

TABLE 5-18
ROAD ALIGNMENT STANDARDS

Speed mi./hr (km/hr)		Min. Radius of Horizontal Curves in ft. (m)		Min. Length of Vertical Curve Each 1% Change in Grade in ft. (m)		Min. Sight Distance in ft. (m)		Max. Grade (%)
20	(30)	100	(30)	10	(3)	150	(46)	12
30	(50)	260	(80)	20	(6)	215	(66)	10
40	(65)	490	(150)	40	(12)	280	(86)	8 - 9
50	(80)	750	(230)	70	(21)	380	(116)	7
60	(100)	1210	(370)	150	(46)	525	(160)	5

Source: Adapted from Lynch and Hack (1984:459-460).

Roads and traffic at the neighbourhood level deserve special attention. Minor roads confer access to individual buildings and define the shape of individual sites. They are an important element in neighbourhood planning. Their layout affects the "buildability" of individual sites, land values, social interaction, privacy, and so on. For these reasons, traffic management on minor roads is a very important consideration. The purpose of traffic management is to lessen the detrimental effects of vehicles on the environment, while retaining convenient access for essential traffic. One of the most widely held principles in traffic management is the exclusion of extraneous traffic from a particular area. But this requires the peripheral major roads to be able to handle the through traffic. Within the area served by the minor roads it is necessary to ensure good environmental conditions as well as accessibility to the various buildings or sites.

A principal method of reducing penetration by through traffic is to reduce the number of entry points from the peripheral roads into an area. But correspondingly, the volume of traffic at these few entry points will be higher. It is important to organize the land use in the area so that those uses which are not affected by, or can benefit from, the heavy traffic be located at these entry points. To further discourage through traffic, the layout of the interior roads should offer no easy route through the area. However, discouraging or restricting automobile access to an area should be complemented by an efficient, reliable, and flexible public transport system.

TABLE 5-19
PARKING STANDARDS

Stall space

Standard	8-9 ft. x 20 ft.	(2.4 - 2.7m x 6.1m)
Small car	8 ft. x 16 ft.	(2.4m x 4.8m)
Handicapped	13 ft. x 20 ft.	(4.0m x 6.1m)

Aisle Width

(30 and 90 degree parking)	12 ft.	(3.7m)
(90 degree parking)	20 ft.	(6.2m)

Overall space per car	250-400 sq.ft.	(23-37 sq.m)
Max. distance to destination	600 ft.	(180m)

Parking Ratio

Residential

Suburban	2.0/dwelling unit
Normal	1.5/dwelling unit
Dense urban	0.5/dwelling unit
Elderly	0.3/dwelling unit

Source: Lynch and Hack (1984:217 and 467).

The only traffic generated internally in a residential area is that of the residents themselves or their visitors. All other extraneous traffic can be kept out by narrowing the roads at entry and exit points or limiting the access to certain vehicles and/or to certain times of the day. Speed controls can be achieved by speed bumps, design of intersections, curbside parking arrangements, signage, and pedestrian controlled traffic lights and crossing. The level of parking provisions can also be used to regulate the flow of traffic in an area. Where a residential neighbourhood is located near a commercial area, on-street parking may be reserved for residents only, thus excluding commuters and shoppers. Some cities do this by selling special permits to residents so that they can park in areas reserved for them on the street whilst all other cars have to use the more expensive parking meters.

Sensitive traffic management in commercial areas can actually help to increase business. Very simple measures can be effective, such as the widening of sidewalks, the rearrangement of pedestrian crossings, the building of pedestrian tunnels or bridges, parking and waiting restrictions, and the arrangement of shop access. Parking for inner city shopping areas is difficult and expensive to provide. The lack of parking in these areas has been regarded as one reason for their decline relative to suburban centres. To counter this, some merchants actually offer to refund their customers the cost of parking if their purchase exceeds a certain amount. It is very important in areas where parking space is at a premium to establish priorities between long-term users (commuters), short-term patrons (shoppers) and those on business. Each group should be treated differently.

More drastic measures such as the exclusion of certain kinds of traffic or partial or total pedestrianization are costly and are not always advisable. Vehicular traffic brings with it a sense of activity and vitality. A large traffic-free area can become bleak, desolate, and even dangerous to pedestrians. To cite Jacobs (1972: 362): "To think of city traffic in oversimplified terms of pedestrian versus cars and to fix on the segregation of each as a principal goal is to go to the problem from the wrong end. Consideration for pedestrians in cities is inseparable from consideration for city diversity, vitality, and concentration of use."

Transit (and Transit Node Development)

Our focus is rail and bus transit. But there are many other ways of moving people (and goods). Para-transits are demand-responsive services, such as taxis, vans and small buses. They are particularly useful in low-density suburbs and small towns, as well as for minority groups such as the elderly and disabled. Carpooling and vanpooling are also transit of sorts, and are getting more attention, especially in highly congested areas, such as southern California. People movers have proven to be useful in activity centres such as airports and amusement parks.

The debate between rail and bus has been going on for a long time. Bus advocates point to the advantage of using existing streets and low capital costs, as well as innovations such as subscription services and exclusive bus lanes. Bus transit has great flexibility, too. Buses can pass each other. Unlike a train, a stalled bus will not affect the rest of the system. A bus route can be started, modified or dropped at any time (although this does not happen often because of the fear of lost ridership). An under-used busway can be converted easily for automobile and truck use. There are also institutional factors. For instance, the automobile, oil, and highway lobby prefers the bus because it is a road vehicle. Senior government subsidies have for some time favoured bus. The U.S. federal funding formulas pay 90 percent of the cost of constructing bus lanes which are part of an interstate highway, whereas the federal government pays only 80 percent for rail facilities. However, if senior governments would pay for capital investment only, then rail projects would be favoured.

Rail transit nearly always requires a new start, whether it is a heavy rail system that gets power from a third rail or a light rail system that gets power from an overhead wire. But rail transit has operational advantages. It is more comfortable, with no stop-and-go traffic. Collision and injury rates are low. Boarding is fast, making it very efficient in high-demand situations. The length of trains can be changed, adjusting to the demand at different periods of the day, week or year. Also, rail transit has a major beneficial impact on land development. Unlike a bus line which can be re-routed or cancelled without much second thought, a rail line is perceived as a permanent facility and major public commitment. Developers like to build next to rail stations, especially when there are other beneficial factors, such as a pro-development government and a good business location.

Some see light rail transit (LRT) as the compromised option between heavy rail and bus. "... it is relatively quiet, thus environmentally unobtrusive; is electrically propelled, thus less dependent than buses on the availability of petrochemical fuels; and can operate effectively along available railroad rights-of-way and street medians, thus is far cheaper, less disruptive, and easier to build than heavy rail. LRT's lack of exhaust fumes and comparatively slow speeds make it particularly compatible with pedestrian settings such as downtown malls." (Cervero, 1984:134)

A typical transit system consists of a combination of three connected systems: residential collection and feeders, which are linked to longer line-haul systems, and which are connected with distribution systems that circulate people within a major commercial or industrial centre. The following table shows typical design standards.

TABLE 5-20
TRANSIT SYSTEMS AND PLANNING STANDARDS

Systems	Service Area	Network	Service	Station Spacing
Feeder systems	High-density urban areas, large centres, or low-density suburban areas	Limited (up to a few miles)	Scheduled	1/4 - 1/2 mile (0.4 - 0.8 km)
Line-haul systems	Areas with population density exceeding 5,000/sq. mile	Linear or radial (up to several miles)	Scheduled	1/2 - 3 miles (0.8 - 4.8 km)
Distribution systems	High-density areas or small centres	Loops or shuttles	Scheduled or on-demand	1/4 - 1/2 mile (0.4 - 0.8 km)

Source: Adapted from Kaiser, Godschalk and Chapin (1995:379, Fig. 15-2).

Transit analysis is a component of total transportation analysis. (Refer to earlier discussion in this section on Transportation.) A region is divided into traffic zones. It is assumed that all trip ends (origins and destinations) in a zone occur at a point, referred to as the loading node or zone centroid. (It is from this point that the average walking time to the transit stops will be estimated.) The analysis is essentially a network analysis, with links and nodes. The links represent segments of transit routes. For rail, a link is a section of track; for bus, a link is a section of the street on which the buses run. Transit nodes are rail stations, bus stops or groups of adjacent stops, and major changes in a route such as when buses enter an expressway and increase the speed greatly. Also, the "friction" of walking time to the transit stop, waiting time, and the fares are estimated for each traffic zone.

As noted earlier, a general transportation analysis has four steps: (i) trip generation, (ii) trip distribution, (iii) modal split, and (iv) traffic (network) assignment. Two types of models can be employed to estimate the share of trips that will use transit. Trip-end models are used after the trip-generation step and before the trip-distribution step (i.e., between steps i and ii). They are based essentially on the characteristics of travelers (e.g., automobile ownership, income, household size, age, and occupation) and place of residence (e.g., population density and distance from the CBD). Trip interchange models are used after the trip-distribution step and before the traffic-assignment step (i.e., between steps ii and iii). They are based on the attractiveness of transit versus automobile, which is essentially, though not exclusively, measured by "friction" (time and cost). The output of the analysis is a listing of estimates of the number of passengers using every link of the transit network, the number of people getting on and off at each transit stop, and the total travel times.

There has been much literature exhorting the development potentials around transit nodes. (Refer also to transit-oriented development in the section on New Urbanism in the Synthesis chapter.) The record of achievement is checkered (Porter, 1998). The necessary conditions for success have remained quite constant over time and across cities. Knight and Trygg (1977) suggest the following: (i) local government policies that encourage development at the station, such as higher density zoning, density bonuses, reduced parking requirements, tax abatements, and public investment; (ii) pressure for development in the region, such as population growth, employment growth, and office booms; (iii) availability of land near the station, such as vacant sites or sites with old buildings that can be torn down at low cost; and (iv) desirable physical characteristics, such as an attractive appearance and reputation of a good neighbourhood.

There are also some location and design criteria (Ontario Ministry of Transportation and Ministry of Municipal Affairs, 1992).

(i) Activity nodes should be developed at focal points in the transit system, such as points where bus routes intersect, and commuter rail or rapid transit stations.

(ii) The size, density, and variety of uses should be directly related to the level and range of transit services provided. Generally, nodes should be of high density with a full range of uses. This will increase transit use as well as justify higher level of transit service.

(iii) Recommended densities for activity nodes are 1.5-2 Floor Area Ratio (FAR) in small municipalities; 2-3 FAR for nodes served by buses, in larger municipalities; and 3-5 FAR or more for nodes served by rapid transit or commuter rail, in larger urban centres.

(iv) Trip-generating facilities, such as regional or sub-regional shopping centres, large employment facilities, high density residential uses and large recreational facilities should be located within the nodes to support transit services. The majority of these should be within 1,300 feet (400 m) or less.

(v) Residential uses can help balance ridership levels in both directions.

(vi) Street patterns should provide maximum convenience and direct access from residences and jobs to nodes.

(vii) Pedestrian accessibility throughout the node is vital. Shorter walking distances act as an incentive for potential transit users.

Pedestrians and Cyclists

The European Parliament adopted a Charter of Pedestrians' Rights in 1988. Although we do not have a similar charter in North America we are, nonetheless, witnessing a tremendous upsurge of interests and activism in the pedestrian (and bicycling) mode of urban transportation. It is worthwhile to note some of the highlights of the European Charter (Tolley, 1990:xvi-xviii).

- The pedestrian has the right to live in a healthy environment and freely to enjoy the amenities offered by public areas under conditions that adequately safeguard his physical and psychological well-being.

- The pedestrian has the right to live in urban or village centres tailored to the needs of the motor car and to have amenities within walking or cycling distance.

- Children, the elderly and the disabled have the right to expect towns to be places of easy social contact and not places that aggravate their inherent weakness.

- The pedestrian has the right to urban areas which are intended exclusively for his use, are as extensive as possible, and are not mere "pedestrian precincts" but in harmony with the overall organization of the town, and also the exclusive right to connecting short, logical and safe routes.

- The pedestrian has the right to complete and unimpeded mobility, which can be achieved through the integrated use of the means of transport.

Much of the discussion of "pedestrianism" is a reaction to the over-dependence on the automobile, and the resulting land uses that have developed. Untermann (1984) suggests the following conditions for a good pedestrian environment: (i) reduction of travel distances; (ii) increase in land-use flexibility; (iii) elimination of pedestrian barriers and obstacles; (iv) leveling of walking routes, including the elimination of stairs and steep grades; (v) continuity of travel routes; (vi) protection from wind, rain, noise, cold and pollution; (vii) elimination of conflict, especially through separation of traffic through space and time; and (viii) increase in character, randomness, visual diversity and amenity.

Willingness to walk is affected by four factors: time, convenience, availability of automobile transport, and land use pattern. People will walk if it is safe (no conflict with cars, no difficulty in crossings, no fear of mugging and other crimes, etc.), convenient (direct access, no obstacles and barriers, etc.), and pleasant (protected from weather, feeling of security, good cityscape and street furniture, adequate space, etc.). The usual minimum width for sidewalks is four feet, which allows three persons to pass or walk abreast. (A "lane" width is three feet, and a sidewalk can have more than one lane.) A three-feet sidewalk is the absolute minimum. Sidewalks can be considered as children's play area and snow storage in the winter. In commercial areas sidewalks are crucial to provide a safe environment for pedestrian shoppers. Protection from the elements has become a great concern in urban areas. In colder climates semi-covered sidewalks in major shopping areas have become an attractive design idea.

One of the most important planning considerations is the provision of a safe walking (and cycling) environment, by reducing the threat of motor vehicles. "Traffic calming" consists of number of measures intended to slow down motor-vehicle traffic in order to minimize this threat. It includes: enforcing a speed limit of 20 mph (30 km/hr), making physical changes to street geometry (e.g. chokers, speed bumps, traffic circles, meandering rather than straight street path, etc.), and reducing the amount of space allocated to motor vehicles (Velo, 1992:15). (See also earlier discussion in the section on Roads and Traffic.)

Street crossings are important for pedestrians. There are three general types. (i) Uncontrolled crossings can be crosswalks with painted lines, pedestrian refuges, raised crosswalks and safe crosses. Pedestrian refuges are raised islands in the middle of a wide (over 30 feet) or busy street. Safe crosses are expanded sidewalks at the four corners of a street intersection. (ii) Controlled crossings use signals or traffic patrol. (iii) Grade separation uses underpasses or overpasses. Underpasses can be expensive and tend to be perceived as dangerous and unsavoury places. If unavoidable they should be wide and connected with shopping or other public facilities. Overpasses may cause pedestrian to abandon the street below, making the street even more hazardous and unpleasant.

A pedestrian environment must be barrier-free. Grades over eight percent begin to present difficulty, especially for people with moving impairments and who have to use canes, crutches, walkers or wheelchairs. Five percent grade is comfortable. Walkways and ramps must be more than four feet wide to allow a person in a wheelchair to pass another person. Also, long ramps have to be broken up by level areas and there should be proper landing areas at the top and bottom.

A "complete" pedestrian system should cater to neighbourhood users as well as recreationists and commuters. It should link all social services (parks, libraries, schools, etc), community services (shopping, medical-professional offices, entertainment, etc.), and amenities (views, forests, streams, etc.) It should pass through the higher density part of a community (where these routes can actually serve as community open space), replace under-used streets, and serve as buffer space between different land uses. In all these, make sure these routes can serve cyclists too.

Bicycle traffic is handled differently under different situations. Where both automobile and bicycle traffics are light, the sidewalk may be used. With increased bicycle traffic, certain streets may be designated as bicycle routes where the maximum motor-vehicle speed is restricted to 20 mph (30 km/hr). As bicycle traffic increases further, a bicycle lane can be designated on a street, with the elimination of one row of parked cars. Sometimes, a two-way street may be turned into a one-way street and the "captured" land used for bicycles. The motor-vehicle lanes on an existing street can be narrowed (say from 12 feet wide to 10 feet wide) in order to provide space for cyclist. This can also force cars to reduce their speed to that more compatible with bicycles. Separate routes are not always possible. The following is a summary of bicycle lane standards. (Vélo, 1992:42).

Here are some general bicycle planning principles. Follow the most direct routes; provide varied access; focus on safety from accidents and criminal acts; remove barriers and reduce delays; minimize conflicts with motor vehicles; avoid streets with extensive parking or large volume of vehicular traffic; incorporate scenic and attractive sights; and provide smooth, hard and easy-to-maintain pavement.

TABLE 5-21
BICYCLE LANE STANDARDS

Volume of cyclists/day	Lane with pavement markings, without parking	Lane with pavement markings, with parking	Protected bicycle lane	Lane between parking and motor-vehicle traffic lanes
1,500 cyclists/day or more				
Unidirectional	7.5 ft. (2.25 m)	8 ft. (2.50 m)	8 ft (2.50 m)	6.5 ft. (2.00 m)
Bidirectional	10 ft. (3.00 m)	10 ft. (3.00 m) 10.5 ft. (3.25 m)*	10 ft. (3.00 m)	n/a
Fewer than 1,500 cyclists/day				
Unidirectional	5 ft. (1.50 m)	6 ft. (1.75 m)	n/a	5 ft. (1.50 m)
Bidirectional	9 ft. (2.75 m)	9 ft. (2.75 m) 10 ft. (3.00 m)*	9 ft. (2.75m)	n/a

Note: *When the bicycle lane adjacent to the parking lane flows in the same direction as the motor-vehicle traffic.

Source: Adapted from Vélo Québec (1992).

Telecommuting and Teleshopping

Telecommuting is "using telecommunications technology to work at home, or at a location close to home during regular work hours, instead of commuting to a conventional work place at the conventional time. It may be part-time or full-time, and need not exclusively involve computers (e.g. cellular phones)" (Mokhtarian, 1994: 749). The popularity of telecommuting is driven on the supply-side by factors such as the changing nature of work, availability of the technology, global economy and corporate climate; and on the demand-side by socio-demographic trends, time pressures, and road congestion and stress. On average, about one to two percent of all workers telecommute on any given weekday in the early 1990s. The majority are part-time telecommuters (one or two days per week). Some, instead of working at home, commute to a nearby telecentre. In that case, commuting is not actually eliminated; it becomes shorter. Sometimes, workers may telecommute for part of the day and work in the workplace for part of the day. The result is a shift in timing for the commute trip.

Because telecommuting is still at an early stage in development, it is still not clear whether the impacts on travel and the environment are completely beneficial. Furthermore, there is uncertainty regarding the future growth of telecommuting.

The current speculation is that it will have some impacts on total vehicle-miles traveled, energy consumption, infrastructure costs, and transportation safety. A recent study (Mokhtarian, 1998) suggests that the impacts of telecommuting on travel would be minimal, even with a considerable rise in the amount of telecommuting. It seems, therefore, that in order to reduce traffic effectively, planners should not only encourage telecommuting, but should also implement other transportation demand management (TDM) strategies.

Handy and Mokhtarian (1995) note four possible implications for planners. (i) Telecommuting can be encouraged as a way to manage traffic demand. This, together with parking charges at work sites, can reduce the demand for commuting. (ii) Decreasing the traffic volume can improve air quality. In fact, the U.S. Clean Air Act encourages the use of telecommuting. (iii) Current zoning practice does not encourage services such as grocery stores, childcare and other home-based businesses to operate close to home, thus constituting a disincentive to telecommuters because they have to make long trips to get to these services. Planners can encourage telecommuting by requiring new development projects to provide telecommunications infrastructure and telecentres. (iv) It is possible that telecommuting can lead to further urban sprawl since there is less need to live close to work sites.

The choice to telecommute involves more than travel. It may depend on psychological conditions, job-related opportunities and difficulties, family-related factors, desire for leisure, etc. In order to estimate the land use implications of telecommuting we need to know the frequency of telecommuting for an individual, the duration of telecommuting, the "workplace" of a telecommuter (at home or at telecentre), and the types of workers who will choose to telecommute (management-level personnel or lower wage workers? male or female? etc.)

Teleshopping may have impact on road travels, too. There are two kinds of shopping--functional and recreational. The former is an activity with the goal of acquiring articles, and the latter treats visiting stores as a form of recreation, a means of social interaction and acquiring general product information without necessarily purchasing. Teleshopping is generally considered as functional shopping. As such, it depends on the type and characteristics of the product, the accessibility of shopping facilities, the method and speed of delivery of the ordered goods, security and privacy, and liability and redress. It also depends on consumer mobility, time availability, and familiarity with shopping facilities.

There are not many studies on the impact of teleshopping on land use and travel patterns. Tacken (1990) reports a study in Holland which indicates that teleshopping reduces the number of shopping trips and decreases the time spent on travel. Because some of the bulky and heavy goods can be ordered and delivered through teleshopping, there is less need to travel by motor vehicle, and many teleshoppers switch to bicycle or walking. The study does not, however, examine the new trips generated as a result of the need for the delivery of goods, some of which may be transnational.

New Directions   Transportation is inextricably related to land use. Trip generation for transportation planning is obviously land-use based (see Table 4-2). However, the relationship has been noted for a long time. Mumford (1963) emphasizes the need to concentrate goods and people within limited areas. Whyte (1958) identifies good planning with the coordination of transportation, land development, and open space. Owen (1968), while advocating highways as convenient forms of transportation, expresses concern over the potential for sprawl. He actually talks about containing growth through the use of road pricing. Even MacKaye (1930), who was one of the earliest proponents of the benefits of expressways, cautions against the strip of endless development along highways, which he calls "road town." As early as 1951, an American Society of Planning Officials (ASPO) report emphasized the value of time to commuters. Wingo (1961) discusses the trade-off between transportation and housing costs, and Alonso (1964) stresses how land values vary according to their accessibility.

The more recent resurgence of interest in the relationship between land use and transportation is driven by a different set of concerns: fiscal and environmental, with public transit as the preferred option. The land use-transportation link has become more focused on the sprawl-infrastructure link. In 1975, the U.S. Environmental Impact Center released a study which concluded that public infrastructure investment has an important impact on the location, type and magnitude of development, particularly for single-detached homes. In 1976, the U.S. Council on Environmental Quality found that little had been done to control the design and location of new infrastructure. Its report argues that regulatory efforts to reduce the negative impacts of unplanned growth have floundered because of rapid changes in land use, aided and abetted by infrastructure expansion. However, it also notes that infrastructure investments on highways, mass transit and sewer lines have helped to shape growth, but they have not caused growth.

In more recent years, infrastructure efficiency and environmental concerns have become paramount issues. The U.S. Clear Air Act Amendments (CAAA) of 1990 attempt to coordinate land use, transportation and air quality. The U.S. Intermodal Surface Transportation Efficiency Act (ISTEA) of 1991 also links transportation, land use, and air pollution. ISTEA has an urban focus which emphasizes a greater role for local officials, more flexibility in spending, increased stress on reduction of urban and suburban congestion, more prominent role for transit, and provision for enhancements of historic preservation, landscaping and pedestrian improvement. "Rather than simply expanding the road system, or ... adding single-occupancy vehicle capacity, the new regulations require a broad look at all the possible measure. These range from intersection improvement, to alternative transportation models--car pools, transit, bicycle, and pedestrian--and more controversial options such as congestion pricing, growth management, and activity centre strategies." (Dunphy, 1994:31) Infrastructure cost is also a concern for both developers and municipalities. A Maryland study puts potential savings of 15% in capital costs by encouraging compact and contiguous development (Kelly, 1994).

The big debate is about the strategic choice between private automobile and public transit. There is a growing momentum among planners to see transit not only as an alternative mode of transportation, but also as a "community builder". Newman and Kenworthy (1996) note that after Toronto successfully avoided the construction of the Spadina Expressway it has experienced an upsurge in its inner city population. The expressway moratorium, together with the city's aggressive transit promotion and transit-oriented land development, results in a transit system that caters for 25% of all passenger travel in the city. Peter Calthorpe is one of the most forceful proponents of "transit-oriented development" (TOD) which is also pedestrian, bicycle and human oriented. It is impossible not to notice that much of the perception about the relationship between land use and transportation is influenced by New Urbanism. (Refer to the section on New Urbanism in the Synthesis chapter.)

Essentially, the land use response has been toward a combination of mixed uses, higher densities, a non-hierarchical road system, and sub-centres. Kenworthy and Laube (1996) have produced "an international comparison of urban transport and land use patterns with implications for sustainability." Most proponents are convinced that the problem is low-density housing and use separation. They argue for densification and mixed uses, which will produce a jobs-housing balance and a pedestrian friendly environment (especially through a non-hierarchical grid system of roads, and improved safety and lighting for cycling and walking). Some find that neighbourhood densities have a stronger influence on the mode of commuting than mixed land uses. It seems that mixed uses will exert an influence only when the shops are within 300 feet (100 metres) of walking, cycling, or the transit stop (Cevero, 1996). All these above measures are supposed to strengthen the central and inner city and develop compact suburban centres. Also, sub-centres will emerge if planning regulations will allow residential, commercial and light office structures to be built in close proximity to each other along transit lines. This will in turn induce a strong transit network that connects these smaller centres to each other and to the CBD, and promote mixed-use development along the transit corridors.

Vancouver has recently developed a Livable Regional Strategic Plan. It calls for the use of four policy instruments to reduce automobile dependence and reverse urban sprawl: land-use controls, demand management, adjusting service levels, and increasing transport capacity. Intensification is the key in Vancouver because of limited land base and high land prices. However, residents are concerned that intensification will result in an increase in traffic through neighbourhoods, over-use of local amenities such as parks, poor site design or loss of heritage through demolition, and loss of green space. Similarly, the Ontario Ministry of Transportation and the Ministry of Municipal Affairs have produced the Transit-Supportive Land Use Planning Guidelines in 1992, which encourage the development of an urban infrastructure based on linked activity nodes and corridors. Since then, the Ministry of Transportation has revised its road subsidy policy. A minimum pavement width of 8.5 metres (28 feet) is no longer required for subsidy purpose, thus allowing municipalities greater freedom in choosing smaller rights-of-way in neighbourhood design.

There is by no means consensus about what to do, or even what really is the relationship between land use and transportation. For instance, Mary Lupa (1995) examines the impacts of land use on transportation by looking at "vehicle miles traveled" against five land use scenarios (dense corridors, dense clusters, growth boundaries, urban infill, and suburb to suburb rail). Her conclusion is that "land use inputs do not respond in a spectacular fashion to regional modeling strategies. The result of making a significant change, like introducing regional corridors, is a minimal change in the output variables." (ibid:94)

Many researchers (e.g. Gomez-Ibanez, 1991; Gordon and Richardson, 1989; Ewing, 1995) realize that automobile use is complex — modal choice is influenced by incomes, gasoline prices, and public subsidies policy, and that there is a strong personal preference for the convenience of the automobile. Some emphasize accessibility over transportation, and believe that travelling can be reduced through improved access and linkages of activities without having to affect density and land use of residential neighbourhoods in the low-density regions. On the other hand, transit use is also complex. Some point out that the relationship between density and transit use is only indirect in that as density increases, automobile ownership decreases, and as automobile ownership decreases, transit use increases (Messenger and Ewing, 1996). There are further problems, too. The coordination of land use planning and transportation planning is difficult because the two functions are carried out by different agencies or departments. There is little practical advice for planners on how to integrate land use and transportation decisions and there are also little numerical standards for the density thresholds for transit services.

OTHER INFRASTRUCTURE

The availability of adequate infrastructure is not only a pre-condition for development; it may induce development (in terms of both the siting and sizing of it). However, over-provision of municipal infrastructure can have adverse effects, too. It lowers development cost to the developer and the consumer (even when the developer pays for the initial capital cost), which can lead to low-density land uses, inefficient infrastructure use and waste of natural resources. It can also degrade the environment and increase the fiscal burden on a municipality. Managing the demand for new infrastructure and maintaining the existing infrastructure properly are important land use planning considerations. (Refer to Strategic Choices in the Synthesis chapter.)

Water Supply
Three factors are essential for a municipal water supply system: quantity, potability and pressure. In North America, municipal water supply is usually designed for average daily consumption of 150-300 gallons (570-1,140 litres) per person. (In Canada, actual consumption in 1994 was about 650 litres per person.) Approximately 35% (or higher) of the water is consumed for domestic use, 50% for non-domestic and public uses, and 15% unaccounted losses and leakage. Leakage, breaks and unaccounted for water (UAW) are big problems. Water audits and leak detection are important management issues. Potability deals with health and safety consideration (organic, inorganic and microbiological hazards) as well as "aesthetics" (taste, temperature, odour, colour, turbidity, etc.). In Canada, provincial governments have jurisdiction over their own water supplies, but most would follow the Canadian Drinking Water Guidelines, set out by a federal-provincial commit-

tee. Pressure in the delivery system has to be maintained at a minimum of 30 psi (30 pounds per square inch or about 2 atmospheres) for fire-fighting purposes. The optimal is between 50-75 psi. Customers will start complaining when pressure falls below 40 psi.

Projected water demand is based on urban growth and consumer behaviour. The quantity, quality and location of demand is affected by land-use types, locations and intensities, and by living standards and life-styles. A municipal system is economically justified when population density exceeds 1000 per sq. mile (suggesting average lot sizes of less than 1.5 acre or gross density of greater than 0.6 dwelling per acre). Age and condition of the distribution system (mains) are very important facts when considering urban intensification. The additional water pressure can lead to more water loss and pipe rupture.

The present trend is to manage demand rather than increase supply. This can be done through technology (e.g., water-saving plumbing fixtures such as faucet aerators, pressure-reducing valves and toilet dams), regulations (e.g., restricted water-use hours, alternating days for watering lawns), and pricing (e.g., metered supply and increased rates). There are more elaborate and costly schemes, such as dual water systems (separate systems for potable and non-potable water), and grey water systems (e.g., use of rain water and wastewater from clothes washers and showers for toilet flushing and lawn irrigation). Another trend is to rehabilitate rather than replace. This is driven largely by the usually lower costs of rehabilitation. But a rehabilitated system usually has a shorter life.

Pollution of supply sources is becoming a big issue. Pollution may come from old landfill sites; application of fertilizers, herbicides and pesticides from agricultural and urban land; road de-icing salts and road litter; bacterial and viral contamination from septic tanks, feedlots and improper sewage disposal. All of these are affected by land use decisions. In most cases, water supply sources are also the receiving waters of our wastes. This is certainly true of downstream municipalities.

Wastewater   The amount of sewage produced is normally related to the amount of water supplied (between 65% and 85%). Another way is to use a daily per capita flow. The U.S. EPA recommends a range of between 100-125 gal. (60% of which is from domestic sources and the remainder from commercial, industrial and institutional sources). A third way to estimate is based on land use. For each land use, the total flow is determined by population density and average per capita contribution of wastewater. Table 5-22 shows some typical flows for residential areas. However, the amount that goes into the treatment plant is often increased by extraneous water that seeps into the collection system through leaks or incorrect connections. At times, this may even exceed the volume of the wastewater produced originally. The situation gets much worse when the sanitary sewage system is also used to carry urban runoff (combined sewers).

Sewerage capacity can influence land capacity for development. It is, in turn, impacted by land development. An impact analysis examines the location and amount of projected development (individual projects and cumulative growth) against the collection and treatment capacity of the system. Sometimes, an impact analysis is needed to examine the impacts of new treatment needs (such as new types of pollutants) or new regulatory requirements (such as new effluent standards). The findings are used to manage urban growth as well as determine the new service areas and trunk line extensions. Inadequate sewerage capacity is reasonable ground to halt urban development (referred to as premature development). The sharing of the costs of capacity expansion (for collection as well as treatment) to accommodate urban growth is a controversial issue. The trend is to require the new development pay the capital costs.

TABLE 5-22
TYPICAL WASTEWATER FLOWS FOR RESIDENTIAL USES
Flow in gal/unit.day (litre/unit.day)

Source	Unit	Range	Typical
Apartment:			
High-rise	Person	35-75 (130-285)	50 (190)
Low-rise	Person	50-80 (190-300)	65 (250)
Residence:			
Typical home	Person	45-90 (170-340)	70 (265)
Better home	Person	60-100 (230-380)	80 (305)
Luxury home	Person	75-150 (285-570)	95 (360)
Older home	Person	30-60 (115-230)	45 (170)
Summer cottage	Person	25-50 (95-190)	40 (150)
Hotel	Guest	30-55 (115-210)	45 (170)
Motel:			
With kitchen	Unit	90-180 (340-680)	100 (380)
Without kitchen	Unit	75-150 (285-570)	95 (360)
Trailer park	Person	30-50 (115-300)	40 (150)

Source: Metcalf and Eddy (1991).

For isolated developments, communal treatment plants can be used, but they are usually limited to a maximum volume of 1 million gal/day. For smaller rural developments, septic systems are used. These use bacterial action to treat the waste on site, with the effluents discharged through underground drainage pipes, and percolated into the soil (septic beds). This is possible only for very low-density development. (The house and the water well must be located sufficiently away from each other, say 100 feet or 30 metres.) In eastern Ontario, where the topsoil is shallow, the optimal lot size with a septic system is one acre. With its optimal shape of 150 feet x 300 feet (50m x 100m), it usually has sufficient separation distances to place a house, a well and a septic bed. Even then, governments have been trying to stop all development on septic systems.

Storm Water The amount of urban runoff is calculated for two purposes: design of channels and conduits and design of flood control measures (including detention and retention facilities). There are two groups of methods.

1. RATIONAL METHOD

It is best used for channel and pipe design in a small catchment basin of less than 120 acres (approx. 50 hectares); that means most subdivisions. The generic equation is Q = CIA. The rate of flow of water (expressed as cubic feet or cubic metres per second) that enters a channel or conduit is a function of the coefficient of runoff (C) of the surface area, the intensity of rainfall (I), and the size of the surface to be drained (A). All of these are influenced by land use decisions.

> **(i) Coefficient of Runoff (C)** Different land uses create different amounts and configurations of impervious surfaces and, therefore, different runoff coefficients (expressed as a percentage). The following table shows the coefficients of some typical land uses. More sophisticated tables would include native soil conditions effects of antecedent storms, etc.

TABLE 5-23
RUNOFF COEFFICIENTS

Surface	Runoff Coefficient
Roofs and pavements	0.9
Gravel road	0.7
Planted area	0.2
Wooded area	0.1
Residential development	
10(25) households/acre(hectare)	0.3-0.5
40(100) households/acre(hectare)	0.5-0.7
Business	
Downtown	0.7-0.95
Neighbourhood	0.5-0.7
Industrial	
Light	0.5-0.8
Heavy	0.6-0.9

Source: Adapted from Lynch and Hack (1984:237 and 462)

> **(ii) Intensity of Rainfall (I)** Channels and conduits are designed typically to handle a high-intensity, short-duration summer storm (single storms, and not successive storms). The intensity of rainfall (expressed as inches or centimetres per hour) can be based on an actual event in the past or a hypothetical statistical probability. Commonly, systems designed for a residential area are supposed to handle the biggest storm that could occur in a 2-year period (referred as a 2-year return period or a 2-year storm event). Sometimes this goes up to a 5-year return period. Two- to 10-year

return periods are used for high value general commercial areas, and 5- to 10-year return periods for high value downtown commercial areas. The choice of return periods is essentially a political decision (based on liabilities, citizen complaints, etc.), informed by land use implications. The main concern is inconvenience and property damage caused by flooding.

(iii) Area to be Drained (A) The size of drainage area (expressed in acres or hectares) is entirely a land use planning decision, based on consideration about land use configuration and topography. The catchment area served by a channel or conduit, the point of entry of surface water into a surface channel or underground conduit, and the points of connection between surface channels and underground conduits should all be governed by good land use siting and sizing principles and the dictates of gravity.

2. HYDROGRAPH METHOD

This method is best used for flood control and design of retention and detention facilities, where the fluctuation flow rates during and after the storm are more important than simply the peak flow rate. It involves constructing a storm profile — the varying flow rates that occur at any "point of interest" (e.g., where the water enters into or leaves a detention pond, and where the water reaches a narrow part in a stream) over the duration of a storm, taking into consideration rainfall intensity and duration, changing capacities of the ground to absorb and retain water as the storm progresses, etc. Again, the flow rate fluctuation is very much a function of land use and topography. Complex modeling can now be done, such as the U.S. EPA's Storm Water Management Model (SWMM), and the U.S. Army Corps of Engineers' Storage, Treatment, Overflow, Runoff Model (STORM).

The recent trend is to deal with the runoff problems (quantity and quality) at the site where they are produced. More and more municipalities require the rate of runoff from new development to be equal or less than the rate prior to the development (referred to as zero discharge increase). This trend has led to the emergence of best management practices (BMP). There are two types of solutions.

> **1. Structural Solutions.** These include the extended use of roofs, parking lots, grassed swales, and temporary (detention) and permanent (retention) ponds to contain the runoff in order to lessen the peak flow. They also include the use of urban forests, constructed wetlands, and bio-filtration to enhance the removal of pollutants. However, these structural solutions take up land, thus removing it from development use. The swales, ponds and wetlands have to be maintained, too. This often requires municipalities to take over the responsibility and cost. More troublesome is the fact that, instead of pollutants being discharged to the receiving waters directly, they now settle on rooftops and ponds. Over time, they will create health and environmental problems.
>
> Some municipal officials and developers see the retention and detention ponds, and constructed wetlands as offering visual and recreation amenities, which will actually enhance the value of the land around them. This

view should be tempered with caution. Some years ago, a "progressive" commercial land developer in the Township of Kingston, Ontario, constructed a large retention pond on his site and turned it over to the local municipality. The Lions Club made it into a nice park, with ducks and boats. The Township Reeve installed a jet fountain in the middle of the pond for the many children who came there to play. A group of researchers who were monitoring the pond found that the fountain was re-aerating all the heavy metals that had settled at the bottom. The fountain was discreetly removed, but there were many red faces.

2. Non-structural Solutions. These rely on land use controls, building regulations, municipal water bylaws (including the regulation of pesticide and herbicide use), fertilization application controls, solid waste management, street sweeping, control of illegal dumping, erosion and sediment source control on construction sites, economic incentives (including water pricing), and public education.

CONCLUSION

The discussion in this chapter includes both city-wide (or area-wide) and site-specific analysis. In practice, most planning situations are site-specific. The following typical analytic questions on site planning have been adapted from Lynch and Hack (1984: 421-425).

(1) General Site Context: geography, demography, ecology and economy.

- Will important locations or resources become inaccessible to the general public?
- Will energy, water, food, or other scarce resources be depleted or degraded?
- Will the health or safety of the surrounding population be endangered?
- Will the development put an undue traffic load on its surroundings?
- Will surrounding political, social, or economic systems be disrupted?
- Will the proposed development have a negative impact on existing businesses or institutions?
- Will its construction or maintenance lay undesirable financial burdens on the surrounding community?

(2) Physical Analysis: geology, water, topography, climate, ecology, man-made structures and sensory qualities.

- Are landslides, subsidence, or earthquakes likely to occur?

- Will the soil be contaminated?
- Can the soil absorb likely wastes without damage?
- Will the topsoil or its nutrient balance be lost?
- Will the purity, oxygen level, turbidity, or temperature of surface waters be affected?
- Will siltation occur?
- Can the drainage system accept the additional runoff?
- Will lands be flooded, erosion induced, or water bodies caused to fluctuate?
- Will the water table rise or fall, affecting vegetation, basements, or foundations?
- Will groundwater be contaminated, or the recharge or drawn-down of aquifers affected?
- Will the landform be suitable for the predominant circulation mode envisaged?
- Will unique or valued landforms be damaged?
- Will the development cause general climatic changes in terms of temperature, humidity, or wind speed?
- Will local microclimates be affected adversely, e.g., wind tunnels, glare, shadow effects, temperature fluctuations, and snow drifts?
- Will the development increase or decrease air, noise, and odour pollution?
- Will the development cause any radiation or other toxic hazards?
- Will important plant and animal communities be disrupted, or endangered species destroyed, or pest species promoted?
- Will the plan remove significant agricultural uses or make it difficult for them to be reestablished in the future?
- Will present and planned roads and other infrastructure serve the site without adverse impacts on adjacent areas?
- Will the development require a substantial investment in surrounding roads and infrastructure?
- Can these new facilities be adequately maintained and operated?
- Will new structures conflict with or damage existing ones?
- Is the new landscape in character with the existing one?
- Are existing views and focal points conserved and enhanced?
- Are the proposed buildings compatible in character with existing structures to be retained?
- Are heritage and historic structures conserved?
- Are archaeological sites and information conserved and developed?
- Will the proposed development disrupt or facilitate current physical changes in the area?

- Will the development destroy or enhance the way that groups and individuals identify with the site?
- Does the proposed development take into account the popular meanings and values of the site?

(3) User Analysis: residents or other users, their activities, and rights, and limitations.

- Will any of the existing population be relocated?
- Will any segment of this population be disadvantaged?
- How will existing jobs and businesses be affected?
- Will the proposed development modify current lifestyles or cultural practices in undesirable ways?
- Will existing institutions or social ties be disrupted?
- Will the development provide a better setting for the user activities than what exists now?
- Will the proposed development destroy important patterns of use without replacing them?
- Will new uses conflict with old ones or endanger safety?
- Is future change and expansion provided for?
- Will the economic values of the site or its surroundings be depreciated or enhanced?
- Will ownerships or customary "territories" be significantly disrupted?

These are questions about the congruence between the locational and space needs on the one hand, and the environmental impact of a particular use and the suitability and capacity of the site to accommodate that use on the other. There are two basic considerations. The first is the proper use of the site within an overall land use pattern. To make this judgment, we need to refer to the plan for the city or the area as a whole, which has been the main focus of this chapter. The second is the congruence between the needs of the user and the site characteristics, and the compatibility with adjacent uses. Since some sites can, if considered in isolation, accommodate a variety of uses and intensities, it is particularly important that a comprehensive city-wide plan is available to provide guidance about the most suitable use and optimum intensity for a specific site. But it is common practice in the comprehensive city-wide plan to give only general norms and a range of uses and intensities to large areas of land. Within the general guidelines, the actual use and development of individual parcels of land over a period of time create unique conditions for site-specific land use decisions. We should be particularly careful to consider the impact of any proposed use at a specific site on the environmental qualities of its neighbour (traffic congestion, health and safety hazards, loss of amenities, and nuisances). This constitutes the bulk of a planner's day-to-day decisions.

SYNTHESIS

S
ynthesis is about matching user needs and land supply within the framework of the public interest. It involves creative thinking and critical evaluation. In this chapter we will discuss substantive principles, that is, what constitutes good land use; and processoral principles, that is, how to make land use decisions intelligently and creatively. We will then explore some strategic choices in land use decisions. To conclude, we will discuss briefly typical contents of a land use plan and graphical presentation of plans.

According to Kaiser, Godschalk and Chapin (1995:251-252) there is a number of "plans": policy framework plans, land classification plans, urban land use designs, and development management plans, each progressively more specific in terms of the goals, facts and recommendations. A policy framework plan is the product of "direction-setting", which involves the description of existing and emerging and conditions and causes, setting of goals, and formulation of general policies regarding land use design and actions. A land classification plan is a continuation of the policy framework plan, with an analysis of land demand and supply, culminating in the designation of land for natural processes, urban use and agricultural production. An urban land use design is a further extension of the above two plans, with more detail analyses of land demand and supply, and a more fine-grain designation of locations for employment and commercial centres, residential communities, and infrastructure and community facilities. Finally, a development management plan is the final stage of all of the above planning exercises, when implementation factors are analysed, procedural goals set, and management programme, standards and procedures specified.

For our purpose all these plans involve the five elements discussed in this book (purpose, information, analysis, synthesis and implementation) and the logic of siting and sizing is also applicable to all. The difference is in the level of detail and size of the planning area, which vary according to the planning issue at hand, the number of people affected or involved, and the amount of resources available to do the task. Simply put, a plan is a statement of policies of what the community wants to do with its land, and how these community goals are to be achieved. It is a document with words and graphics. The following elements are usually included.

(i) A background study describes the general conditions of user needs and land supply and the physical, social, economic, and institutional context within which these needs and supplies are to be matched. It also explains the methods used for the investigation and analysis.

(ii) The plan itself usually begins with a brief summary of the background findings leading to a statement about goals. These are the items of public interest such as health, safety, social, economic, and environmental concerns which are to be pursued by land use development, transportation, and other special policies in the plan. It is important that these goals are stated in a way that has meaning in land use. For instance, a social goal such as affordable housing does not make sense if it cannot be related to residential land use policies regarding minimum lot sizes, housing types, densities, and so on; or an economic goal, to promote tourism, which does not relate to commercial land use policies such as the location and permitted types of recreational and commercial uses.

(iii) Various kinds of policies are then proposed to pursue the community goals. These usually cover land use, development, transportation, and certain special concerns. Land use policies deal with the type, location, and amount of land uses, and the criteria employed to decide the appropriateness of different uses for certain land or the suitability of different parcels of land for certain uses. These policies can be organized according to geographic areas, land use types, or a combination of both. A city can be divided into planning zones or functional areas such as the city centre, the inner ring, and the outer suburbs, with different land use policies for each of these areas. Alternatively, policies can be established for each land use category, such as residential, commercial, industrial, and recreational. Development policies deal with how and when development should occur. They are used to pursue goals such as the preservation of the urban fabric and the resolution of conflicts between environmental concerns and developmental needs. For instance, in preserving the urban fabric, development policies will state the choice between rehabilitation and renewal. Similarly, development policies on the phasing of land release or the programming of infrastructure construction are used to ensure the balance between environmental concerns and development needs. Transportation policies regarding road hierarchies, public transit routes, road construction maintenance and repairs, and so on, are used to pursue public interest goals such as safety and efficiency. Finally, policies can be developed for special areas such as the city centre, heritage districts, and squatter areas, or for special concerns such as sewage treatment, student housing, and urban design.

(iv) The last major element in a plan is a statement on implementation. Usually there are two kinds — control-oriented measures such as zoning and property maintenance codes, and action-oriented measures such as infrastructure programming, land assembly and development corporations.

Some land use planners have a strong aversion to their work being called "mere" physical planning. They want "social" planning to be included. Land use planning has little to say about such things as pension schemes, education programmes, and health care. But, on the other hand, many social services have physical expression in terms of land and buildings such as schools, hospitals, clinics, senior citizen housing projects, government offices, and group homes. The proper siting and sizing for these according to the criteria of a good city is very much a land use planning matter. The challenge is, of course, what is a good city?

Hok-Lin Leung

THE GOOD CITY

Society in general, and planners in particular, have always been searching for the good city. There will never be consensus. In this section we will examine several perspectives that have been clearly and forcefully articulated.

The Modernists   The "proposals" formulated by the International Congress for Modern Architecture (CIAM or Congrès Internationaux d'Architecture Moderne) in 1933 is the modernist manifesto of city planning. It is easily the most maligned of all the declarations about what a good city is. Its critics have faulted it in the last five decades on the following grounds:

- Lack of appreciation of socio-economic and political factors.
- Lack of social conscience.
- Static and lack of appreciation of change.
- Lack of appreciation of interdependence and organic growth, and especially lack of a holistic regional outlook.
- Lack of human scale.
- Isolating workplaces from residential places.
- Destroying heritage and communities.
- Putting cars before people.
- Subordinating the individual to the collective, or subordinating the common good to individual liberty.
- Physical (architectural) determinism.

The following is a shortened, but unedited, version of the manifesto (Sert, 1942:246-249), and I will let our readers be the judge, keeping in mind that it was proclaimed in 1933 — a time of deep pessimism and chaos, everywhere in the world.

THE TOWN-PLANNING CHART, FOURTH CIAM CONGRESS, ATHENS, 1933

1. Definitions and preliminary statements.
Town and country merge into one another and are elements of what may be called a regional unit. Every city forms part of a geographic, economic, social, cultural and political unit (region), upon which its development depends. Towns or cities cannot, in consequence, be studies apart from their regions, which constitute their natural limits and environment.

The development of these regional units depends on: (a) their geographical and topographical characteristics--climate, land and waters, natural communications both within the region and with other regions; (b) their economic potentialities--natural resources (soil and subsoil, raw materials, sources of energy, flora and fauna), technical resources (industrial and agricultural production), the economic system, and the distribution of wealth; [and] (c) their political and social situation--the social structure of the population, the political regime, and the administrative system......

The basic factors governing the development of cities are therefore subject to continual changes. It is the uncontrolled and disorderly development of the Machine Age, which has produced the chaos of our cities.

All these essential factors taken together constitute the only true basis for the scientific planning of any region. They are: (a) interdependent, the one reacting upon the other; [and] (b) subject to continuous fluctuations that are due to scientific and technical progress, and to social, political, and economic changes. Whether these fluctuations are forward or backward, from the human viewpoint, depends upon the measure in which man's aspirations toward the improvement of his material and spiritual well-being are able to assert themselves.

2.The four functions of the city.

The following statements of the actual conditions of life in cities and what is needed to correct their deficiencies relate to the four functions of the city: dwelling, recreation, work, and transportation. These four functions constitute a basic classification for the study of modern town-planning problems.

3. Dwelling, the first urban function.

The density of the population is too great in central districts; in many cases it exceeds 400 inhabitants to the acre (1,000 to the hectare). Overcrowding is not only to be found in the central parts of our cities. It also occurs in the vast residential areas, which developed as a consequence of the industrial growth of the past century. In overcrowded districts, living conditions are unhealthful. This is due to the fact that the land surface is overbuilt, open spaces are lacking, and the buildings themselves are in a dilapidated and insanitary state....

The more densely populated areas are frequently those sites which are least appropriate for dwellings, such as those having northern exposures on hilly ground, lowlands subject to inundations or fog, or sites too close to industrial districts and consequently disturbed by noises, vibrations and smoke. Districts of a low concentration of population have been developed on the best sites, favored by good climatological and topographical conditions, sheltered from industry, and easily accessible by roads. This irrational location of dwellings is still permitted by legislation that does not take into consideration the health factors that are thereby jeopardized....

Modern suburbs have often developed rapidly, without planning and without control. Consequently their later connection with the metropolitan center (by rail, by roads, or by other means) has met with physical obstacles which might have been avoided if suburban growth had been considered as part of a regional development....

The distribution of buildings intended for community services is of an arbitrary and heedless nature. This is notoriously true of schools, which are often situated on the most congested thoroughfares and too far from the dwellings they serve....

Residential districts ought to occupy the best sites. The climatological and topographical conditions of those sites intended for dwelling purposes must be carefully considered, as well as their proximity to existing unbuilt land surfaces suitable for recreation purposes. The possible future location of industry and business in the immediate vicinity should also be considered....

4. Recreation.

Open spaces in cities today are generally insufficient. Open spaces are often poorly situated and consequently difficult of access to many people. Since most open spaces are situated in outlying and suburban areas, they do not benefit the inhabitants of the unhealthful central districts....

It should be required that the general sanitation of too densely populated districts is improved by the razing of slums and other buildings, the cleared sites to be devoted to recreational purposes; that open spaces near kindergartens or playgrounds be used as sites for nursery schools, and that certain sites in parks be devoted to general community purposes, with branch public libraries, small neighborhood museums, or auditoriums....

5. Work.

Places of work (industrial, business, governmental) are not situated in the city structure according to their functions. The absence of a planned coordination of the locations of work-places with those of dwellings creates excessive traveling distances between the two. Traffic is overtaxed during rush hours, on account of disorganized communications.

Owing to high land values, increasing taxation, traffic congestion, and to the rapid and uncontrolled expansion of the city, industry is often forced to move away, bringing about a decentralization which is facilitated by modern technics. Business districts can be expanded only through the costly action of purchasing and razing surrounding dwellings.

Possible ways of solving these problems....Industries should be classified according to their character and their needs, and should be distributed in special zones throughout the territory comprised of the city and the region they influence. In delimiting these zones, it will be necessary to take into account the relation of the different industries to each other and their relation to zones intended for other functions. The distances between dwellings and work places should be direct and traversable in a minimum of time. Industrial districts should be independent of residential districts (indeed, of other districts as well), and should be isolated by means of green bands, or neutral zones. Certain small industries intimately related to urban life and not the source of any inconvenience or nuisance should remain within the city, serving its different residential districts....Business districts should enjoy favorable means of communication linking them to residential districts and to industrial zones.

6. Transportation.

The street systems found in most cities and their suburbs today are a heritage of past eras (the Middle Ages in many European cities, and later periods in America), when they were designed for the use of pedestrians and horse-drawn vehicles. As such, in spite of successive alterations, they no longer fulfill the requirements of modern types of vehicles (automobiles, buses, trucks) or modern traffic volume. The insufficient width of streets causes congestion. The lack of space in our streets and the frequency of crossings make the new possibilities of locomotion almost useless. Traffic congestion, which is the cause of thousands of accidents, is becoming increasingly hazardous to everyone.

Our present streets fail to exhibit any differentiation in terms of their possible functions, a circumstance, which excludes an efficacious approach to the modern traffic problem. The solution of this problem is unattainable through present corrective measures (street widening, traffic restrictions, or others), and can be reached only by means of new city planning.

A certain type of "academic" city planning, conceived in "the grand manner" and striving mainly toward monumental effects in its layout of buildings, avenues, and squares, often complicates the traffic situation. Railroad lines are often obstacles to urban development. Encircling certain districts, they separate them from other parts of the city with which they should have direct contact and easy communication.

Changes necessary for the solution of the most important transportation problems. The universal use of motorized transportation, bringing speeds unknown only a few years ago, has violently agitated the whole urban structure and fundamentally affected living conditions within it. A new street system designed for modern means of transportation is therefore required.

For the purpose of providing a new street system corresponding to modern traffic needs, it is necessary that accurate statistics be available for the rational determination of street dimension requirements. The speeds to be provided for in each street will depend upon the function of the street and upon the nature of the vehicles it carries. These speeds therefore are also factors of classification, determining the features of those thoroughfares intended for fast moving traffic and those intended for trucks and other slow traffic, and differentiating these from tributary or secondary streets. In the proposed network of restricted streets, provision should be made for pedestrian lanes, designed for the convenience of pedestrians and therefore not necessarily following vehicular routes....

7. Buildings and districts of historical interest.

Buildings or groups of buildings that are remnants of past cultures should not be demolished: (a) when they are really representative of their period and, as such, may be of general interest and serve for the instruction of the public; (b) when their existence does not affect the health conditions of populations living in the area; [and] (c) whenever it is possible to route main thoroughfares so that the presence of these old districts does not increase traffic congestion and so that their location does not affect the organic growth of the city.

All attempts at adapting new districts to these old layouts (which is often done under pretext of preserving local characteristics) have had bad results. Such adaptations to the past should not be tolerated in any case. By a planned clearance of slum areas, which are frequently to be found in the neighborhood of these monuments of the past, it is possible to improve the living conditions of the residential areas near-by and to safeguard the health of their inhabitants.

8. General requirements.

One might summarize the analysis of urban functions....by saying that the living conditions found in most cities today do not correspond to the most elementary biological and psychological needs of great masses of their populations.

Since the beginning of the Machine Age, these conditions have been an expression of the ceaseless growth of private interests. The growth of cities has been caused by the increasing use of the machine--the change from the manual labor of artisans to big industry. There is apparent in most cities a disastrous rupture between the economic resources and the administrative and social responsibility of the municipality.

Although cities are constantly changing, it may be stated as a general fact that changes are not anticipated and that their development suffers because of the absence of control and the failure to apply the principles recognized by contemporary town planning. The magnitude of the work to be undertaken in the urgently needed reconstruction of cities, on the one hand, and the excessive division of urban land, on the other, represent two antagonistic realities. This sharp contradiction creates a most serious problem in our time: that of the pressing needs to establish the disposition of the land upon a basis that will satisfy the needs of the many as well as those of the individual. In case of conflict, private interest should be subordinated to public interest.

The city should be examined in the economic ensemble of its region of influence. A plan of the economic unit, the "city-region" in its totality, must therefore replace the simple city plan of today. It will be necessary to fix the limits of the plan in accordance with those of the region defined by the scope of the city's economic influence: (a) to produce an equitable layout, with respect to location and areas, of the various districts intended for dwellings, for work, or for recreation, as well as to establish traffic networks; (b) to establish plans that will determine the development of different districts according to their needs and their organic laws; [and] (c) the town planner should also establish the relationship between places of dwelling, work, and recreation, in such a way that the daily cycle of activities going on in these various districts may occur with the greatest economy of time....

In establishing the relations between the different urban functions, the town planner must not forget that dwelling is the first urban function, a primordial element in the city pattern.

The urban unit should be able to develop organically in all its different parts. And each phase of its development should assure a state of equilibrium among all its respective functions. It should therefore assure, on both the spiritual and material planes, individual liberty and the benefits of collective action.

To the architect engaged in town planning, human needs and the human scale of values is the key to all the architectural compositions to be made.

The point of departure for all town planning should be the cell represented by a single dwelling, taken together with similar cells to form a neighborhood unit of efficacious size. With this cell as the starting point, dwellings, places of work, and recreation areas should be distributed throughout the urban area in the most favorable relationship possible.

To solve this tremendous problem, it is necessary to utilize the resources put at our disposal by modern technic and to procure the collaboration of specialists.

The course to be taken in all town-planning projects will be influenced basically by the political, social, and economic factors of the time and not, in the last resort, by the spirit of modern architecture. The dimensions of the component parts of the functional city should be estimated on the human scale and in relation to human needs.

Town planning is a science based on three dimensions, not two. It is in admitting the element of height that efficacious provision can be made for traffic needs and for the creation of open spaces for recreation or other purposes.

It is of the most urgent necessity that each city should provide itself with a town-planning program, coordinated with the programs of its region and of the nation as a whole. The execution of these programs on a national, regional, or urban scale must be guaranteed by the necessary legal arrangements. Every town-planning program must be based upon accurate researches made by specialists. It must foresee the different stages of urban development in time and space. It must coordinate the natural, sociological, economic, and cultural factors that exist in each case.

Many of the concepts, techniques and standards used in current practice are based on the modernist approach. However, progress and failures in city planning cannot be attributed to the modernist approach alone. So much of what we see and experience in our city environment and city life is the result of many, many factors. But one thing is certain; the physical quality of city life has improved enormously, especially with respect to public health, crowding and congestion, the very ills that were identified in the CIAM manifesto. In that way, one can say that these successes correlated with modern planning.

But planning goals are moving targets and the status quo are always questioned. It is only "natural" that the modernist approach heralded in CIAM is challenged. However, post-modernists have at least one thing to learn from the pioneer modernists--their optimism in the human spirit and their faith in reason. I want to highlight two branches of this modernist tree: Kevin Lynch's contribution to "reason", and Christopher Alexander's contribution to "the human spirit".

Lynch (1981) argues that it is difficult to express the difference between a really good plan and a merely ordinary one. He proposes five basic criteria of a good city. They are probably the most coherent set of practical guidance for city planning to date.

>(i) Vitality. This is measured by the degree to which the physical form of the city protects the survival and supports the vital functions, the biological requirements and capabilities of human beings.

>(ii) Sense. This is similar to Lynch's earlier idea of imageability (1960); that is, the degree to which the city can be clearly perceived and mentally structured in time and space by its residents and the degree to which the mental structure connects with their values and concepts.

>(iii) Fit. This is the degree of congruence between environment and activities, including the adaptability of the environment to future needs.

>(iv) Access. This is the ability to reach other persons, activities, resources, services, information, or places. Included here is also the idea of choice.

>(v) Control. This refers to users' control over the provision, use, access, and management of spaces and activities.

Besides these five criteria Lynch added two metacriteria: efficiency, which includes both the real cost and opportunity cost; and justice, which has to do with the distribution of benefits and costs among the people.

Alexander (1982) gives us another view of the good city. For him, the good city is "whole" and good city planning is "to heal." "The kind of growing wholeness is not merely that existed in old towns. It exists always in all growing organisms (which is why we feel that old towns are somehow organic...simply because they share, with organisms, this self-determined, inward-governed, growing wholeness)." His overriding rule is that "every increment of construction must be made in such a way as to heal the city...Every new act of construction has just one basic obligation: It must create a continuous structure of whole around itself." (ibid.:22) Alexander's message covers a whole spectrum of city planning and design situations, from a small site to the whole city. He suggests seven rules.

>(i) Piecemeal growth (in terms of size, mix of sizes, and mix of functions)

>(ii) The growth of larger wholes.

(iii) The importance of a vision of an individual building as well as a vision towards the whole. Such a vision is "a product of the inner shouting of the site, not a product of whimsy or fantasy." (ibid.:63)

(iv) Creating positive urban spaces — buildings surrounding public spaces, and not spaces surrounding buildings.

(v) Making the layout of large buildings — entrances, main circulation, division of function parts, interior open spaces, day-lighting, movement within building, etc. — "coherent and consistent with the position of the building in the street, and in the neighborhood." (ibid.:77)

(vi) Relating structures and details to their larger as well as smaller wholes.

(vii) Creating "centers" — "a loosely connected system of local symmetries, always relaxed, always allowing necessity to guide it, in such a way as to produce the deepest possible structure of centers, at every scale." (ibid.:95)

Over time, "modernism" has become the status quo. But the status quo is not a bad thing in itself. In fact, there must be a lot of good about something for it to become accepted and entrenched. However, after the tremendous creative outburst that resulted in near-universal success, the pioneering spirit was dimmed, and second and third generation modernists are often second- and third-rate modernists. The status quo has become complacent and lazy and, when challenged, defensive. For some people, modern planning has come to mean planning by the rulebook, with the rules being hopelessly out-of-date. They do not believe modern planning has the capacity to improve and regenerate. They want, or think they want, a revolution. A number of these alternatives are introduced in the following.

New Urbanism

It all began with suburban sprawl. Most post WWII suburbs are large tracts of low-density residential areas separate from commercial and industrial activities. The prevalence of the private automobile reinforces sprawl, which in turn increases travel distance. Many critics suggest that all these have led to increased traffic congestion, air pollution, vast use of land, decay of the inner city and reduced interaction in community (e.g., Calthorpe, 1993; and Christoforidis, 1994). Several planning approaches have emerged in the 1980s as alternatives to address the "ills" of suburban sprawl.

High-profile movements include the Traditional Neighbourhood Development (TND) pioneered by Andres Duany and Elizabeth Plater-Zyberk and Transit-Oriented Development (TOD) introduced by Peter Calthorpe. TND and TOD are rather similar in both intent and results, and many planners and architects have embraced their principles under the name of New Urbanism (Kelbaugh, 1997).

Advocates organized a conference that established the Congress of the New Urbanism (CNU) in 1993, dedicated to promoting these alternatives. CNU endorses the restructuring of public policy and development practices to support the restoration of urban centres and towns, the creation of a diversity of neighbourhoods, and enhancement of transit and pedestrian use.

The emphasis in TND is "urban design" (Krieger and Lennertz, 1991). The growth of a town is to be contained by a greenbelt. In the town, there is a wide variety of housing types to encourage a diverse socioeconomic mix. The development of a new community begins with a master plan that provides a network of interconnected streets and convenient walking distances. Neighbourhoods are to have a 1/4 mile radius, which means a five-minute walk from edge to the centre. Street blocks are generally not bigger than 230 by 600 feet, with integrated building types and uses. Pedestrian routes are provided throughout, with paths and sidewalks. Each street has its own distinguishing alignment of trees and other plantings. Squares and parks are evenly distributed, with community buildings placed on prominent sites. All these are controlled by a design code that draws on the architecture of the region. It regulates building use, building placement, building shape, landscape, and street types. One of the hallmarks of TND is the revival of alleys to provide for a whole range of activities such as garbage removal, meters, mailboxes, car storage, storm water inlets, etc. It has been observed that much of New Urbanism's goal of pedestrianization and social interaction have been achieved primarily on the back-side of the house (Martin, 1996). The best-known TND developments are Seaside, Florida and Kentlands, Maryland.

A typical TOD is mixed-use community with an average walking distance of 2,000 feet (or 10 minutes) to a transit stop and core commercial area (Calthorpe, 1993). Transit station spacing is about 1/2 - 1 mile. Travel time on a feeder transit line (joining a neighbourhood to a trunk line) is no more than 10 minutes. There are multiple and parallel routes between the core commercial, residential and employment areas so that local trips are not forced onto arterial roads. In a TOD, streets are designed for travel speeds of 15 mph (25 km/h), with 8-10 feet (2.5-3m) wide traffic lanes, on-street parking, 5-foot (1.5m) sidewalk, and street trees spaced at a maximum of 30 feet (10 m). Parking standards are set at 2-4 spaces for every 1,000 sq. ft. (100 sq. m) of office, 3-5 for retail, and 1-3 for light industry.

Average density for a TOD residential area is between 10 and 25 dwellings per acre (approx. 25-60 dwellings per hectare). All TODs have mixed uses. At the centre, core commercial uses must occupy at least 10% of the total area, with a minimum of 10,000 sq. ft. (1,000 sq. m) of retail space adjacent to a transit stop. Within one mile of the core new competing retail uses are limited. Community buildings and services are located in central areas. School and community parts are located at the edges, where the residential density can go as low as six units per acre (15 units per hectare) (referred to as "secondary areas", which are also used to accommodate other uses that are more automobile-oriented).

Local plants are used for landscaping and prominent stands of heritage trees are preserved. Existing drainage ways and wetlands are protected, and swales and surface drainage are encouraged over storm drains. Urban growth boundaries are established at the edge of metropolitan regions to protect the natural resources.

Table 6-1 shows some defining characteristics of Traditional Neighbourhood Development and Transit-Oriented Development (Southworth, 1997).

TABLE 6-1
CHARACTERISTICS OF NEW URBANISM DEVELOPMENTS

	Traditional Neighbourhood Development	Transit-Oriented Development
	Kentlands (Duany Plater- Zyberk)	**Laguana West (Peter Calthorpe)**
Description	- Designed in 1988. - 356 acres and 1,600 units. - Construction completed 1996.	- Development began in 1990. - 1,018-acre site with a projection of 3,300 dwelling units. - 550 homes built, by 1997.
Character	Historic image of white picket fences, porches, and alleyways. Incorporated topography in design.	Strong sense of streetscape. Houses have front porches and yards, and garages set at back or side yard.
Land Use Patterns	Mix of housing types. Average Density: 4,78 d.u./acre Density: Single family 5-8 d.u./net acre Row houses 17 d.u./net acre	Mix of housing types. Average Density: 3.24 d.u./acre Density: Single family 1.28-6.5 d.u./net acre Carriage home 15 d.u./net acre Apart./Condo. 17-25 d.u./net acre
Public Open Space	100 acres or 28% of site is open space.	205 acres or 20% of site is open space.

Source: Adapted from Southworth (1997)

Nelessen's hamlets and MacBurnie's metropolitan purlieus are two other variations of New Urbanism. Nelessen (from Knack, 1991) emphasizes the participation of citizens and public officials in the design process. His hamlets resemble traditional eastern U.S. small towns that are made up of a common town green and single-detached homes. These homes have porches, small lawns, and common open space in the rear. MacBurnie (1992) uses a combination of TND, TOD, garden city and garden suburb ideas. Metropolitan purlieus are transit-oriented, regionally based, small communities separated by greenbelts and connected by rail lines, bus routes, and bicycle paths. A purlieu would be located on a 150-acre (60 hectare) site, accommodating 7,000 residents and sustaining 3,000-4,000 jobs. There is a variety of housing types, from single-detached homes to high-density garden apartments.

The New Urbanism concept faces several challenges: persistent consumer preference for lower-density housing; dominance of the automobile and an established infrastructure that is automobile-oriented; and existing municipal plans and zoning regulations which limit the mixing of land uses. Some critics question if the ubiquitous front porch will necessarily increase the sense of neighbourliness, given the power of television and people's mobility. Some express concerns about the safety of alley ways. On a social level, critics are worried about the loss of industry and feel that the predominance of the service sector in New Urbanism communities will encourage a white-collar mono-culture.

There is also increasing skepticism with New Urbanism projects. Many have been built on greenfield suburban lands, thus perpetuating the very sprawl they are supposed to halt. Most are targeted toward high-income homebuyers and are thus viewed as elitist. However, the U.S. Department of Housing and Urban Development's HOPE VI has more recently embraced it as a tool to developing public and affordable housing (Fulton, 1996), and the Canada Mortgage and Housing Corporation has also undertaken studies to examine its potential as mainstream housing option (CMHC, 1998).

Douglas Kelbaugh (1997) is perhaps one of the most ardent apologists of New Urbanism. He believes that the movement is not simply recycling old principles and practices, but represents a new and total attempt to find a unified design for entire regions. For him, New Urbanism is not a new suburban design but a regional strategy that can, and should, be applied to downtown and inner city neighbourhoods. He believes that it is not elitist because there is a point where a movement must move on from discussion and questions in order to put theory into practice. It is not formulaic but can be refined through practice. Although the projects are fairly separate from other existing residential areas, it is only because it is easier for planners and designers to work on a new site rather than modify the existing social fabric of a neighbourhood. While it is true that transit and walking will never replace car use, New Urbanism designs can at least reduce the number and length of trips. Finally, the fact that New Urbanism projects have not had a great deal of marketing success is because the public needs time to appreciate the nature of the projects; then it will embrace the concept.

My own question is whether these "designer suburbs" are really affordable and sustainable as a mainstream option (Leung, 1995). The "higher" densities do not necessarily translate into lower housing costs. The dwelling types (more attached houses and smaller lots) and layouts (narrower streets and smaller setbacks) may suggest compactness. But we should not confuse built form with density. The built-up part is often surrounded by, or interspersed with, generous open spaces. This makes the actual land consumption much higher than the look the development suggests. The neighbourhood density (number of dwellings divided by the total area) of a neo-traditional or eco-village development is often quite comparable to that of a conventional subdivision. With no savings on land, housing prices will not come down. New Urbanism suburbs are not meant to be affordable.

In a way, these "designer suburbs" can be interpreted as an effort by the elite to reclaim the earlier suburban ideals of democracy and community, lost through the invasion of the masses. Nowhere is this more clearly illustrated than in its conception and treatment of open space. There is a shift from yards to parks, that is, from individual private open space to communal open space. This is aimed at catering to the life cycle of the old and lifestyle of the young. There are fewer children and fewer parents who stay at home. The emphasis is on larger open spaces rather than "fragmented" ones--spaces that celebrate the community spirit and protect natural habitats. If these suburbs catch on in a big way there may be significant regional consequences.

Imagine all the new developments to have compact buildings in the centre and generous open spaces around them. Development sizes will vary according to site sizes, which, in turn, vary according to the pattern of private land ownership. And, the pattern of private land ownership bears no necessary rationale to either ecology or community. There will be clusters of compact housing, from a few units to a few hundred, separated by open spaces, the shapes and sizes of which are governed more by property lines than by the dictates of natural or social relations. These clusters will also be linked by roads and other infrastructure. Thus, instead of Corbusier's "towers in the park" we will now have "horizontal towers in a sea of green" — picturesque sprawl that will take up just as much land and use up as much energy as the conventional suburban sprawl of old.

Ecological Perspectives

In an ecological approach, two principles define the good city: integrity and connectivity. Whether it is resource management for human use, maintenance of ecosystem integrity, or preservation of the intrinsic value of nature, the unifying principle is perhaps "sustainable development." The chief land use concern is the fragmentation of natural lands by urban development, and all the implications that come from it. The challenge is about dealing with the conflicts between natural processes and urban processes.

Inter-connected lands are essential for natural processes. But this interconnectedness is threatened by the urban processes (activities and networks). Since the natural environment does not automatically resist the urban processes it becomes fragmented. This fragmentation can be avoided only if the planning of urban activities and networks takes on an ecological perspective. In this perspective, the natural and urban patterns are seen as two different layers superimposed on each other. The natural patterns must remain sustainable and the urban patterns must accommodate and work around the natural landscape. Vrijlandt and Kerkstra (1994) suggest two principles. (i) Where the urban pattern is very dense with small meshes, it should be molded around the integrity of the natural pattern. (ii) Where the urban pattern has large meshes, more room is available for the natural pattern, and both can be laid out following their own requirements, with provisions given to maintain the continuity of both patterns.

The ecological perspective also "reinforces" the connectedness between man and nature — an integration of urban activity with ecology. Michael Hough (1995) suggests a number of principles.

(i) Process. Human beings have to understand that natural processes are not always "attractive", but necessary, ecologically. For example, when rocks fell to the bottom of the Niagara Falls, many spectators were concerned that this would change the fall's appearance.

(ii) Economy of means. Always use the least effort, where the least amount of resources and energy produce the greatest environmental, economic and social benefits. For example, in the Netherlands, fruit growers keep sheep in their orchard in order to maintain the grass. This keeps the grass short, which helps minimize competition for nutrients and moisture, and provides the grower with two sources of income from the fruit and sheep.

(iii) Diversity. Diversity provides choice, especially with respect to energy sources.

(iv) Connectedness. One needs to understand the local environment in the larger context in order to understand how local activity affects the larger environment, and vice versa.

(v) Environmental education begins at home. Learning about one's immediate surroundings and recognizing its potential is a necessary first step to appreciate the inter-relationships between human and natural life.

(vi) Human development and environmental enhancement. Current practice is to minimize negative environmental effects. This implies that degradation is inevitable. One must go beyond this and focus on how development can contribute to the environment, such as recycling.

(vii) Make visible the processes that sustain urban life. We must eschew the philosophy of "out of sight, out of mind." For example, draining storm water as soon as it falls on the ground hides the environmental consequence of urban development.

Central to the ecological perspective is sustainability. Sustainable development is the balance between economic, community and ecological development. Maclaren (1996) lists a number of characteristics of sustainable development.

- An individual's well being depends on meeting the individual's basic physical and economic needs.
- The needs of future generations are as important as the needs of the current generation.
- There has to be fair distribution of costs and benefits of resource use.
- Waste discharges should not exceed the capacity of the ecosystem to process them.
- Use of renewable resources should be within the capacity of the ecosystem to regenerate them.
- Minimize the use of non-renewable resources — minimize use, reuse, recycle and seek substitutes.
- Increase land use efficiency by reducing sprawl and encouraging compact development.
- Aim at long-term economic development.
- Diversity in the economic, biological and cultural domains of an urban system increases its ability to adapt to change.

Essentially, there are three components in sustainable development: ecological integrity, economic viability, and social equity (Grant, Darrell and Manuel, 1993). There are three types of indicators.

(i) Environmental quality. These measure the connectivity and productivity of the landscape, such as species viability, open space conservation, and environmental conditions of water, air and land.

(ii) Effects of development. These measures the harmful effects of development, such as acres of habitat destroyed, habitat loss, species loss, volume of runoff, volume of soil loss, percent of land covered by impermeable surfaces, percent of flood plain modified by development.

(iii) Environmental policies, practices and regulations. These measure the potentials of policies, practices and regulations in curbing harmful development, such as those concerning the designation of areas for protection and control, environmental review prior to development, environmental monitoring, management of natural areas, and municipal purchase of conservation lands.

There are also some practical suggestions (Ewing, 1996).

1. Best environmental practices to incorporate design with nature.

    *   A systems approach that goes beyond individual sites to the larger region.
    *   Channel development into areas that have already been disturbed.
    *   Preserve high-quality patches, as large and circular as possible, feathered at the edges and connected by wildlife corridors.
    *   Protect wetlands by designing around them.
    *   Protect wetlands and natural water bodies from erosion, nutrient overload and loss of species by using natural upland buffers.
    *   Preserve uplands in order to maintain biodiversity at a regional scale.
    *   Restore and enhance environmental processes previously disturbed by human activities.
    *   Minimize runoff by siting development on the least porous soil, and use infiltration devices and permeable pavements to reduce the risk of flooding and spread of pollutants.
    *   Detain runoff with open, natural drainage systems, such as swales and filter strips.
    *   Design artificial storm-water lakes and ponds to increase wildlife habitats. (A mix of shallow and deep water to help remove pollutants; littoral shelves with aquatic plants to help absorb metals; vegetation along the shoreline to increase habitat activity; irregularly shaped ponds to provide space for vegetation; sandbars and mudflats to provide feeding areas for wading birds; islands to provide space for low-nesting waterfowl; and ponds located at the edge of a residential area to prevent cats and dogs from disturbing the wildlife.)
    *   Use reclaimed water on large landscaped areas.

- Use integrated pest management instead of pesticides by introducing natural enemies to local pests, and growing disease- and insect-resistant grasses.
- Design landscaping that minimizes maintenance (xeriscapes).

2. Best land use practices for sustainable development.

- Design to higher density to reduce vehicle miles per capita (more difficult for outlying developments).
- Strive at jobs-housing balance in an area by aiming at 1.3 to 1.7 jobs per household.
- Encourage mixed land uses (and include civic uses in the mix) at the finest grain that the market will bear in order to reduce trip distance to commercial areas, and increase property values and street security.
- Develop in small clusters and reduce lot sizes in order to provide for more open space, less landscape irrigation, and less runoff.
- Place higher density and seniors' housing near commercial centres, transit lines, and community facilities in order to provide better access for the less mobile.
- Phase commercial and recreational facilities to keep pace with housing in order to sustain commercial activity and reduce travel outside of the immediate area.
- Turn subdivisions into neighbourhoods with well-defined centres (to improve social interaction and sense of community) and edges (to define the neighbourhood identity).
- Reserve (and donate, if necessary) school sites to attract new schools in order to maintain a more supportive learning environment, higher student achievement, higher rates of participation in school activities, and more walking and biking.
- Concentrate commercial use in compact centres (as opposed to strips) in order to reduce shopping stops, increase the functional relationship among stores, and deter crime.
- Make shopping centres and business parks into all-purpose activity centres in order to increase pedestrian movement in the area, reduce the number of trips, encourage alternative modes of travel (such as carpools and transit use), and moderate peak demands.
- Tame auto-oriented land uses, such as big-box retail, to be more pedestrian-friendly by limiting the setbacks, locating parking at the back of buildings, and designing buildings to be compatible to neighbouring shops.

Because sustainable development stresses the balance between economic, community and ecological development, it emphasizes partnership among all the stakeholders in building a community vision, and use of local knowledge and experience. As such, sustainable development planning usually involves three components: (i) goals which the community wishes to work toward; (ii) targets and triggers which set a time-frame for the targets to be achieved; and (iii) strategies and commitments by stakeholders to ensure continual partnership in achieving the objectives (International Council for Local Environment, et al., 1996).

Other Approaches

1. Multiculturalism

American and British literature have focused on the segregation and discrimination of blacks and ethnic minorities, and poverty and need for revitalization of the inner city. Canada has focused on equity issues concerning the relationship between built forms and cultural preferences.

In the U.S., there is a higher concentration of blacks and ethnic minorities in the inner city. The out-migration of affluent white and black households from the inner city has increased the rate of unemployment and poverty in this area. Difficulty for blacks to obtain loans to purchase a home further reinforces segregation. As a result, "the spatial concentration of black households in poverty areas is much higher than any other group" (Blakely and Deka, 1996:118). The challenge is equal access to resources with which to improve one's surroundings, or to move to a different location. The U.S. has placed greater emphasis on encouraging community-based development and private entrepreneurship. Housing policy in the U.S. favours those who can take out a loan to buy a home (tax deductions for mortgage interest and property tax), and developers who provide suburban homes. Advocates argue that governments should ensure lenders are responsive to the credit needs of low- and moderate-income neighbourhoods, and assist low-income black families in moving from public housing into private apartments (Squires, 1994).

The U.K. has a stronger welfare-orientation than the U.S., but the decline in urban investment has a greater impact on those living in the inner city. U.K. policies have been placing greater emphasis on generating employment and providing affordable housing. But urban development efforts have declined over the last three decades, and there is an increasing welfare-dependence among residents on the inner city (Blakely and Deka, 1996). On the other hand, there has been more effort by planning authorities to include minorities--equal opportunity policy in hiring, training, media liaison, monitoring of planning application, consultation with minorities, and research into minority needs (Davies, 1996).

Canadian multiculturalism has a different complexion. The identity of Canada as a "mosaic of culture" acknowledges the diverse cultures that have built neighbourhoods, businesses, and community. The Charter of Rights and Freedoms of 1982 and the Canadian Multiculturalism Act of 1985 have ensured that urban policy is free of racial or cultural discrimination.

During the 1980s, almost two-thirds of Canada's immigrants came from Asia, Latin America and Africa; most settled in the three largest metropolitan cities of Vancouver, Toronto and Montreal. As ethnic neighbourhoods began to emerge and grow, so did the demand for planning standards and policies that recognize the preference of the various cultures. For example, the preference in size and location of residential trees varies among cultures, and becomes a source of dispute among residents with varying tastes in landscaping. My colleague,

Mohammad Qadeer (1997), argues that multiculturalism should serve two functions: fulfilling the social needs of ethnic communities, and addressing the diversity of activities and built forms that compete in the community planning process. There has been a shift from the invasion-succession paradigm of neighbourhood change toward a multicultural response, which stresses mutual accommodation. Therefore, the planning system in a multicultural context must be able to separate out public policy issues from interest group agendas. The emerging idea is "communicative planning" which makes the participation by stakeholders, with their divergent (ethnic) interests, a necessary condition of good planning (Innes, 1998).

What has become evident in Canada is that planning standards that were once considered neutral are now recognized for their cultural biases, since a standard may appease one cultural preference while refusing another. Ethnic concentrations have resulted in new planning practices. Qadeer (1994) has documented many interesting examples. For instance, in one of the cities he studied Chinese shopping centres usually required extra customer parking because they included restaurants and banquet halls. The cumulative site-specific zoning amendments generated by these projects eventually resulted in an amendment to the city-wide parking standard.

Under multiculturalism the planning processes must also be able to deal with pluralistic interests among cultures as well as within a culture. This has modified the scope and procedure of citizen participation. Qadeer (1997) has observed that when Vancouver developed its city plan, ethnic community groups and individuals were invited specifically, and phone-lines were set up in four languages to provide information and receive comments.

2. Feminist Perspectives

Feminist theory has defined gender as a socially constructed role — "the result of political arrangements and is amenable to social and political analysis" (Tobias, 1997:1).

In the first wave of the feminist movement, women worked to achieve the right to vote in the late 19th and early 20th century. By the 1960s, the second wave of feminism focussed on equal employment opportunities, equal pay and education. But countless "grass roots" groups emerged, resulting in the fragmentation of the movement based on division between class, race and ethnicity (Little, 1994). By the 1970s, academics, planners and activists began analyzing the role of the built environment and how it reflected and reinforced gender inequality. Feminists (e.g., Hayden, 1984; and Little, 1994) have argued that the layout of cities has influenced the degree of control that women have over their daily activities. The separation of residential areas from employment and the dominance of suburban sprawl have increased the need for travel, and thus have increased the demands on women's mobility, given the nature of their multiple responsibility. Greed (1994) notes that current transportation planning focuses on accommodating the journey from home to work, without combining other activities such as childcare, school, and shopping. Also, public transit has not accommodated travels during off-peak times of the day for those (mainly women) who work part-time or shift work. She suggests that planning should try to decrease the need to travel by increasing land use mix; providing a greater distribution of localized, small-scale, friendly, and safe facilities, shops and amenities; providing better public transit; and centralizing facilities such as hospitals, schools, and government offices.

There are some general features of a "feminist city" (Andrew, 1992).

- A well-developed network of services dealing with the issue of violence against women and children.

- A public agency whose mandate is to ensure the elimination of violence against women.

- A wide variety of services.

- Friendly neighbourhoods through mixed use of spaces, and lively pedestrian-oriented streets.

- Close physical relationship between services, residences, and workplaces, through mixed land uses.

- Public transportation that is safe, cheap, and efficient.

- Social housing policy which includes co-operative housing, housing for women leaving transitional homes, and special housing for women with disabilities.

- Good daycare, from drop-in centres to full-daycare.

- Active encouragement of community-based economic development, with meaningful jobs for women, coordinated with daycare.

- A feminist planning process — working with the population rather than about the population.

- Public art that is representative of women and women-centred activities.

At the site level, there are also suggestions about land use and design that will meet women's needs. Mostly, these focus on increasing accessibility and safety in the built environment (Hayden, 1984; Little, 1994; and Wekerle and Whitzman, 1995). The built environment should provide good visibility and eliminate enclosed environments such as multi-storey parking, alleys, and walled estates. Safety may be enhanced through women-only sections of car parks, women's transportation schemes, and any environment that increases informal surveillance. Also, feminists' concerns are not only about women, but include children and the elderly. They advocate making space more accessible for parents (including the provision of a children's play area in department stores); seating for children with the availability of small furniture in banks, stores and restaurants; baby changing places; and windows at children's eye level. "Play spaces can add a sense of joy for people of all ages, especially when they are organized to incorporate trees and flowers, public art or local landmarks such as ruins of old buildings, traces of past settlement patterns, or artifacts conveying economic history" (Hayden, 1984:214).

A Concluding Remark

Much of planning practice today is based on the modernist idea of the good city. However, there is now a sense of restlessness about the future. There are two obvious directions that the planning profession, and society at large, can take. There can be a rejuvenation of the modernist faith in reason and the human spirit. In practical terms, this means a revisit of the first principles that justify planning, a reexamination of the social, economic and technical bases of planning concepts, norms and standards, and a de-ossification of planning procedures and bureaucracies. The other is to throw out everything and start afresh; somewhat like the pioneer modernists did in the first half of this century. So far, I see the many new-isms as essentially "reactions" to modernism; some are actually extensions of modernism; and all use modernism as their point of reference.

THE DYNAMICS OF IDEAL ENVIRONS

People seek environments that are congruent to their images of the ideal, much of which were formed during their growing-up years. Yesterday's aspiration is today's reality. But aspirations differ between the social and economic elite and the common people. Since ancient Greek and Roman times the elite has always desired the suburbs. In the second half of the 19th century the Industrial Revolution brought new reasons and opportunities for the escape into the suburbs. Extreme urban congestion and uncontrolled industrial pollution, combined with improved transportation and rising incomes made it desirable and possible for the urban elite to find refuge in the suburbs. The middle class followed their social betters in the exodus. These early suburbs were small, seldom accommodating more than 10,000 people, and were clustered neatly around the train stations that were spaced three to five miles apart, each surrounded by country greenery. Here is how Frederick Allen, the editor of *Harper's Magazine*, writing in 1925, described what these early suburbanites, including himself, were looking for (from Strauss, 1968:417-418).

"They want air that does not reek of motor exhaust, light instead of the grim shadow of apartment houses, quiet instead of the clatter of riveters by day and the squawk of taxicabs by night, neighbors whom they know and to whom their existence is not a matter of utter indifference, and a life whose tempo is less nerve-racking than that of the city...

I live in one of the most attractive suburbs in New York. It is built on rolling hills and interloping ledges; excellent trains reach it forty minutes from the city; the houses were mainly designed by architects, rather than contractors, with fortunate results; and there is not a tenement, a three-decker, or a factory within its limits. The house which I occupy looks over several acres of open country, where on a June evening one may walk beside a little brook and hear wood thrushes singing in the thickets; and I can reach my office in a little over an hour."

The common people did not, and could not move. But suburban living became their environmental ideal, especially when they experienced further decline in economic opportunities and further deterioration in living conditions during the Great Depression of the 1930s. The end of WWII saw an economic boom: steady jobs, shorter hours, and better wages. There was also a baby boom. These, together with the mass production and use of the automobile, ushered in a period of unprecedented suburban expansion. The American dream of your own house in the suburbs was being realized by millions of people. These suburbs of the lower-middle classes and the newly affluent working classes appeared almost "overnight". The rush was on, and has continued since. Study after study has shown that the success of the post-WWII suburbs was based on their congruence with the images of good living held by great masses of common people regardless of race, family and background (e.g., Wilson, 1962; Cooper, 1972; and Marans and Rodgers, 1973).

Since then, the image of good living for the elite has also changed. At first there was resentment to the invasion of the suburbs by the lower classes, again as illustrated by Frederick Allen's own observation, this time in 1954 (from Strauss, 1968:417).

"The days are passing (if indeed they are not already passed) when one could think of a suburban town outside of our cities as a village in the country. It would be much wiser today, to think of it as a more or less comfortably spaced residential area or residential and business area within the greater metropolis."

Then there was a reevaluation of the suburban ideal. While the masses were fulfilling their dreams of a single-detached home, fresh air, safe and quiet streets, a wholesome environment to raise children, and a retreat from the drudgery and roughness of the workplace, the elite were becoming increasingly ambivalent. Suburb became "suburbia": a twilight zone — a sprawl of undifferentiated dwellings, street blocks and subdivisions. Suburban living became "escapism". There was also bitter disappointment about the realities of suburban living. Instead of the expected friendliness and democracy of an ideal small town they found false friendliness, mock neighborliness, castes of snobbery, and the deadening rounds of sociability that left little time for genuine leisure (Strauss, 1968).

New environmental ideals for the elite have begun to emerge. One of them is moving further out into exurbia where the lots are larger, nature more abundant, and the locale more prestigious. Another is the "designer suburbs" which recreate the "ambience" of the 19th century American small town. At the same time, the idea of inner-city living reentered the competition for the hearts of the elite as soon as the commoners invaded its suburbs. However, while the elite have to decide among the new alternatives — moving to exurbia, reviving suburbia, or rejoining the city, the common people are sticking to the mass-produced suburban single-detached home based on the stereotypical images of good living that have been handed down to them through books, advertisements, media and visits.

What we are witnessing today among the elite is a reaction to, and among the common people an affirmation of, the suburb, each according to their image. Once upon a time, the elite gave up the city for the suburbs. Now it is giving up the suburbs, or at least the kind of conventional and mass-produced suburbs that give it no satisfaction or status. Its place in the suburbs is being taken up by the common people. But new images of good living are already being created by the elite, whether these are exurban colonies, designer suburbs, luxury condominiums, or gentrified houses.

For the wave of people who moved to the post-WWII suburbs of the 1950s and 1960s, it had taken them a long time to earn enough money to buy the dream home with three bedrooms and a large backyard, in a neighbourhood with identical and well-maintained houses. For those who grew up in these post-WWII suburbs, they perhaps want another dream home in another dream neighbourhood, except this time they want a house with a Jacuzzi, an entertainment room, and a solarium, in a suburban neighbourhood that has quality daycare, exciting social events and bicycle paths.

Today, potential suburbanites are constantly reminded by messages that conventional suburban living is destroying the environment, depleting agricultural land, and squandering energy resources. At the same time they are told that old buildings are neat, gentrified housing is status, and urban living is exciting. For the near future, at least, most will hold on to the image of the good suburb, but the time will come when the suburb is so vilified that it will be replaced by another icon of the ideal living environment anointed by the elite, abetted by planners, and mass-produced by developers. The irony is, though, by that time the elite may wish to move on and this icon may be condemned for some yet-to-be-discovered sins.

STRATEGIC CHOICES

Planning requires making choices. We cannot have two uses and two buildings occupying exactly the same space at the same time; and we cannot spend the same dollar twice. There are several strategic choices that have far-reaching effects on the match between use and land. We will examine those that influence urban texture, siting priorities, land use mixes, the choice between rehabilitation and redevelopment, and the choices in infrastructure use and investment.

Urban Texture   Modern city planning is rather blind to aesthetics. We have thrown out the formal and abstract design principles of the past but have yet to replace them with demonstrable and practical guides. We must realize that when people object to the removal of a corner store, the building of a subway station, or the construction of a high-rise apartment, their real objection is often not so much about finances, traffic, or some such things, but aesthetics — something they feel strongly about and yet are unable to articulate.

The great visual congruity of old cities that people admire is achieved through the adherence to a small range of building materials and similar building techniques. The shapes, colours and textures of the building materials which usually came from nearby, echoed the vegetation and geology of the site. Today, we deal with building materials that come from all over the world, and we have many more building types and building techniques. Therefore, planners should focus particularly on the visual congruity of buildings: plans, sizes, height and shapes; the arrangement and proportion of solids (walls) and voids (openings); building materials; details of building facades; and the forms, shapes, colours, and textures of various components of the building, landscaping, and environ.

According to Keeble (1983: 21-34), the texture of a city is influenced by three elements: the layout of the various land uses; building heights, especially the location of taller buildings; and the layout of open spaces.

The siting and sizing requirements of the different land uses can often be satisfied at a larger number of locations in the city. This means that there are always a number of layouts to organize them, each of which will confer a different urban texture on the city. The following are some of the strategic choices.

(i) A city can be strung out along lines of communication, with vehicular access being the major determinant and a magnet to draw other kinds of uses towards it. The resulting land use pattern is often formless and characterless.

(ii) Topographic constraints such as marsh lands, and steep terrains, or natural features such as a river and a cliff could force the concentration of land uses which have more stringent locational requirements to be lumped together. Such a layout would create distinctive areas with very different appearances. It confers good accessibility to a very few and restricted accessibility to most.

(iii) A balanced approach between the totally random and highly segregated layout would involve hierarchies of commercial and service centres, schools, and open spaces. This type of land use pattern balances maximum accessibility with minimum service unit size. This will ensure adequate service on the one hand and substantial and interesting clusters of urban elements on the other. The spatial distribution of the use hierarchies follow functional considerations such as trade areas or service catchment areas, and aesthetic considerations such as unique topographic features or vistas. Variety and vitality are achieved through the clustering of compatible uses. This also means controlling the growth of some large centres so as to allow other centres to become financially viable. In a way, this is analogous to Christopher Alexander's idea of "wholeness" and "centering". (Refer to the section on The Good City.)

The strategic choices regarding the location of tall buildings also have significant influence on the texture of the city. Again, there are a number of approaches.

(i) Even height and density for the whole would give an urban silhouette, which suggests stability and monotony at the same time.

(ii) Locating tall buildings at the edge of the city will dramatize the boundary between city and countryside. The tall buildings function visually as a city wall. The occupants of these buildings will also get an unimpeded view of the landscape beyond the city.

Figure 6-1: Strategic Choice in the Location of Tall Buildings

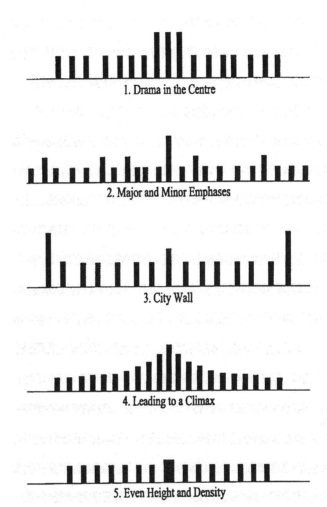

1. Drama in the Centre

2. Major and Minor Emphases

3. City Wall

4. Leading to a Climax

5. Even Height and Density

Source: Adapted from Keeble (1983: 30)

(iii) Locating tall buildings at the city centre will highlight the core of the city and allow a large proportion of the population to live or work very close to the city centre and all its facilities and services. A gradual increase in building heights towards the centre will accentuate the visual climax.

(iv) Tall buildings can be located to give visual identity to major and minor centres. They can be located adjacent to open spaces to provide visual contrasts between horizontal and vertical elements; and to give adequate daylight and privacy, and good views to the occupants. Tall buildings can also be placed to accentuate prominent sites or strategically located to break the monotony of a sea of low buildings.

Figure 6-2:
Strategic Choice in the Location of Urban Open Spaces

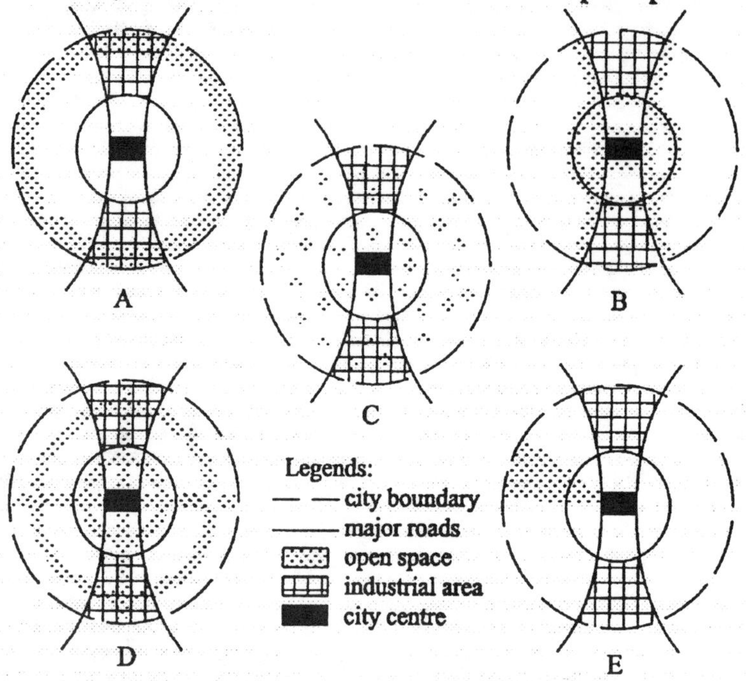

Source: Adapted from Keeble (1983: 28)

Notes:
1. The circular shape and stylized layout patterns are schematic diagrams only.
2. Open space all around the edge of the city condenses the built-up part of the city and establishes a definite edge to it (A).
3. Open space adjacent to main roads and industrial areas acts as a horizontal "buffer" against noise, smell and ugliness (B).
4. Small open spaces throughout the city, so that wherever you are there is an open space nearby (C).
5. Open space in strips in a ring and radial pattern provides a coherent continuous system associated with walking and bicycle and horse-riding tracks, separated from, and as comprehensive as, the road system (D).
6. One, or a very few, really large worthwhile lumps of open space which make a strong visual impact, are convincing illusion of "rus in urbe". This approach is especially desirable near the city centre (E).

The strategic layout of open spaces can influence the urban texture. Open space around the edge of a city helps to concentrate the built-up area and define its edge. Open space along main roads and adjacent to industrial areas can act as a visual buffer and a noise and smell barrier. Strips of open spaces can be organized into a functionally and visually coherent scheme for walking, bicycling, horseback riding and so on. The open space scheme should be coordinated with the road system. Small open spaces throughout the city will ensure that people will always find one nearby. But it is worthwhile to consider also the provision of one or very few really large open spaces, especially in the city centre, which have a strong visual character and which are large enough to give an illusion of being in the country. Such open spaces offer visual and psychological relief to the intensity of urban life.

The semi-public or private open spaces in a city can be used creatively to improve the quality of urban life. Schools, hospitals and large institutions are usually located on large parcels of land. Although the land is publicly owned the public does not have an unrestricted access and use of it. Proper policies regarding access (visual and physical), landscaping and maintenance should be devised to enhance the public use of such spaces.

Finally, the choice of scale is important. When we say that a building, street or space is out of scale, we usually mean that it is too big or too wide. But in relation to what? A cathedral has a monumental scale that belongs to God, a high-rise office building has a repetitive scale that belongs to the corporation, and an aircraft hangar has a functional scale that belongs to the machine. None of these buildings uses the human body and its senses as fundamental units of measurement; hence none has a human scale.

We use a range of innate capabilities to measure the external world. The Roman architectural writer Vitruvius observed two thousand years ago that public buildings and squares should be designed within the specific limits of human sight and mobility. It is always satisfying to see an object as a whole, at a single glance, to comprehend its unity, but seeing is determined by the physiology of the eye, its rotation angles and sight distances. The optimal rotation of the human eye is 27 degrees up, 30 degrees down and 60 degrees across. This means the distance one stands from a building to see it as a whole, at a single glance, is about twice the building's height. Assuming a typical street width of 60 feet (18 m) and an eye level at five-feet six-inches (1.7 m), human scale means buildings of about 35 feet (10.7 m), or three to four storeys. At this height, tops of trees can also be seen over the roofs, a touch of nature and relief to the eye.

Recognition distance of our fellow citizens is about 70 feet to 80 feet (21-24 m). At about 50 feet (15 m) we can read facial expression. This should be the "normal" width of a neighbourhood street where acquaintances and friends should be able to see one another's face across the road. Four hundred and fifty feet is about the maximum distance to distinguish the general outline, colour, clothes, sex, age and gait of a person. This is a good norm for the maximum length of a city block, park or other urban open space. The maximum length of the much-praised Piazza San Marco in Venice is 425 feet (130 m). Manhattan's West Side has 800-foot (245 m) street blocks, and Jane Jacobs calculates that these long blocks fail esthetically and socially.

Scale is also defined by mobility. Moving in a car, one sees things in a very different way from walking. One misses the usual nuances and subtleties. Once I was working with a small tourist town to identify visual assets which could be used to promote tourism. The townspeople were very enthusiastic about a bevelled clock tower that they used on the cover of their promotion brochure as the local landmark. Though it was in the centre of town, visitors hardly noticed it. When you are driving through a town in a hurry, looking for some place to park or some important interchange, your eyes are not going to pick out the unique features on top of a tower located right next to the pavement.

We measure our environment with other senses too. For example, we cannot have an outdoor conversation at more than eight feet without having to strain our voices. Of course, it is dangerous to generalize too much, but urbanites do share stereotypical "scalers" such as doors, windows, and trees, which they use to define the urban environment and locate themselves in it. If these design "set-pieces" are distorted people become disoriented and uncomfortable.

Buildings are social artifacts. They tell how a society views itself, and how it wants to be viewed. A cityscape that does not respect human scale does not respect the individual.

Siting Priorities

Open space allocation should be the first consideration in any comprehensive land use plan for two reasons: (i) critical environmental processes are vulnerable and their siting and sizing requirements do not allow a large margin for error; and (ii) if a mistake is made about the location or size any remedial measure will be very expensive. These reasons apply to large open spaces for the purposes of environmental protection and enhancement as well as to small urban open spaces for recreational use. This approach differs from the traditional approach which leaves open space allocation to the end, where any land not usable for other functions is coloured green and declared an open space. The allocation of large open spaces is especially important because their characters are so different from built-up areas that they are important elements in defining the boundaries of areas and determining the texture of the city.

Large industrial uses have requirements which are also quite inflexible, such as proximity to major transport routes or a level site. They should also be allocated as early as possible. After industrial uses is the allocation of regional-serving businesses such as major shopping centres or large institutions such as educational, cultural and recreational facilities. In the siting of these industrial, commercial and institutional uses we should consider not only their needs but their environmental impact in terms of traffic, noise, activities, and so on, which will determine the appropriateness of the general area for other uses. Finally, residential uses and local-oriented functions such as primary schools, local shops, and playgrounds have much more flexible siting and space requirements and can be considered after the other uses have been properly allocated.

In the siting and sizing of open space it is well to consider the "sky factor". The sky makes up one-fifth to one-half of our field of vision. But we take the sky so much for granted that we become aware of it only through its absence. In fact, one can measure the degree of urbanness by the amount of sky obliterated.

Buildings and the sky relate in two ways--the sky as a backdrop for the buildings, or the buildings seen as carved out from the sky. Yet even the best-designed buildings look awkward and inanimate against the colour, texture and mood that is the sky. The post-modern Greek pediments and Roman columns that adorn the tops of skyscrapers are not intended for any ordinary mortal on the street; they are supposed to be seen from a helicopter, or from a couple of miles out in the water. For the pedestrian, the prevailing experience is the concrete canyon-- dark, deep and gloomy.

The high-rises are here to stay. After all, even though people want to see the sky and enjoy its beauty, they also want to be protected from its malevolence: shade from glare, cover from rain or snow, and shelter from heat and cold. But we should make the buildings compensate for our loss of the sky. Cities have customarily allowed developers to build higher in exchange for some public open space at the street level. The idea is that these open areas will give a breather to the harried citizens, providing a bit of fresh air, sunlight and greenery. Clearly, however, an open space can only mean open to the sky, while these spaces are made so that the developer can build even more storeys and block out more of the sky. And since the open areas are usually the size of postage stamps, the effect is that of deep wells of urban shadows. Even the sturdiest of trees are anemic from lack of sky exposure.

The city and its citizens will fare much better if we can exchange such haphazard and ineffectual half-measures for a few centrally located and adequately sized open areas. Not every city can have its Central Park, but the strategy should be to place quality above numbers. Perhaps instead of having individual developers "dedicating" token open spaces which, in effect, represent nothing more than a few feet of street-widening, cities should allow developers to trade their obligations with one another, or pay cash, so that with some planning and a lot of patience we may end up with a few larger and accessible areas where citizens can take back the sky.

While tall buildings have robbed us of the sky, they can also return some of it by reflection. Citizens have every right to resent a cityscape dominated by look-alike high-rise boxes. Designers respond by dressing up their boxes with a great variety of claddings--brick, stone, marble, steel, aluminum, glass and concrete. Few, however, have made use of the sky as an active design element. Yet well designed walls can mirror, with mesmerizing effects, the changing composition of the sky, with all its intensity and changing hues. Simple considerations such as orientation of the site, the tint of the glass and angle of the windows can bring life to an otherwise nondescript building by reflecting the sky's colour and drama. Today we have "smart" buildings, whose facades can be programmed to open and close, rotate and change colour in response to temperature, humidity, lighting, ventilation and a host of other environmental factors. We can certainly introduce the sky factor, requiring such buildings to play to the moods of the sky with the people on the street as audience.

Separation Versus Mixing

The separation of incompatible uses is a basic consideration in land use planning. Those uses which by their nature produce large amounts of traffic, noise, smell, vibration, smoke, or mess, ought to be separated from other uses which they may adversely affect, especially residential. But physical separation may not always be a viable answer, and it often operates against the principle of accessibility. It is sometimes necessary to confine the negative effects generated by any use to the site on which they are produced. The costs and benefits of separation versus those of containment should be carefully compared.

The principle of separation is applicable sometimes to quite small uses. For instance, a pub is what some people would like to have close by, but would find it a nuisance if located next door. In this case, careful siting is needed to ensure that it is close to many people but not immediately adjacent to any house.

Separation of incompatible uses is a good principle but we should realize that not too many uses are really incompatible and some incompatible uses may be located in the same area if they are carried out at different times of the day or at different times of the year. A sensitive and innovative approach to "mixed uses" such as putting residences in the central business district or, better still, "integrated uses" such as putting worker housing adjacent to the workplace can contribute to the efficient use of the land and the vitality of urban life.

But how much mixing? Take the extreme case of the city centre. The replanning of many city centres has been based on the assumption that the natural behaviour of shoppers is incompatible with the moving car. From the point of view of a driver, pedestrian shoppers pay little attention to moving cars and, for that matter, their own safety. They move about haphazardly and unpredictably. But given the significant role of shopping in many city centres, the safety and comfort of shoppers is of paramount importance. This consideration has become the basis for the redesign of many city centres where motor vehicles have been removed from shopping areas, partially or completely, part of the time or all of the time.

Pedestrianization may be complete or partial, and could be achieved either through layout or regulations. But delivery vehicles have to be allowed at least for certain times of the day. Instead of total pedestrianization, one-way street systems can be used. But if there are shops on both sides of the one-way street the need for shoppers to move haphazardly across the street remains. The usually higher speed of the one-way traffic flow only makes pedestrian crossing even more dangerous. Moreover, one-way systems can be very confusing to strangers. When multi-storey car parks are added to one-way systems, especially when direction to their entrances is inefficient, more congestion will result.

With respect to the mixing of land uses in the city centre, there are two different schools of thought. One argues that the essence of city centres is a rich mixture of interrelated uses, This argument suggests that people and uses do not locate in a city centre unless they need to be there. It is therefore unwise and impossible to disentangle them. The other argues that it is desirable to segregate because different uses thrive in different physical environments, and attract and generate different traffic, both vehicular and pedestrian. Some uses are more appropriate to a bustling environment, such as a supermarket, while others are more compatible with a quiet ambience, such as a professional office. Zones of selective uses will promote good neighborliness between uses and facilitate effective and economical provision of streets, intersections, and parking. Both arguments can be valid, depending on the situation, and it requires skill and creativity to strike the best balance.

Redevelopment Versus Rehabilitation

In planning for an existing urban area, Keeble (1983: 52) points out that we have three kinds of decisions to make. (1) What existing good features must be preserved even if preservation conflicts with other planning requirements? (2) Which existing bad features must be removed? (3) What bad features are impossible to remove and must be included in the plan with as little adverse effect as possible? A strategic choice has to be made between redevelopment, rehabilitation, and conservation, especially with respect to old structures in poor condition.

Redevelopment is the revision or replacement of the existing land use and population of a built-up area through the acquisition, clearance and rebuilding of the area. The crucial question is whether the area is so bad that redevelopment is the only alternative. Then a decision has to be made about the new use and density. Rehabilitation, on the other hand, is the improvement or restoration of a blighted area through the acquisition and clearance of scattered deteriorated buildings, the repair, upgrading or installation of facilities and services, the provision of street, park or other public amenities, or clean-up and maintenance work by property owners. Conservation is the preservation of predominantly built-up areas that are in "good" condition and are substantially satisfactory in terms of land use and population density, but which require vigorous code enforcements and some public improvements to ensure that private investment will continue to maintain the condition.

For a long time redevelopment was considered the only solution to deal with the problem of urban blight, especially in the older residential areas. Now, rehabilitation and conservation have gained currency, partly because the housing stock has renewed itself more or less in the last 40 years. But some of the following arguments in favour of redevelopment remain. (1) The condition of the buildings may be so bad or the cost of rehabilitation so high that redevelopment is the only solution. (2) Redevelopment will bring a more significant improvement in the quantity and quality of the buildings than rehabilitation. (3) Local government has easier and more comprehensive control over redevelopment than over any other form of action. (4) The argument that existing residents are always opposed to redevelopment may be ill-founded if they can be convinced that their living/working condition will be significantly improved and the disruption to their lives will be avoided by careful phasing of the redevelopment programme.

Parallel to the choice between rehabilitation and redevelopment of land is the choice between the rehabilitation and replacement of the physical infrastructure. Most planners seem convinced that maintenance and rehabilitation is a better choice, especially when given the financial and environmental constraints of the day. There are two reasons: good maintenance saves money; and expansion only creates more demand.

But when to rehabilitate? "Historically, for an urban street system, strategies involved 'worst first' prioritization of candidate rehabilitation projects, along with routine maintenance strategies.... This approach — giving attention to streets that look bad — has a certain logical appeal. This methodology, however, is not consistent with current pavement management research. Rehabilitation costs for maintaining street systems in good condition may be as much as four to five times less than if pavements are allowed to reach poor or failed conditions before rehabilitation takes place." (McRae, 1987:347) It is also true that expanding a system to accommodate "apparent" demand often leads to more demand. A study by the Royal Commission on National Passenger Transportation (1992) shows that where a highway is realigned to remove substandard curves and grades or improve intersections (all of which are aimed primarily at relieving congestion) the time savings soon disappear as additional traffic volume brings the operating speed back that existed before the alignment.

However, it is not always possible to divert funds from new construction to maintenance and rehabilitation. In most municipalities, the locations of urban growth (e.g., suburbs) does not coincide with the locations of maintenance needs (e.g., inner city). As a result, new expansion often takes place while existing system continues to be used below capacity. Besides, new construction (expansion) is politically "glamorous", and usually has identifiable constituencies (motor leagues, trucking associations, land developers, etc.) as opposed to the "silent majority" who use the existing system.

It is safe to assume that all levels of government now recognize and question the fiscal ability of governments to sustain the physical infrastructure. In the past it was increasing the supply, now it is improving the "productivity". While old habits die hard there are genuine efforts aimed at enhancing the productivity of infrastructure by managing demands and/or providing adequate maintenance and timely rehabilitation. This requires us to tackle what Fields (1992) identifies as generic questions in a general infrastructure management process: What is in the ground (inventory)? What can it provide (service capacity)? And, how can we upgrade it (repair versus renewal)?

To optimize existing capacity we need asset/inventory management systems that include an inventory of conditions, capacities, and state of repair; on-line instrumentation and processing of data; geographic information systems; simulations; real-time modelling, etc. We also need maintenance/operations management systems that include modelling, simulations, predictive operation control strategies, rating and prioritization strategies, etc. The question of "turf" can be serious because different infrastructure overlap physically and jurisdictionally, creating competition for control and funds. The new emphasis is to redirect attention and resources away from day-to-day crises and corrective and emergency activities, which are driven by complaints and politics, to "preventative" maintenance (Phillips et al., 1991). Advance planning is needed. The focus is on the integration of land use and infrastructure planning. There is also renewed emphasis on coordinating the planning, financing and delivery of services. Of special interest is "forecasting and backcasting" which means doing "forecasts" based on anticipated uses rather than past trends, and then to make "backcasts" from the desired futures (Tate, 1990).

Finally, planning and investment decisions take place within the budgetary process which is largely political. Today, public investment decisions in infrastructure will usually consider life-cycle costs. Sometimes "total costing" is used to evaluate intangibles such as future operation and maintenance, risks, secondary benefits (e.g., contracting out to charitable organizations which have greater tendency to hire the unemployed), and social costs (e.g., the speed of response to complaints, "accountability" to the public, degree of cooperation in reducing inconveniences, and level of disruption to the public and environment during work).

Demand Management or Capacity Expansion

Should we increase the capacity of infrastructure to accommodate (and sometimes induce) growth; or should we manage the demand (without stopping growth)? Managing demand (especially reducing it) has been advocated as an alternative to the conventional approach of increasing the supply to meet rising needs.

Demand is not simply consumption. Take water. Brooks and Peters (1988) suggest that demand should be defined as the amount of water consumed plus the degree to which wastewater is degraded. Therefore, water demand management is defined as measures that reduce average or peak withdrawals from surface or groundwater sources without increasing the extent to which wastewater is degraded. Those who only consume small amounts of water but return badly contaminated wastewater are considered to have "demanded" as much from a water resource as those who consume large quantities. Thus, the setting of effluent standards becomes a demand management measure, because it encourages reuse of water as well as reducing pollution in return flow.

Demand management is driven by two overlapping motivations which are not always compatible: fiscal constraint and revenue generation on the one hand, and conservation and optimization on the other. Fields (1992: 31) explains these as follows. "Suppose there is genuine shortage of supply and citizens have to endure odd-even lawn-watering days and disrupted supplies during summer, the population is therefore made aware of the value of water when costs for system expansion are debated. Demand management becomes a viable alternative to the tax increases needed to finance supply expansion. On the other hand, there is the environmental lobby for sustainable development. It is made up of people who feel waste of any resources — water, energy, natural resources--compromises the long-term survival of Mother Earth. Its action is typically directed at the political level. It questions the public works and engineering administration: Why are we treating, pumping and delivering all this water when we really do not need it? This is different from the pressure coming from the taxpayers or customers who are asking why it costs so much to water their lawn everyday.

There are three approaches to demand management: technical, economic and planning.

1. Technical Approaches. These tend to be infrastructure-type specific. Managing water-demand is perhaps more advanced than other infrastructure types. The general idea is that though managing water supply we are also managing the demand on the wastewater system. Efficient water use practices include use audit, leak detection and repair, reduction of water pressure, erosion control, valve exercising, reuse and recirculation, retrofit, etc. Road demand management focuses on reducing the volume and spreading the time period of road use, including such techniques as centralized and computerized traffic control, Intelligent Vehicle Highway Systems (IVHS), telecommuting, etc. Urban runoff volume can be reduced and controlled by on-site retention and similar measures generally known as "best management practices." (Refer to Storm Water Management in the Analysis chapter.)

The problem with these approaches is not technology per se, but technology uptake. There is inadequate procedure for assessing, approving, implementing, monitoring and reporting of application. There is also the question of user/consumer expectations and behaviour, such as the acceptance and continuation of retrofitting, and acceptance of local temporary flooding.

2. Economic Approaches. These rely on some form of pricing to reflect "real" costs. The assumption is that historical low prices have led to undervalue and overuse, overbuilt, and reduced quality as well as transfer of costs and benefits without political discussion. Some form of "market" pricing is therefore beneficial for the rationing of resources (allocation to highest-valued users and to uses with highest return), and for production motivation (by indicating consumer willingness-to-pay in relation to levels of service). For water pricing there are schemes such as lifeline rates (i.e., a lower first rate for a basic volume of consumption, then higher rates will apply), hookup charges (to reflect marginal costs of new connections), peaking rates (peak load pricing to cut peak consumption), and charging excessive use. For roads, demand management schemes include paid parking, removal of parking subsidies (and economic benefits), road pricing at peak periods or long distances (including pay-as-you-drive insurance), and greater reliance on incentives and market forces to expand transit system. Besides pricing there are other economic incentives such as rebates, tax credits, and give-away of conservation devices, as well as economic disincentives such as penalties and fines.

3. Planning. There are two kinds of planning challenges: planning the services so as to optimize the capacity, and integrating infrastructure planning and land use planning. The former is about supply efficiency (productivity). It is the latter that offers the best long-term solution. Fields (1992: 22) observes: "The framework exists to carry out community planning on the basis of population, zoning, and proposed development. Taking it the next step, determining the need for new infrastructure and the impact of this on existing infrastructure, is less established." (Refer to the discussion on planning issues regarding transportation, water supply, storm water, and wastewater in the Analysis chapter.)

"Education" can make a difference. It can include public education (e.g. water-use index in local newspapers, conservation tips in utility billing, tagging of conservation fixtures), school programmes, training of managers and system planners, education programmes for industrial employees, etc. But enforcement is very important, whether it is water/wastewater bylaws, plumbing codes, parking restriction, or traffic control. "A great deal of enforcement can be purchased for the cost of an expressway..." (Soberman, 1987: 311).

THE INTELLIGENT AND CREATIVE PLANNER

Plan making (for a whole planning area as well as for an individual site) requires, on the one hand, skills to balance the competing needs and aspirations among the different users against the supply of land and, on the other hand, an ability to create and evaluate solutions that can exploit technological advances and the unique qualities of the land. In the following, we will discuss ways to appreciate and evaluate various user needs as well as to create workable solutions.

The traditional rationalist and incrementalist approaches to plan making deal with only partial truths. Rationality is a necessary element in any planning exercise yet most of the planning decisions are incremental in nature. There are no inherent conflicts between the two and any purist deba te is futile. Geoffrey Vickers' (1965) approach is like a breath of fresh air when he suggests that rather than thinking in terms of means and ends in a simplistic manner we should try to appreciate the relationship between perceptions and actions and between people who have different perceptions and scopes of action. In another book I have dealt at some length with the subjective nature of people's values and the way in which plan making can accommodate these values (Leung, 1985). It is sufficient to say here that while plan making should be based on the logic of efficient land use it should be sensitive to differences in people's values, perceptions, abilities, and resources, that is, to embrace Lynch's (1981: 221-230) metacriteria of efficiency and justice.

Since there are always a number of probable answers to a problem, the exploration and evaluation of alternatives becomes crucial. Fortunately, a planner's experience should be sufficient to help him/her to filter out alternatives which are totally absurd, although at an early stage of plan making, the planner should entertain as many imaginative alternatives as are practicable.

The analysis of alternatives should generally produce a limited number of valid choices. In each of these alternatives it is important to relate explicitly the solutions to the goals. The planner or the planning team should come to grips very quickly with the meaning or implication of any planning goal in land use terms or the potential for a land use solution. Ideally, plan making is a collaborative effort between various departments such as planning, housing, health, recreation, and education. But in reality departmental territories are jealously guarded. A realistic planner should have a good sense of what is possible within the institutional division of powers and resources. This appreciation of institutional relationships is essential to successful plan making, and even more so to plan implementation.

Most of the public interest elements which planning is supposed to defend or promote can be defended or promoted by other means. For instance, proper health service may be more dependent on government policies regarding funding than on the proper siting of hospitals or clinics. A planner must realize that his/her professional mandate is not to debate funding policies for health services but rather to provide the best site in terms of access and accommodation. Much of the frustration of the profession is caused by an inflated notion of what it should, and can, do. Although any land use solution would have all kinds of social, economic, or management implications, it is essentially a set of recommendations for physical change, involving such things as the designation of land use to an area, application of certain development control measures and design guidelines, making of traffic management schemes, programming of public investment and development, and phasing of private development.

The choice of alternatives is not solely the result of public participation. It is based on a combination of independent and related actors involved in the decision-making process: elected representatives, interest groups, the public, government agencies, as well as the planner. The planner's role in this is to ensure that these actors understand the relationships between solutions and goals, and the advantages and disadvantages of the various alternatives.

Informed and impartial presentation of alternatives is a very practical means of attracting informed, sensible, and helpful expressions of public opinion about what alternative to adopt. But we must avoid two fatal defects: (i) an insufficient discrimination in the selection thus resulting in a large number of half-baked and poorly evaluated alternatives; and (ii) a biased presentation in favour of the alternative preferred by the planner thus resulting in a misinformed or antagonized public.

The following are some suggestions about how to generate land use decisions innovatively. (1) Use stereotypes. Stereotypes are tested solutions and therefore they are usually good for normal, stable situations and can be readily related to by the user. For instance, cul-de-sacs for residential layout, sidewalk cafes for an entertainment area, the corner grocery store, the industrial park, the office village, the everything-under-the-same-roof giant shopping mall, and the more recent "new urbanism" layouts. (2) A problem can be turned upside down and become a solution. Instead of trying to solve a problem one can make use of the problem situation, such as making a steep terrain a dramatic backdrop for buildings perching on it, turning an unsightly drainage retention pond into an artificial lake for recreation, and converting a dilapidated market building into a studio and specialty retail complex. (3) Instead of the traditional approach of identifying a problem first and then finding a solution to it, a planner may examine innovative financial, technological or legislative instruments to determine what profitable ends can be served by these. He/she may look at senior government programme funding criteria and then identify what local goals can be best pursued by these programmes. The same approach can be used to exploit new building techniques, laws, market conditions, and so on. This approach suffers from a lack of direction and conviction and the city might end up spending a lot more on items that may not be essential. But as a tool to stimulate the mind it can be useful.

Making sound planning synthesis is really a question of good habits. We have to be constantly observant and alert, to explore with all our senses, to empathize with the users, and, most importantly, to bridge the gap between lines, shapes, and words on paper and lives as lived.

PLAN EVALUATION

Planning alternatives have to be evaluated so that the "best" choice can be made. There are two kinds of evaluation. In an ex ante evaluation the focus is on choice, and in an ex post evaluation the focus is on performance. But both the choice criteria and performance indicators have to relate to the planning goals.

If a planning proposal is based on clear goals and careful analysis, it is technically sound. But this does not guarantee its being chosen because the goals may not be accepted by everyone or the proposal may produce adverse effects on someone. So, the question comes down to: who pays, who benefits, and who decides.

There are essentially two kinds of evaluative techniques: goal-explicit techniques which compare alternatives on the basis of explicit goals and goal achievement, and goal-implicit techniques which analyze actual or predicted consequences of different alternatives based on implicit value premises. These techniques are used to assist in the choice among alternatives as well as to evaluate the implementation of the chosen alternative. With goal-explicit techniques, the determination of the goals to be included in the evaluation is overtly political. With goal- implicit techniques the debate about goals is subsumed under technical jargons, such as what constitutes the "benefits" and "costs" of a proposal.

Goal-Explicit Techniques

Hill's (1968) goals-achievement matrix is perhaps a typical example of the goal-explicit techniques. It seeks to compare alternative courses of action on the basis of their relative achievement of established goals. The advantages and disadvantages of the alternatives are expressed in terms of progression toward or retrogression from the specified goals. All goal-explicit techniques deal with some or all of the following methodological issues: ranking, rating, or weighing of goals; the probability of implementation of the various alternatives; and the ordering of the alternatives in terms of how well or how effective they serve each of the goals. Sometimes, as a recognition that different people have different perceptions about the utility of the different goals, their valuation of the goals and their relative importance as a socioeconomic group are also taken into consideration. There are also different methods of summing up or integrating the overall achievement of an alternative with respect to all the different goals. These range from simple addition of scores to complex mathematical equations.

Another goal-explicit technique is optimization. Optimization (linear programming) is the maximization of some advantages or the minimization of some disadvantages within certain constraints. It offers the planner an immediately useful way to test various alternatives of matching needs and supply. The following is a typical example of what the technique can be used for. Suppose there is a piece of land which can be developed for only two kinds of housing which are defined in terms of density, housing price and the property tax revenue to the government. The constraint is the total development cost that can be spent. The technique can be used to determine the proper mixture of the two housing types which would give the maximum property tax revenue to the local government. Even for such a straightforward question the calculation is quite involved. In real life problems, many more variables and constraints are present. A computer will be needed to find the solution. But a more difficult problem is about the assumptions used and the difficulty in defining the "objective function" (that is, deciding exactly what we are trying to maximize or minimize). This technique has been criticized by Perry Lewis (1969) as having the following problems. The choice of aim (the objective function) is itself subjective, but even if we have chosen to minimize, let us say, the journey to work, we must ask how to measure it. Do we do it in time, distance, cost, some mixture of these, or what? Do we take mean time along a route or modal time? Do we pay more attention to time spent by certain kinds of workers? Do we value time saved on a five-minute journey as much as on a twenty-minute journey? It is possible to go on listing more questions of this type. What we have to realize is that whether we ask the questions or not, we do in fact imply answers to all of them by our very choice of the objective function. We are simplifying away the question but not the answer.

Environmental impact assessment is yet another goal-explicit technique. It is the assessment of a development proposal against its potential environmental effects. As such, the goals are explicit. It helps us to appreciate the environmental consequences of any mismatch between needs and supply. The assessment results can be made to assist the making of a rational decision based on the likely environmental loss due to the development, the benefit of the development, and the possibility and cost of mitigation. This can be done by using a simple checklist with a weighting scheme to a complex network approach which simulates the cumulative direct and indirect effects. But this perfectly reasonable technique has been abused by those who try to include everything from physical to cultural, social, and economic considerations. Since there is no convenient and convincing way to compare and evaluate the trade-offs between these various dimensions, the exercise has become a highly frustrating one for planners and developers alike.

Goal-Implicit Techniques

A typical example of a goal-implicit technique is social cost-benefit analysis (Dasgupta and Pearce, 1979). Certainly, the definition of what constitutes a cost or benefit is value-laden but the technique does not require an explicit recognition of what, or whose, values are represented by the various costs and benefits. Cost-benefit analysis is a generic name for those techniques which try to put a monetary value to, or at least to quantify, the costs and benefits of a development proposal and to use them as a basis for deciding whether that proposal is acceptable. Such a technique devotes great effort in measuring and aggregating costs and benefits and in refining the decision criteria which may be benefit maximization, cost minimization, maximization of the benefit-to-cost ratio, or some other such formulae. Here the questions of time-horizon, accounting prices, discount rates for future costs and benefits, and the basis for choosing between alternatives are even more complex than in the case of optimization. Besides, different groups disagree on what constitutes the potential costs and benefits of a proposal. Lichfield, Kettle and Whitbread (1975) propose a planning balance sheet technique which deals with values more explicitly by examining the costs and benefits from the points of view of both the provider and the consumer (user). But this compromise has serious methodological consequence in that overall costs and benefits of a scheme can no longer be aggregated, leaving the balance sheet technique nothing more than an account of the valuation by different interested parties, without any decision crite-rion. A limited but often used approach is fiscal impact analysis which examines the direct current public costs and revenues associated with a development pro-posal to the local jurisdiction. These costs include various municipal capital and operation costs, as well as those incurred by school boards, public utilities com-missions, etc. The increased revenues include property tax and transfers and grants from senior governments as well as user fees, lot levies, parkland dedications, etc. The main problem with this approach is that it takes a very narrow view of what should be evaluated. Besides, it also has many difficult methodological issues to deal with, such as the choice between average and marginal costs, and the differen-tiation between one-time revenues and recurring revenues.

Another goal-implicit technique which was in vogue for a while is "threshold analysis" (Kozlowski and Hughes, 1972). Essentially, it is a technique to work out the timing for the release of land for development. The basic idea is that the development of a city can be supported satisfactorily and economically by the existing infrastructure up to a certain point. When the point is reached, that is the threshold, further development can only be considered after the provision of a package of infrastructure projects involving substantial capital expenditure, such as a new sewage treatment plant, and a major highway. Since such infrastructure projects are usually indivisible and cannot be provided incrementally, some choice has to be made as to when to implement a particular project or when to proceed with development in a particular area. This choice may depend upon the relationship between the capital costs involved for each project and the quantity of new population that each completed project can service satisfactorily.

Another technique is called "planning games." These are actually role-playing games in which a planning situation is simulated, such as a proposal to redevelop a disused railway yard for a commercial and shopping complex, and people play the roles of various parties who would take part in the negotiations and decisions, such as planning officials, politicians, developers, and various interest groups, thereby learning insights about how a planning situation may evolve in real life. But real life situations are very different from games; the rules may change as events unfold. It seems that this technique may help planners to be more sensitized to the needs and intentions of the various actors, but it is doubtful whether in the end it will make better land use.

It must be emphasized that neither the goal-explicit nor the goal-implicit techniques are widely used except in the case of some transportation studies in the late 1950s and early 1960s and some large facilities location studies. Systematic planning evaluation remains more an exception than the rule.

Perhaps the simplest evaluation method that most planners employ is the ubiquitous checklist which is widely used in land use and transportation planning and environmental impact studies. In essence, the checklist method evaluates alternatives against a set of criteria according to some ranking, rating or scoring schemes. The simplest checklist may consist of only a few criteria and each alternative is judged as either positive or negative with respect to each criterion. The more sophisticated application involves weighting of the different criteria, ranking or rating of alternatives against each criterion, aggregation of total ranking or rating scores, and successive iterations to eliminate alternatives. In order to be meaningful and effective the criteria must be related to the goals to be pursued;

they must be measurable at reasonable cost; and they must not have a bias in favour of any particular alternative. Table 6-2 is an example of a checklist developed by McHarg (1969:33) for the evaluation of alternative highway routes.

Table 6-2
CHECKLIST FOR THE EVALUATION OF ALTERNATIVE HIGHWAY ROUTES

BENEFITS AND SAVINGS	COSTS
price benefits	**price costs**
reduced time distance	survey
reduced gasoline costs	engineering
reduced oil costs	land and building acquisition
reduced tire costs	construction costs
reduced vehicle depreciation	financing costs
increased traffic volume	administrative costs, operation and maintenance costs
increase in value (land & buildings)	**reduction in values (land & buildings)**
industrial values	industrial values
commercial values	commercial values
residential values	residential values
recreational values	recreational values
institutional values	institutional values
agricultural land values	agricultural land values
non-price benefits	**non-price costs**
increased convenience	reduced convenience to adjacent properties
increased safety	reduced safety to adjacent populations
increased pleasure	reduced pleasure to adjacent populations
	health hazards and nuisance from toxic fumes, noise, glare, dust
price savings	**price costs**
non-limiting topography	difficult topography
adequate foundation conditions present	poor foundations
adequate drainage conditions present	poor drainage
available sand, gravels, etc.	absence of construction materials
minimum bridges, structures, etc., required	abundant structures required.
non-price savings	**non-price costs**
community values maintained	community values lost
institutional values maintained	institutional values lost
residential quality maintained	residential quality lost
scenic quality maintained	scenic quality lost
historic values maintained	historic values lost
recreational values maintained	recreational values lost
surface water system unimpaired	surface water system impaired
groundwater resources unimpaired	groundwater resources impaired
forest resources maintained	forest resources impaired
wildlife resources maintained	wildfire resources impaired

Source: McHarg (1969:33).

CONFLICT RESOLUTION

Given the wide array of stakeholder values and interests in land use decisions there are bound to be conflicts. Sometimes such conflicts lead to more responsive and balanced decision, but often they create hostile, polarized and adversarial situations. Susskind and Cruikshank (1987) have identified a range of techniques to resolve conflicts: (i) direct, or unassisted, negotiation where the parties resolve the conflicts on their own; (ii) facilitation that involves a third party who helps with procedures, communication and logistics; (iii) mediation that requires a third party to be a go-between to resolve the conflict and develop acceptable solutions; and (iv) arbitration that involves a third party who listens to both sides and then suggests a binding, or non-binding, solution to the conflict.

There is no agreement on whether conflicts can be headed off through preliminary reviews or early consultation. But there are some general criteria regarding successful conflict resolution. The most important is "principled negotiation." It emphasizes consensus building and joint gains, and separates real interests from aggressive positions. It involves four principles (Fisher, Ury and Patton, 1991). (1) Separate the people from the problem. This ensures a clear focus on the tough substantive issues while creating a productive problem-solving relationship between the parties. (2) Focus on interests, not positions. This moves the parties beyond positional statements to their underlying interests. (3) Invent options for mutual gains. The emphasis is on creating options that will broaden the benefits and beneficiaries, and on identifying complementary interests. (4) Use objective criteria. The emphasis is on verifiable objective criteria that apply equally to all parties. This ensures fairness between the parties and increases the likelihood of the agreement being honoured.

To be an effective contributor to conflict resolution a planner needs to understand the stakeholders, their interests, positions and options. Each stakeholder has a distinct set of mandates and interests with which to measure gains and losses. These will determine what it will accept or not accept as a solution. Each operates within a different time line and time frame. These will determine its sense of urgency in finding a solution. Each has different information about the issue and about one another. These will determine its perception of obstacles and possibilities as well as the scope of alliances. Each has different options. These will determine the range of trade-offs and compromises that can be entertained. Many stakeholders are related to one another on other issues as well as the particular issue at hand. This will introduce new barriers or opportunities for a solution.

GRAPHICS

The use of graphics is to show the relevant facts, the precise proposal, and the connection between facts and proposals. There are usually five considerations.

(i) The level of detail. A drawing without a lot of details is much easier to understand but adequate details are needed to convey sufficient information.

(ii) The number of drawings. It is not possible to put everything on one drawing and still convey the information clearly. But it is equally confusing to have a drawing for each different aspect of the same subject.

(iii) The existing versus the proposed. Showing only the proposed situation makes it difficult to appreciate and appraise the changes. Showing both on the same drawing will help in the assessment of the desirability and practicability of the proposal but may be difficult to present graphically.

(iv) Colour or black-and-white. A black-and-white master copy requires a lot of thought in the use of graphical symbols and is very time-consuming to prepare, but reproduction can be made very easily and cheaply. Colour drawings can show a variety of information more clearly and are more attractive (an important consideration if we want people to be interested). The production of a colour master copy is usually quicker but the reproduction is costly.

(v) One size or different sizes of drawings. This depends on the purpose for which the drawings are to be used, whether they are for working on, for hanging on a wall, and for reproduction in a publication. It is nearly always better to redraw the detailed working drawings if they need to be reduced for publication or distribution. In this way, we can remove the illegible and unnecessary details as well as highlight certain parts or certain information.

Here are some small, but sometimes rather crucial points about maps.

(i) A map can be amended from time to time. Visually an amendment can be very minor but the real implication on the ground can be quite significant. It is good practice to have the completion date for each successive version of a map.

(ii) Maps are usually oriented with the north direction pointing upwards. But it is still necessary to draw in the north point every time. The omission of a north point can lead to great confusion, especially when the map relates to a small part of a much larger area.

(iii) All maps should have a scale. The worst situation is to have a ratio scale, like 1:2500, and then to have the map enlarged or reduced with the ratio scale on it. It is always good practice to include a bar scale.

Hok-Lin Leung

(iv) When a part of a map is taken out and enlarged to a larger scale and to form a separate map, it is good practice to show the main features such as roads, rivers, and major land uses beyond the boundary of the subarea so as to show the relationship between the subarea and the larger area.

(v) It is good practice to have reference numbers on the maps and relate these to the written document which forms part of the plan. This cross-referencing assists understanding of the plan greatly.

(vi) Diagrams may be good to illustrate planning philosophies or schematic ideas but their imprecise character may lead to confusion, especially when they are treated as maps.

In recent years there has been a trend to play down the importance of maps and drawings and to emphasize the written word. Words can be made very indefinite and subject to all sorts of interpretation. The retreat from clear and precise maps and drawings betrays a lack of commitment. Plans have become more a legal and administrative document than a commitment to a vision of the future.

There is now a great variety of materials and techniques for graphic presentation. Maps and drawings are becoming more attractive and sophisticated. The biggest stride in graphic presentation is perhaps made in the area of computer aided design and drafting (CAD) (Brown and Schoen, 1987). Planners can use CAD programmes to produce drawings and maps that illustrate planning proposals. A building, a group of buildings, or a landscape can be examined three-dimensionally and from a variety of viewpoints. These programmes also allow the planner to edit and interact with drawings so as to explore and test planning ideas. Many planning offices have installed microcomputers that can easily accommodate CAD. At the same time CAD programmes are becoming more capable to interact with other databases, thus allowing the planner to integrate graphic presentation with data analysis. Recent advances in CAD have seen a convergence of CAD and GIS technologies (Erwin, 1998). The conventional view that GIS is more suited to deal with large-scale existing conditions whereas CAD is more suited to deal with small area proposals has blurred. The biggest advantage of CAD/GIS graphics is its ability to allow scale-less three-dimensional models to be displayed or printed at any selected scale for design or presentation purpose.

Real or virtual three-dimensional models are now used much more widely. For the laymen politicians and the general public, models, even rough models, are more effective than the best maps. A topographic model is a good device to show contour consideration in land use allocation, and a massing model is a good way to show building heights and volumes in urban design proposals. A planner can also use videos, slides, overhead projections, or "computer graphics" to make a presentation. But the public is also becoming more sophisticated. For a plan to look good, it has to be good.

TYPICAL CONTENTS OF A LAND USE PLAN

The scope of a land use plan may vary between only the physical aspects of land and its use to all aspects of government functions. The degree of detail can range from broad-brush sketches of the whole city to detailed prescriptions of the external appearance of buildings. Its functions can vary between policy guidance to civic education. There is really no such thing as typical contents. However, Jack Kent's classic work (1964) on the format and content of a city-wide or area-wide land use plan is perhaps still the most logical and precise statement of how a land use plan can be organized. In fact, the organization and contents of most of the municipal general plans we have in North America can be readily related to Kent's prescription. Site-specific, land-use-type-specific, or function-specific plans may also have similar logic and organization. The following is a very brief outline of his recommended format and content of a plan.

1.Introduction

> (i) The agency responsible for drafting the plan, the purpose of the plan, and the organization of the contents.

> (ii) The mandate and the limits of power of the local government in development and redevelopment of land.

> (iii) A brief description of how the plan is to be implemented (this section may be placed later).

> (iv) Present situation, issues and problems.

> (v) The function of planning.

> (vi) The scientific basis of planning. This includes the analysis of the present situation and prediction of the future. The following topics are usually included: history, geography, population, economy, environment, land, housing, and public facilities and infrastructure. Only the major findings should be reported here. The relevant data and analytic techniques used should be placed in an appendix.

2. Summary

> This is a brief outline of the plan. It should be as complete, precise, and simple as possible. Both text and graphics should be used.

3. Social and Economic Goals to be Pursued and the Planning Concept Used

4. The Text of the Plan

(i) Basic development policies, including programming and design considerations.

(ii) Living and working area plan.

(iii) Community facilities plan.

(iv) Urban design.

(v) Transportation plan.

(vi) Utilities and infrastructure plan.

(vii) Others.

5. Conclusion

(i) Implementation, including control regulations, capital works programming, and inputs from, and actions by, other levels of government and agencies.

(ii) Amendment procedure.

(iii) Appeal procedure.

6. Appendices

(i) The legislative text of the plan.

(ii) Background studies.

(iii) Supplementary reports such as documents of consultation with other agencies and records of public participation.

(iv) Planning techniques employed.

As planning implementation and shorter-term programmes became more emphasized, the contents of medium- and short-term plans would have the following additional considerations, as suggested in A Model Land Development Code. (American Law Institute, 1976).

(i) Land to be purchased and retained.

(ii) Relocation required (residence, shops, factories, etc.) and the social, economic, and environmental impacts.

(iii) Implementing agency and personnel needs.

(iv) Programme funding and source.

(v) Coordination with environmental, social and economic factors.

(vi) Future development prospects.

(vii) Procedures for consultation, reporting, and amendment.

The plan should really be directed to three interested parties: (1) the local government for which it will be a policy guidance to its own investments and the control of private action; (2) the general public for whom it will be an information and discussion document; and (3) developers for whom it will be a guide and a brief of what can or cannot be done. Both written texts and maps or other graphics should be used to describe the planning area or subareas, to outline the policies as they affect the various areas, to show the coordination with other government policies, plans, and programmes, to show the relationship between planning areas, and to indicate the phasing and implementation of the plan.

CHAPTER SEVEN

IMPLEMENTATION (CONTROL-ORIENTED)

L and use control, often referred to as development control, is perhaps older than land use planning. When we speak of land use control as a tool to implement a plan, we are assuming that control is guided by a plan and that it does not precede nor replace planning. This may seem obvious but, as we shall find out, it was and still is in some cases, not so.

The scope of development control is extraordinarily wide, from regulating the siting of an international airport to requiring a permit to cut down and replant a tree. Development control has often been described as "negative." It is only negative to the extent that it prevents some development from happening, which may be a very positive means to implement a plan.

Generally speaking, development control covers all aspects of siting, sizing, and environmental impact of any type of land use. The rationale for control may include a full range of "public interest," from health and safety to economic viability and social desirability. And in the ideal state of affairs these rationales should all be clearly expressed in the plan.

The predominant development control instrument in the United States and Canada is zoning. These will be the focus of this chapter. Although there are numerous other planning instruments such as subdivision control, and site plan control, these are really extensions and refinements, both in substantive and procedural terms, of zoning. Then there are instruments such as building codes, traffic bylaws, and property maintenance bylaws, which are also control measures but which generally fall outside the jurisdiction of the land use planner.

DEVELOPMENT CONTROL IN THE UNITED STATES

Zoning as a development control tool is used extensively in the United States and Canada. The idea was first used in Germany at the end of the 19th century, transferred and adapted for use in the United States in the early 20th century, and later extended to Canada.

Zoning in the United States is a form of "police power." This means that the government, in protecting the public interest, can apply certain limitations to the use and development of private land without the need to compensate for the owner's loss due to the limitations. However, if the limitations are so severe that the land loses its development possibility, then "police power" has been exceeded and the government must pay reasonable compensation. Both the boundaries of "police power" and the amount of compensation are matters for the court to decide.

Zoning ordinances, as they are called in the United States (or bylaws in Canada), are laws enacted by the local legislature (municipal councils) which delineate zones for the entire municipality (hence called comprehensive zoning) and specify the uses that are permitted within each zone. These ordinances are not necessarily based on, or related to, any land use plan and they are applied with little or no flexibility.

When zoning was first introduced in Germany, at the end of the last century, two schools of thought were prevalent. The first argued that, because there was no control, developers were building at very high densities. This pushed up the price of land, making it impossible to improve the housing conditions of the working class. Therefore, the government should legislate density limits in order to control land price. The second argued that the problem of high land prices, and therefore urban congestion, was caused by high land taxes, strict construction regulations and rigid control of the movement of capital and working population. Therefore, if the government would relax these controls the marketplace could be freed to decide on the appropriate development and the housing problem would be solved. These arguments sound very familiar today, which goes to show how little has changed in nearly a century of theorizing and debate.

Zoning was first introduced in Frankfurt in 1891 and was used primarily as an instrument to control density and bulk. The control of land use was crude and was only a secondary consideration. As the practice spread in Germany, pioneers of modern planning from the United States such as Marsh, Olmsted and Freund watched the development with great admiration.

Although the idea of "zones" as a tool to discriminate against certain uses had been in practice for some time in the United States (such as in San Francisco and Boston), the first comprehensive zoning ordinance originated in New York City. In 1905, a group of owners of fashionable shops on Fifth Avenue organized itself to oust the ever-increasing garment factories in the district. They thought that, given the high land prices in the area, if building heights were restricted then factory development would become uneconomical. Through their lobbying efforts, New York City enacted the first zoning ordinance in the United States. The city

Hok-Lin Leung

was divided into three kinds of zones: residential, commercial, and uncontrolled use. Building heights were also regulated by reference to the width of the streets. There were five height categories, from "the same as" to "two-and-a-half times" the street width.

The idea of comprehensive zoning, that is zoning covering the whole city and all uses, spread very rapidly across the country. In 1927, the Commerce Department promulgated the first Standard Zoning Enabling Act, to streamline the procedure whereby state governments could delegate to local governments the power to enact zoning ordinances, and to unify the format and content of these ordinances. In 1926, the United States Supreme Court had decided that zoning ordinances which were based on the protection and promotion of the public interest did not exceed the boundary of "police power" under the United States Constitution. This firmly enshrined the legal status of zoning. By now, few municipalities have no zoning ordinances.

It is best to remember that zoning as originated in Germany had been intended as a tool to improve the living conditions of the working class but in the United States zoning has been regarded as a panacea for all sorts of urban ills, which include the following.

(i) To improve living conditions by reducing development density.

(ii) To assist the city government in the distribution of public facilities.

(iii) To limit the development of skyscrapers.

(iv) To promote fire safety, hygiene, and traffic efficiency.

(v) To stabilize land prices.

(vi) To segregate industrial use from residential use or, in fact, to exclude any undesirable use.

A hidden agenda in most of the early zoning ordinances was to protect the homogeneity of the socioeconomic character of established areas so as to maintain the value of the land and to exclude the intrusion of "lower class outsiders." Although not a lawful purpose, this was the thrust behind the early spread of zoning across the country and was perhaps the cause for much of the later disappointment about the efficacy of zoning. The Mount Laurel court cases in New Jersey is a celebrated challenge to this exclusionary practice of local government.

Mount Laurel, New Jersey, had imposed minimum lot size restrictions along with other restrictions that effectively excluded low-income families and other groups, such as the elderly and racial minorities. The zoning policy was challenged by a number of public-interest groups. The case eventually reached the New Jersey Supreme Court in 1975. The court (Southern Burlington County NAACP v. Township of Mount Laurel, 67 N.J. 151, 174-75, 1975) determined that local land use regulations had to provide a "realistic opportunity for the construction of its fair share of the present and prospective regional need for low and moderate income housing." This is known as "Mount Laurel I". The municipalities did not change much in their actual zoning practice and provision of affordable housing, and the case was brought to court a second time in 1983 (Southern Burlington County NAACP v. Township of Mount Laurel, 92 N.J. 158, 456 A. 2d 390, 1983).

This is known as "Mount Laurel II". "In response to widespread municipal noncompliance and governmental inactivity, the court endeavored in Mount Laurel II to aggressively implement the constitutional obligation, prescribing an arsenal of remedies and procedures aimed at providing a meaningful chance for the construction of 'decent housing for the poor'" (Franzese, 1991:60). Mount Laurel II gave developers the tools (known as the "builder's remedy") to challenge exclusionary zoning ordinances in order to build lower- and moderate-income housing. Mount Laurel II is significant in that the court determined that judicial intervention was limited and that legislative action was needed in order to secure the provision for fair housing share. The New Jersey Fair Housing Act was enacted in 1985. It prescribed the formation of the Council on Affordable Housing (COAH) which would ensure that the provision for fair housing was carried out by local governments. COAH had the power to determine the regional need for affordable housing, establish the guidelines for municipalities to determine fair share, and approve or disapprove proposed municipal plans to satisfy the housing needs. The Act also sets out provisions that enable municipalities to pay their way out of 50% of their Mount Laurel responsibilities through the "regional contribution agreement" under the Act. In a 1986 case, known as Mount Laurel III (Hills Development Co. v. Township of Bernards 510 A.2d 621 N.J. 1986), the court upheld the Fair Housing Act. It ruled that many of the lower court cases could be transferred to the Council on Affordable Housing, which had the authority to reduce a town's fair share quota, density levels, and builder's remedy agreements. Mount Laurel III has been criticized for accommodating municipalities and thus limiting the progress in addressing the issue of affordable housing (Lovejoy, 1992).

The form and content of zoning ordinances vary widely. For very small towns they may consist of only a very few simple provisions against noxious industries. For bigger cities there are very detailed regulations and procedures. The following is a brief description of the general content. There are usually two parts: regulations and procedures.

Zoning Regulations

1. USE

Use regulations specify land use categories and the uses permitted under each category. Generally there are three main ones: residential, commercial, and industrial. Other categories include rural, recreational, environmental protection, institutional, open space, community, and mixed uses.

Each category can be divided into subcategories. For instance, the residential category can be divided into single-family, row housing, apartments, and mobile homes, and the commercial category into general commercial, highway commercial, central business districts, recreational commercial, shopping centres, and neighbourhood commercial. Within each category or subcategory, there are specifications of "permitted uses." This can be a very elaborate affair and any use besides the permitted ones is allowed only after a long and costly process of zoning amendment.

At the beginning, land use categories were organized in a "pyramidal" way, with residential use at the top and industrial use at the bottom. This meant that residential land could only be used for residential purposes while commercial land could be used for both commercial and residential purposes and industrial land could be used for all purposes. The idea was to protect residential areas against the intrusion of commercial and industrial uses. The attitude was that it was contrary to the public interest to have industrial and commercial uses in a residential area, but if people wanted to live in an industrial area it was not a violation of the public interest. Obviously, this essentially "elitist" approach of protecting residential areas was not going to help improve the living conditions of the working class. Later on, land use categories became more specific and exclusionary. Some people have claimed that by ignoring the interrelatedness of land uses this approach has been responsible for the promulgation of monotonous residential suburbia and the creation of desolate commercial areas after office or shopping hours. The present emphasis is on the promotion of mixed uses but this is still quite a distance away from the idea of integrated uses.

2. DENSITY (OR "INTENSITY" IN THE CASE OF NON-RESIDENTIAL USES)

There are two kinds of regulations: density ratios and lot size requirements. For residential use it is the number of dwellings or population per acre or hectare. For other uses it is the number of employees or workers per acre or hectare. The assumption is that through controlling the density, a match between user needs and land supply can be achieved and maintained, because density is directly related to infrastructure, service needs, and environmental stress and degradation.

A floor area ratio (floor space index in Canada) can be used to regulate density. This is the ratio between total building floor space and the area of the site. For example, if the site area is 1000 square feet, a six-storey building with a floor area of 750 square feet per floor would have a floor area ratio of 4.5 (750 multiplied by six and divided by 1000). Another ratio standard is the site coverage, that is, the proportion of the site occupied by the building. In the above example, the site coverage is 75 percent. When applied to commercial and industrial uses these two ratio standards can control the intensity of the uses, that is, the number of workers, employees, customers, visitors, etc. In this way these standards seek to ensure a minimum amount of daylight and air to the occupants as well as to the neighbours, a maximum volume of traffic generated by the use, adequate space for parking, loading, and waiting of vehicles, and an acceptable environmental impact by the use on the site and its neighbours.

Density is also controlled by regulating lot sizes. A maximum lot size may be required to maintain high density development or a minimum lot size to ensure low density development. Sometimes, in the case of residential use, housing type is used as a density control; for instance, single-detached housing is assumed to have a lower density than row housing. Finally, in a mixed housing development, the number and proportion of the different housing types can be fixed.

However, density control by itself does not ensure that land will be "used" in the way the density standards assume, but it gives a false impression of precision. In some ways a density standard is a lazy form of control, a shortcut which tends to perpetuate traditional forms of design and does not make allowances for innovation or special circumstances. Residential densities in particular assume certain lifestyles and family structure. They may not bear any useful relationship to the services, facilities, and other uses that are needed to support the residential development. For instance, two areas may have the same density of 100 persons per acre but may have actual populations of completely different age mix, hence having very different services and facility needs, such as a primary school in one case and a geriatric clinic in the other. In fact, some of the public interest concerns, such as safety and health, which have been the *raison d'être* of density controls, are now being more effectively handled by specific regulations regarding open space, noise, pollution, daylight, and so on. Some other concerns will never be satisfactorily handled through density control, such as aesthetics and landscaping. In fact, density controls are often used for dubious purposes such as protection of the socioeconomic status of an area or discouragement of certain kinds of development.

Density standards are often the bone of contention between developers and the city. Developers usually want to put as much building onto a site as they can, while city governments (by no means always for good or even explicable reasons) often want to keep the density down. The way that density controls are expressed can lead to dispute. For instance, a standard of a certain number of people per net acre of residential land may mean one type of housing for some and another type for others. Even when the housing type is specified, say for instance, single-detached houses, the size of the houses in terms of the number of bedrooms will be different depending on assumptions about the number of persons per bedroom.

City governments are often sympathetic and agreeable, at least in the early stages of development and/or redevelopment of an area, to proposals which have densities higher than those set out in the zoning and may even be willing to amend the zoning in order to "attract development." But while there are plenty of people eager and willing to develop at above the average density, there are none willing to develop at below the average. When this happens, as it often does, the population of the area would, when it is fully developed, be very substantially higher than that planned for, with consequent overstraining of local facilities.

More recently, some municipalities want to promote new urbanism, with mixed densities and housing types. But most developers want to stay with the more conventional lower density housing types (e.g., single-detached). They will try to get the maximum number of these conventional units in the subdivision agreement with the municipality. Then they will build and sell these units first, leaving the rest of the land which has been designated in the agreement for higher density or more unconventional housing types undeveloped, or re-negotiating for more lower density units.

3. BULK

These regulations control the area and dimension of front, side, and rear yards, and interior courts; number of storeys; dimensions of building floor plans; and building heights and volumes. Site coverage and floor area ratio are also used. These controls can be in absolute dimensions or ratios. Set-back from streets or dimensions of yards or courts are often functions of the height and bulk (especially length of walls) of the building. The main purposes of these regulations are to ensure that enough daylight and air can penetrate into the building itself and that neighbours are not deprived of their fair share of daylight and air, to provide for privacy especially in terms of noise and sight, and to control the bulk and proportion of buildings for aesthetic reasons.

Figure 7-1: Floor Area Ratio (F.A.R.)

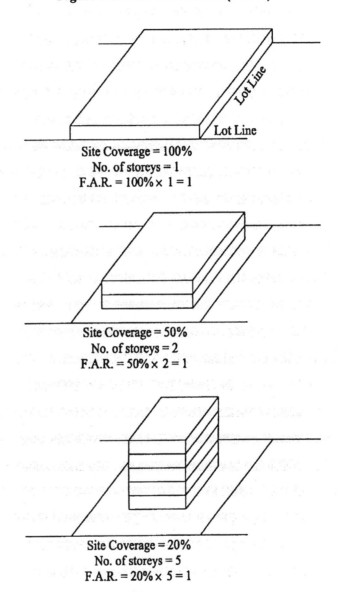

Site Coverage = 100%
No. of storeys = 1
F.A.R. = 100% × 1 = 1

Site Coverage = 50%
No. of storeys = 2
F.A.R. = 50% × 2 = 1

Site Coverage = 20%
No. of storeys = 5
F.A.R. = 20% × 5 = 1

4. PARKING

These regulations are based usually on the number of dwelling units, number of population or users, or the amount of floor space. For example, one parking space may be required for every dwelling unit or for every 300 square feet of leasable commercial floor space. Such standards are normally related to the type of land use, the characteristics of the area (e.g., city centre or suburbs), land values, and the availability of public transit. Originally introduced to provide convenience for the users and to alleviate traffic congestion, especially in city centres, these provisions of off-street parking are now believed to be responsible for attracting even more traffic into the city centre.

5. OTHERS
The following are some common examples.

(i) The minimum floor area of a dwelling unit, so as to ensure a reasonable quality of living environment.

(ii) Space for loading and unloading of goods.

(iii) Maximum permitted grade to ensure safety and maintenance and to protect against erosion.

(iv) Landscaping standards.

(v) Design and siting of signage and advertisements.

(vi) Protection of special scenic places and vistas.

(vii) Control of building exterior.

(viii) Control of accessory uses, for example, home occupation and cottage industries in a residential use.

Besides these, there may be performance standards for industrial uses to control the emission of pollutants and spread of noise, odours, and smoke. Although performance standards can be used for other land use categories, they are seldom employed.

Maps as well as texts are used to specify the location to which the various designations and regulations apply. These maps cover the whole planning area and show the "zones" for different uses and densities. The type, number and the size of each zone varies from place to place. The principal consideration in drawing the boundaries is the "compatibility" of the uses. Generally speaking, zones tend to be defined by the predominant existing use or form of development. As such, zoning has a tendency to protect and reinforce the status quo.

The fact that the zoning map covers the whole planning area is very important. Without this comprehensiveness, zoning becomes an arbitrary and *ad hoc* control, losing the essential quality of fairness and predetermination. But sometimes, in order to allow time for more thorough planning studies to be carried out, or to wait for a clearer indication of future growth patterns to emerge, or to prevent premature development, an area or a specific site may be designated a "holding" zone. The permitted use and density for the area may actually be assigned but development of the land is prohibited until such time as the "holding" designation is removed and substituted by the proper land use designation.

Sometimes the city may want to impose more limitations or conditions on a specific site in addition to those already stated in the general regulations, or a developer may wish to have specific concessions or considerations. This can be incorporated through an amendment to the existing zoning by creating a "special exception" category. But this has led to abuse. Sometimes on account of shortsightedness, laxity, or fastidiousness on the part of the city, a zoning map may be full of special exception sites making a mockery of its supposed predetermination.

Even more damaging, the municipal government may deliberately designate land on the urban fringe under low-density categories, such as "rural," so as to prepare an advantageous position for bargaining when such land is brought forward for development. The government then negotiates with the developer about the permitted uses and densities while requiring the developer to comply with some special conditions or to make contributions (for example, the developer may be required to construct public roads at his own cost or to dedicate land for community open space). The negotiated uses, density, and conditions are then written into the zoning ordinance through an amendment. This approach is called "spot zoning." It violates the fundamental justification for zoning as law: predetermination, fairness, and consistency.

Finally, if zoning is to be based on comprehensive planning there will always be some existing uses which are inappropriate in the planning sense. These "nonconforming" uses are usually allowed to continue. Upon redevelopment, expansion, or sale, these nonconforming uses must be brought in line with the general zoning regulations governing the area. However, if the existing use is too incompatible, then the city will have to consider purchase and demolition.

Zoning Procedures

Zoning is law. Any contravention is an infraction of the law. The government can stop uses and development, impose fines and/or other penalties, and remove or demolish structures and recover the costs from the violator.

All new constructions and changes in use must comply with zoning regulations. A developer needs to apply for permission from a myriad of government agencies (Health, Commerce, Environment, Transportation, and so on), especially in the United States. Each of these agencies will refer to the zoning ordinance but as they have different mandates and powers they will see zoning in different lights (as an obstacle, a bargaining tool, or a heavy stick). Often there are loopholes and discrepancies in the regulations or in their interpretation, which are temptations for bureaucratic corruption or petty tyranny.

In theory, zoning requirements for any site in the whole city are predetermined, but in reality a number of problems exist.

(i) Insufficient consideration may have been given before a new regulation is introduced, resulting in its being inadequate or too Draconian for some actual circumstances. This is particularly true in cases where zoning regulations are hastily enacted as response to some crisis.

(ii) Changing time and circumstances may have rendered certain regulations obsolete. This is especially true when there is inadequate monitoring, review and evaluation.

(iii) Societal changes, technological progress, and theoretic development may have brought about new conceptions about land use categorization, the relationship between different uses, the effects of different densities, and so on. Examples include changing social perceptions about the environment, energy conservation, and the use of public transit; technological innovations in waste treatment, housing prefabrication, industrial automation, and telecommunication; and new theoretic insights into the process of urban gentrification, the segregation effect of large lot zoning, and the effects of land use segregation on women. As a result, zoning regulations may have to be revised to reflect new realities and insights.

(iv) Land transactions and urban growth may have changed the size and shape of land parcels and their development potential. Since these cannot be accurately predicted, detailed and exact predetermination of use and density in zoning can be rendered obsolete.

(v) The municipal government may want to leave the way open for later bargaining, thus will not commit itself to clear and definite zoning regulations.

Some of the above are more "legitimate" reasons than others but the fact remains that rezoning, or zoning amendment, is an inevitability. In truth, zoning is the most frequently changed of municipal laws. It may be totally revised or partially changed in the text, map, or procedure. Most of the time, though, zoning ordinances are revised to accommodate "spot zoning" and the creation of "special exceptions."

Minor changes, or "variances" as they are sometimes called, may be granted in recognition of site difficulties such as size, shape, and gradient, or hardship to the owner in complying rigidly to the regulations. As a rule-of-thumb, such changes should not be more than a ten percent deviation from the norm, for instance, an expansion of less than ten percent of the existing floor area, or a reduction of ten percent of the minimum separation distance. Such changes are normally handled by a committee appointed by the City Council and do not involve any legislative procedure.

Bigger changes will require an amendment to the zoning ordinance. This is a legislative process and must comply with established "procedural law" which specifies the requirements of the legislative framework, and procedures for consultation, public participation, review, registration, and so on. Depending on the nature of the change, this process may take from a couple of months to years. Presently, except for minor infill developments, nearly all new development proposals require a zoning amendment, which means the principle of predetermination has been seriously eroded in recent years.

An amendment cannot be applied retroactively to remedy any anomalies of the past. If the city refuses to amend, or if the amendment is unacceptable or unsatisfactory to the developer or to any agency, group or individual, they can appeal the decision to the courts.

In rendering its judgment, the court will normally consider the following:

(i) Does the zoning decision contravene the Constitution, especially with respect to social, economic, and racial discrimination?

(ii) Does the decision exceed local "police power" and amount to the taking away of property without compensation?

(iii) Are all the conditions imposed legal?

(iv) Is there too much "discretionary power" given to officials?

(v) If the decision involves the total ban of a certain use, then is the ban reasonable and will it lead to the demise of a particular trade or industry?

(vi) Has the municipal government considered only the impact of the development on local finance (such as increased tax revenue, and decreased expenditure in public infrastructure and facilities), and ignored the appropriateness of the development and other aspects of the public interest?

In the administration of zoning there is an interesting but alarming contradiction. Both the regulator (government) and the regulated (developer) want zoning to be detailed and comprehensive. Through these, the government hopes to have overall and tight control of the pattern of development, and the developer hopes to have clear and definite laws within which to plan his activities. Yet, at the same time, they both want to have more flexibility so that they can bargain to their respective advantage.

Zoning Variations

The basic concept of zoning has not changed since the beginning. The following are some more significant extensions and variations of the idea.

1. PLANNED UNIT DEVELOPMENT REGULATIONS

This approach breaks away from the traditional rigid density control in order to promote more comprehensive and integrated large-scale residential development. It is now also applied to commercial development. The regulations control only the overall land use character and density leaving the exact locational mix of land uses, housing types, lot layouts, and building designs more flexible and responsive to market and site conditions.

2. PERFORMANCE ZONING

Instead of specifying the permitted uses, density, and design, this approach seeks to control the physical, social, economic, and environmental effects of the development such as traffic flow, air quality, and environmental impacts. A number of municipalities have attempted this approach and it is applied primarily to large-scale projects. (Refer also to discussion on planning standards in the Analysis chapter.)

3. SPECIAL ZONES

Certain special districts such as university and hospital areas have peculiar characteristics and functional needs. The activities in these areas may affect the environmental qualities (quietness, traffic, etc.) of the surrounding areas. A "special zone" designation will enable specific regulations to be made to reduce the conflict between these areas and the surrounding communities as well as to safeguard the compatibility of the uses within these areas.

4. BONUS REGULATIONS

These regulations give certain types of development advantages and conveniences (including more permitted uses and higher densities) over and above the normal, in order to encourage the pursuit of certain community goals. For instance, if a developer leaves a portion of the ground area for public use or sets aside the ground floor for retail uses, then he may be allowed a larger and taller building in recognition of these "public contributions." Of course, what qualifies for public contribution and how much bonus will be given depends on the sociopolitical climate of the time. Unfortunately, bonus regulations are often not accompanied by careful design control and monitoring, to ensure that the public contributions are effective and useful and not just a gimmick for the developer to gain more floor area or use types.

5. TRANSFER OF DEVELOPMENT RIGHTS

To preserve buildings of architectural and historic significance or to protect districts with special character, such as the theatre district, the city may designate these as heritage buildings or districts and prohibit renewal or redevelopment. But such a designation would have exceeded the normal, acceptable limits of development control, especially when these are located on high value land in city centres. To compensate for the owner's loss of development value and to avoid the financial burden on the city if it were to purchase the land, the concept of transfer of development rights is employed as follows. Under normal zoning, the owner is entitled to a higher density than what is presently used up by the existing building. The owner can transfer the excess density (normally calculated in terms of floor space), which he is not able to realize because of the designation, to another site or sell to another developer. This transferred or purchased density can then be used on the other sites to build larger or taller buildings than what is normally permitted. This scheme can be used for other purposes, such as to exchange residential space in one location for office space in another. It can be managed in different ways, such as to dispose of the transferable rights through an auction. There are some major theoretic and practical problems involved. For example, if densities can be transferred from one site to another what was the basis of the original density regulation? How can the true value of lost development potential be accurately measured? What prevents the city from extending this scheme to become a means to create revenue?

6. NEGOTIATED DEVELOPMENT

An important purpose of comprehensive zoning is to provide predictability. But comprehensive zoning also means that some nonconforming uses within a zone have to be allowed or that some variances have to be given, if the existing property owners are not to suffer unnecessary hardship. Besides, the shape and direction of urban growth is difficult to predict, which means that rezoning becomes necessary. As a result, the development approval process has become increasingly dependent on special permitting procedures which require case-by-case review of development proposals rather than allowing them as a matter of right. The power to control development has also given governments the leverage to "exact" certain concessions from developers in the pursuit of community interests. Communities can also offer incentives such as use and density bonus, favourable tax assessment, and provision of services to entice certain types of development, usually those which would increase jobs and the tax base. The combination of these necessities, aspirations and powers has made the development approval process one of negotiation. Most negotiations are done in rather formal administrative hearings that mimic the adversary process of the courts. Opponents argue that negotiated development involves ad hoc decisions, the cumulative effects of which may be contradictory and inefficient as a whole. There are other problems, too, including the abuse of discretionary power, the exclusion of people most likely to be affected by the negotiated outcome such as the residents of a housing project which is being negotiated as a linkage to a commercial development, and the concern that the adversary process tends to prevent creative solutions.

Zoning, as used in the United States, has a built-in bias to protect the *status quo* through controlling the uses and densities which are not compatible with the existing ones. This idea was the force behind the rapid spread of the adoption of the zoning concept in the 1920s, and it has not changed much today. By law, zoning has to be based on comprehensive land use planning and, in theory, zoning is a tool to implement the land use plan, that is, planning provides the rationale for zoning control. But in reality planning and zoning are often unrelated.

Planning is forward looking and has traditionally emphasized those land uses which are usually ignored by the market (such as open space, greenbelt, visual amenities, and community facilities), or those people who cannot compete in the market (such as the low income, elderly, and handicapped). These concerns run contrary to the idea of zoning which emphasizes compatibility with existing use, that is, with established interests. The outcome of this conflict can be seen in the legislative history of planning and zoning. The first Standard Zoning Enabling Act in the United States was promulgated in 1924 which was taken up immediately and spread widely but the first Standard Planning Enabling Act had to wait until 1928. This means many areas had zoning first before they had planning. Take New York for instance. It was the first city to enact a zoning ordinance (in 1905) but its first planning commission was established 21 years later and there was a 55-year lapse between its first zoning ordinance and its first comprehensive plan. Even now, some people in the United States still believe that city planning is "socialist" and has no place in America. Some cities have only zoning ordinance and no plan and sometimes even the courts have used zoning maps as comprehensive land use plans, thus making zoning maps a basis for zoning regulations!

DEVELOPMENT CONTROL IN CANADA

Both the concept of zoning and the form of zoning bylaws in Canada were imported from the United States. The scope and level of detail of the regulations are very similar. The major differences are in administration and amendment procedures.

In the United States, zoning authority is based on "police power," and the interpretation of the scope of this power is in the hands of the courts. The substance and procedure of zoning are the subject of countless legal battles both at the local and state levels, although in recent years the Supreme Court in the United States has not taken an active interest in zoning matters.

In settling disputes, courts in the United States base their decisions on precedence, but the United States is a huge country with vastly different patterns and history of urban growth and management styles. Since court decisions are often based on specific circumstances of the site or issue involved, the appropriateness of precedence is often challenged and decisions appealed, involving much time and cost.

In Canada, zoning is a power generally delegated by the provincial government to the local municipalities. But the structure of government in Canada is based on the principle of "the supremacy of Parliament" and is more similar to that of Britain than the United States. The judiciary is independent but its powers are much more restricted than those enjoyed by its counterpart in the United States. This arrangement means that zoning disputes can be settled in a less complex, cumbersome, and legalistic way by referring or appealing to a provincially appointed tribunal (such as the Ontario Municipal Board). In addition, planning officials in Canada have more discretion in interpreting zoning bylaws, but this is balanced by the fact that zoning bylaws are themselves very detailed and specific thus reducing the danger of bureaucratic abuse. Finally, government bureaucracy in Canada is much less susceptible to political influences or changes ("the Minister may come and go but the Assistant Deputy Minister will stay on"). This is true at all levels of government. Therefore, zoning administration is more consistent.

Development control in Canada follows a "one-window" approach, that is, the planning department is both a reviewing authority of a development proposal, as well as the coordinator of consultation and review by other relevant government agencies. This does not necessarily mean that the process is faster because many of the reviewing agencies do not follow statutory response time. Also, a developer and the reviewing agencies may enter into negotiation without involving the planning department, although the result of the negotiation still needs to be channelled through the planning department to the municipal council. But all in all, the "one-window" approach has, at least in theory, more advantages than disadvantages, and is also advocated by some planners in the United States.

Zoning amendment in Canada follows a legislative process which seems to be faster than that in the United States. Most of the zoning disputes are settled in quasi-judiciary tribunals. Courts do not normally take on zoning disputes, and when they do so it is always on a matter of law or procedure and not on the substantive issues in dispute. Canadian jurisprudence recognizes that any delineation of land according to use and density would necessarily "differentiate" certain areas or socioeconomic activities from others. Tribunals and courts will not, therefore, entertain arguments based on any "discrimination" resulting from this "differentiation." Instead, when considering disputes the focus is on whether the zoning regulation was based on public interest, whether there has been comprehensive planning consideration, and whether the interpretation and administration of the zoning regulation has been impartial.

DEVELOPMENT CONTROL IN PRACTICE

When a planner works exclusively on development control for a long time he/she begins to forget that the object of control is to implement the plan. Likewise, if a planner does not do any development control he/she loses the distinction between the ideal and the practical.

The standard bureaucratic routine in development control is to check the development proposal against the provisions in the plan and, where zoning and other control instruments exist, against these provisions. Soon, the rationale behind the plan and development control provisions are forgotten and the letter of the law replaces its spirit. This is particularly serious where municipal governments have chosen to avoid making specific and detailed commitment either in their plans and/or in the development control measures. Under such circumstances any development proposal would require some change, adjustment, or at least refinement in the permitted uses and densities. The following list of questions by Keeble (1983:106) is designed to help the planner to refocus his/her examination on the planning merit of the proposal.

(i) Should the existing use of the land in question be properly changed at all, in light of the plan for the area as a whole?

(ii) If so, is the proposed use suitable for that land?

(iii) Is there some other land more suitable for the proposed use and is it possible to divert the proposal?

(iv) Are the proposed building density and the layout of roads, buildings, and open spaces satisfactory?

(v) Are the design and landscaping proposed satisfactory?

(vi) What are the public interests or legitimate private interests which will be protected or enhanced by the proposal?

(vii) If the proposal is refused, what public interests or legitimate private interests have been served?

To these must be added the environmental impacts and infrastructure impacts of the proposed use, especially at the micro-level. (Refer to appropriate sections in the Information and Analysis chapters.) If the proposed use and density fit in with the land use plan then the following finer issues have to be examined in some detail. First comes traffic, both vehicular and pedestrian, followed by noise, smell, and garbage. Then there are the "good neighbourliness" issues which include intrusion into privacy (especially visual privacy), reduction of daylight or sunlight, and general nuisance and distress. Last, but not least, is aesthetics.

TRAFFIC

It is usually quite straightforward to calculate the traffic generated and/or attracted by the proposed development. What is more difficult to determine is whether or not the additional traffic is acceptable. It is obvious that any additional traffic would have some effect on the time and convenience of other road users, but it is irresponsible to refuse a development proposal on traffic grounds, if the capacity of the existing road system and the effects of the proposed development have not been explicitly and methodically evaluated.

NOISE

Traffic also produces noise, but if the traffic volume is acceptable for the road capacity, traffic noise is likely to be no greater than that expected and tolerated within any normal road system. One exception, though, is that if there is an unusual amount of traffic during the night then more careful study is required.

There are sources of noise other than traffic, such as children at play, religious ceremonies, and machinery. The effect on neighbours depends upon the kinds of activities, the number of people involved in them, the distance between the source of noise and those affected, the difference in levels between the noise source and the recipient, and the presence or absence of screening. A good principle to remember is that it is often futile to try to control the behaviour or activities which produce the noise and it is more effective to try to mitigate the adverse effect on the neighbours.

SMELL

The problems of smell and garbage are more difficult to measure and to deal with. Careful site layout can hide garbage but cannot contain smell. If the smell comes from the garbage then efficient garbage removal from the site may be required as a condition of approval.

PRIVACY AND DAYLIGHTING

The issue of privacy and daylighting is normally dealt with through separation distances, yard sizes, setbacks, and all other regulations controlling building bulk. Privacy for both the proposed users of the site and the neighbours should be considered. Not only separation distances and building heights are important, but also the positioning of windows both horizontally and vertically can help to enhance privacy in a highly urban environment. The location and orientation of buildings, the positioning and size of windows, and the choice of external building materials should be sensitive to the microclimate at the site and the solar paths.

NUISANCE AND STRESS

Development types which cause general nuisance and distress to neighbours are the most difficult to deal with because people are generally not well informed or have exaggerated imaginations about these uses, and local politicians are easily swayed by vocal representations in council meetings. Nothing can be more biased than local opinion and the planner has a professional duty to maintain objectivity in such deliberations. Typical among such "controversial" proposals are high-rise blocks, bars, wrecking yards, low-cost or low-rent housing, conversion of single-detached houses into apartments, halfway houses or group homes, mobile homes, funeral homes, and houses of worship for minority religions.

(i)Many of the objections are based on a snobbish attitude towards certain socioeconomic classes or lifestyles. These are often masked by planning arguments such as traffic and parking, changes to the predominant character of the area, increased noise and activity especially late at night, and increased population leading to an overstraining of local services and facilities. In most situations, the road system and the capacity of local services and facilities can handle the additional demand quite readily. However, it is dangerous to consider such proposals in isolation. For instance, approval given to the conversion of a single-detached house into apartments may open the floodgate for similar conversions, thus altering the essential land use character of an area, especially in a university town where there may be great demand for student housing in residential areas. The issue of conversion should not be dealt with in a piecemeal fashion.

(ii)Few people would really like to live next door to a funeral home. Most people also have an aversion to the physically and developmentally handicapped, but if the location of such uses is acceptable on planning grounds then they should be allowed. Another thorny issue is the location of gambling houses, adult cinemas and shops, and "houses of ill repute." There does not seem to be a generally applicable solution. They are like sanitary sewers--unsightly but serving a function. Some cities have tried to group them together in a specific area for better control and others have tried to disperse them in order to make them inconspicuous. However, through dispersal they may look inconspicuous on the map but can be very conspicuous on the ground.

AESTHETICS

Most aesthetic controls are undertaken in a half-hearted way because they are considered as regulating the public taste and regarded as paternalistic and elitist in a democratic society. This is a myth for three reasons. (1) All of our controls (use, density, and bulk) have an aesthetic implication on the built form and the relationship between buildings. For instance, side yard requirements mean that there is no continuous streetscape and building height restrictions mean a certain urban silhouette. (2) All controls can be considered elitist. The question is not so much that planners suddenly feel less elitist when it comes to aesthetic controls but that they are less familiar, poorly trained, and feel least competent in the case of aesthetics. (3) Aesthetics are important to the "ordinary people" and there are identifiable collective perceptions and images about urban form and urban landscape, although most people are not able to verbalize their sensuous perceptions accurately and adequately.

The general kinds of aesthetic control include the following: building designs in terms of their size, height, and external appearance; plantings of various kinds; and paving, walls, fences, and other means of enclosure. Aesthetic control can extend to outdoor advertising, pylons and power lines, individual trees, groups of trees, and areas of woodland, individual buildings, and a whole district.

Most aesthetic controls are more in the form of guidelines than laws and they are often administered by committees of lay people. This approach, it has been pointed out, has helped to avoid some disasters but has not encouraged good design. Some cities are relying on "architects' advisory panels." There is yet no satisfactory way to resolve disagreement between equally qualified people.

It seems the most significant achievement to date is in the area of urban design. This includes streetscaping such as furniture, signage, paving and planting; small urban open spaces such as plazas, playgrounds, tot lots; and shopping precincts, bazaars, and marketplaces. It seems that while municipal governments are reluctant to control the aesthetics of private development they are more conscious of the need for visually pleasant urban spaces that are in their charge.

ADMINISTRATIVE ISSUES

City governments are becoming more management-conscious but good management is more than a chart on the wall or an elaborate diagram composed of boxes and arrows. Management is defined as "skillful handling." It requires a commitment to the success of the plan, a confidence in the validity of the policies, and the trust of the public in the planners (Loew, 1979: 76).

One of the purposes of development control, in addition to the implementation of the plan, is to protect people from annoyance caused by the activities of unsuitable neighbouring uses. Most municipal governments do not go out of the way to look for trivial breaches of development control regulations. However, neighbours are often much more alert and, if their complaints are factually correct, government has to take action. But in development control, and indeed in any planning deliberation, we have to assume that one is dealing with ordinary, reasonable, and decent people who will be a little noisy, untidy, lazy, and inconsiderate. Any activity which, when carried out in an ordinary way, does not seem likely to cause great annoyance to neighbours should be allowed.

But planners can become very inflexible when it comes to their "sacred cows," such as "greenbelt is inviolable," and "strip development is bad." It is very important that planners should take time to reflect and that politicians should give planners the opportunity to do so. Ideally a planner should rotate between plan making and development control.

The most publicized problem about development control is delays. Delays in the development approval process have now become an accepted way of life for developers. The process may take a few weeks to a few years. There are many reasons for this, one of which is certainly that there is now much more public review of development proposals before they are approved. There are more issues that need consideration now than in the past, especially energy conservation and environmental impact. But these do not exonerate the complex compartmentalization and lack of coordination in the approval process. In fact, much of the planner's job in development control is not so much to evaluate the merit of the proposal but to guide the developer through the labyrinth of officialdom.

In Canada, a subdivision application may be referred to 30 or more agencies for comments. Although there can be statutory response time required of the referred agencies, this is easily bypassed by a note sent within the required response time stating that more time is needed! The one-window approach in development approval may help a little, in that the developer does not have to deal with the various agencies and departments separately, but the question of delay still persists. A recent study (Leung, 1998) that examines a representative city in each of the ten provinces of Canada finds that in the worst-case city the total average time to secure a development permit, when the development proposal necessitates an amendment to the city plan, can be as high as 63 weeks. A developer has to develop and submit a concept plan which is received by the planning department; the planning department then prepares a draft amendment to the city plan which is circulated to other departments and interested parties for review and comment; then the planning department prepares a proposal to the planning commission; the planning commission then presents the proposal to city council; the city council holds a public hearing before making its decision; only then can the developer apply to the city's "corporate planning application group" for a development permit; the application is circulated to referees for review, including relevant community associations; the group makes a recommendation to the planning commission; the planning commission approves the application; the approval is advertised to allow for appeal; and at the end of the appeal period the developer can begin developing. There is some indication that processing time increases with the number of steps, the involvement of more senior staff reviews, the need for provincial approvals, the number of formal public meetings and reporting, and the lack of concurrent reviews and processing of the application.

CONCLUSION

We started this chapter with the assumption that development control is a tool to implement the plan but we will conclude with the suggestion that development control tends to have a life of its own. In the United States zoning preceded planning. Because plans are often not good enough to give guidance to development control, the cumulative effect of development control decisions in the past sets the context for planning of the future. In a way, development control is the tail that wags the dog. So much so that development control has been accused of being responsible for high land prices, segregation between the rich and the poor and between different racial groups, and the inefficient distribution of social services and facilities. David Ervin and others (1977) have raised some very interesting questions about the conventional-wisdom justifications for development control, especially through zoning.

(i) Conventional wisdom for control has assumed that development control can reduce the negative externality of certain patterns of land development, such as the smoke and noise generated by certain industrial development for the adjacent area. It can also reinforce the positive externality brought about by certain types of development such as fresh air and visual amenities brought about by a university campus to an adjacent area. To challenge this assumption, it has been suggested that land as a commodity in a market economy means that its price would accurately reflect how the market values the particular characteristics of the land and its environ. Land affected by positive externality will have a higher price, and that affected by negative externality will have a lower price. The price of every piece of land will reflect its highest and best use in the market sense. The market mechanism, through demand and supply, will automatically adjust the positive and negative externalities of the whole city to their optimal levels, without the need for development control. In fact, it can be argued that development control only disrupts this balance.

(ii) It has been assumed that development control can guarantee the optimal use of land from the point of view of the public interest, especially in the provision of open space and the preservation of agricultural land. However, we have yet to determine whether the allocation and distribution of such "public interest" is fair and reasonable, especially in light of who is the beneficiary and who pays the price.

(iii) It has also been assumed that development control can reduce the cost of infrastructure and social facilities. But given the way that development control is practiced, the crucial question is whether or not it can effectively concentrate the demand for the various public facilities and services and thereby reduce the cost of these facilities and services (from the transportation network to school location, and from drainage and water supply to parks and greenbelts). Moreover, it is also necessary to determine which of development control measures are the most effective. Is it use and density control, or those measures used to safeguard the homogeneity of an area?

(iv) The cost of control is also a relevant question. In particular, we should be concerned about the relationship between development control and land prices, especially residential land; the human, material, and time resources needed in the formulation and execution of development control; the fairness and efficiency of processes and procedures; and the conflict between development control measures and the land use plan. It has been noted that development control affects the development potential of land and therefore its price. Some prices will go up and others will go down. This "artificial" pattern of land value distribution will bring windfalls to some and wipe-outs to others. This has been a central concern in the application of development control and has often been used to argue against planning or at least argue against the efficacy of planning. Much research and experimentation has been done in this area, from the betterment and compensation discussion in the Uthwatt Report (Great Britain. Expert Committee on Compensation and Betterment, 1942) to the compendium compiled by Hagman and Misczynki (1978), and from the simple capital gains tax to land assembly by government. It is beyond the scope of this book to go into these but it should be emphasized that the social costs and benefits of development control, and indeed of planning, are still a controversial issue.

CHAPTER EIGHT

IMPLEMENTATION (ACTION-ORIENTED)

A ny form of development control will be of little practical value in implementing a plan if there is no development forthcoming as a result of the control. In a mixed economy where private development will occur only in response to market demand, planning must seek to provide the condition and stimulation for the desired development. Peter Headicar (1974:836) observes "First, they (the planners) must create those features in the plan (for example highways or car parks) which they themselves have planned. Second, they must influence the activities of the private sector so that developments of the kind indicated in the plan materialize in the time and place specified." This may be done through negotiations and incentives, as well as through direct actions aimed at promoting development.

Chapin and Kaiser (1979: 59-60) talk about "priming decisions" and "secondary decisions." Priming decisions can be made in the public sector, such as decisions on major highway locations or utility locations, and in the private sector, such as decisions on locations of major industries, shopping centres, or large residential subdivisions. They set the stage for secondary decisions such as small-scale subdivision, mortgage financing, lot purchasing, or home building. Together they account for the pattern of land use. Therefore, by selective use of priming decisions in the public sector, the private sector will respond in such a way as to produce a desired pattern of land use. In this chapter, we will describe briefly some tried tools for plan implementation.

CAPITAL WORKS PROGRAMMING

There has long been recognition of the relationship between land use planning and the programming of major physical infrastructure. In fact, the early land use plans were done as a requirement to secure senior level government funding for major capital works such as highways and urban renewal. Most plans today claim that they give guidance to the programming of capital work in the city. A standard clause in the plan is that no public capital works can proceed which do not comply with the plan and that the programming and budgeting of the capital works should synchronize with the phasing of urban development envisaged in the plan. This means that the construction of roads, sewage trunks, schools, and so on, will go hand in hand with land development. In this way, the plan is implemented through the location, timing and capacity of the major urban infrastructure.

In practice this has not worked. More often than not capital works planning dictates land use planning rather than serving it. Even when capital works planning and programming is centralized in a municipal government (in reality, senior government departments have a great deal of influence), the decision-making process involves negotiations and compromises among different departments, commissions, and boards, each of which tries to secure as large a share of the total municipal budget as possible, while conceding as little autonomy as necessary. But since by law whatever is decided would have to comply with the land use plan and these departments, commissions and boards are supposed to become involved in the land use planning process, they will seek ways to make the land use plan conform to their wishes rather than the other way around. They may try to provide the land use planner with very vague and ambiguous statements about their intentions or adopt an uncompromising stance regarding their demands. Given the fact that most departments with significant capital works programmes are usually also politically powerful and resource-rich, the planner would have to swallow his/her pride. The result is that the land use plan will either have enough vagueness for these capital works departments to exploit or will contain the provisions that these departments desire. Thus, capital programming is not implementing the land use plan but rather legitimizing the wishes of powerful capital works departments, boards and commissions.

There is also the jurisdictional problem. Boards and commissions involved in the provision of major physical and social infrastructure do not always have the same boundaries as the planning area. In fact, the rationalization of infrastructure has been a main reason for the creation of regional or metropolitan governments. Thus, we may have one public works commission in charge of the trunk sewers and a number of local boards in charge of the branch sewers; or with the regional government providing sanitary drainage and the subregional governments providing for storm drainage, both using the same trench. Also, there can be a regional land use plan prepared by the regional government and a set of local land use plans prepared by the subregional local governments. Under such circumstances, using capital programming as a tool to implement the land use plan, especially by a lower level government, is almost a hopeless task.

The problem of jurisdiction is vividly illustrated by the following real life example in Ontario, Canada. A house was on fire and the neighbours called the nearest fire station. The firemen refused to come to the scene because, they claimed, theirs was the township station and the house was within the city limits. The city's fire department should be called. The nearest city fire station was about three times the distance away and by the time the firemen arrived, the house was burned down. It was found out later that had the fire occurred a year earlier, the firemen from the nearer station would have responded to the call because at that time the city had contracted firefighting in that area to the township. However, because the land in the area was undergoing rapid development and needed better firefighting service and also because the township had raised its service fees, the city decided to build its own fire station. But the new fire station was actually further away from much of the land to be serviced than the township fire station. The city's decision to terminate the contract and locate the new fire station must have made some political, bureaucratic, and technical sense for those involved in the decision, but the example illustrates how difficult and complex it is to try to coordinate capital works programming with the land use plan, let alone using it to implement the plan.

Capital works can also include social and welfare oriented projects such as housing, conservation and parks, and community facilities. These have been referred to as "soft" services. The implicit bias is that hard services such as roads and sewers are concrete and obvious and a city cannot function without them, while soft services are less tangible and at times controversial and can be trimmed without significant impact on the quality of urban life. As a result, the programming of these capital works has not received adequate attention. The only exception may be schools, which are an important consideration in large-scale residential development.

In theory, the programming of capital works offers a very powerful tool to implement the land use plan, because these are priming decisions which will trigger responses from the private sector (developers, individual households, and other users) towards a planned pattern of development. However, there are serious institutional and political constraints, which prevent planners from using this tool effectively. Also, most planners are not trained to converse with engineers and accountants to convince them of the relevance and importance of land use planning to their work. As a tool to implement the land use plan, capital programming remains an unfulfilled promise.

LAND ACQUISITION AND ASSEMBLY

Astute land developers began assembling land soon after the Second World War. In the 1950s and early 1960s they were, with the encouragement of planners and other government agencies, responsible for the huge tracts of suburban development, making huge profits in the process. In the decade of the 1960s, housing construction and housing prices were increasing at an unprecedented pace and governments wanted to get into the act for a number of reasons.

(i) Private land ownership has been considered the major obstacle to planning implementation. Short of compulsory purchase (eminent domain in the United States) at usually a very high price, the municipal government cannot get rid of an existing use which it does not want or introduce a use it does want. Besides, the legal process involved is cumbersome and the planning rationale required to justify such an action has to be very serious. Comprehensive development or redevelopment of an area cannot proceed if some individual owners decide to hold on to their land. This has made urban renewal very expensive, time-consuming, and controversial. Most "progressive" municipal governments would want to avoid this, especially at the urban fringe and along the locus of anticipated urban growth.

(ii) High housing prices are the result of high land prices, at least that has been the thinking since the 1960s. Therefore, it has been argued, affordable housing for moderate- and low-income people may be made possible if governments can acquire land and then release it to housing developers at a price which is lower than that of the market. This saving can then be transferred to the consumer in the form of lower housing prices. It has never been made quite clear why this is a better way to help low- and moderate-income households than say, a direct subsidy to them. One possible reason could have been to ensure a steady supply of land to the development industry. There is also the housing location consideration. Cheaper land is usually available but its location may not be good for access to services and work. Land assembly by government ensures suitable housing location for the low-income.

(iii) Finally, there is the reason of land value recapture. The recovery by government of increases in land value (betterment) has a venerable tradition (Leung, 1979). One of the main goals of the watershed Town and Country Planning Act of 1947 in Britain was to ensure that it was the community and not the individual landowners who would benefit from the rise in land values. The argument is highly ideological and therefore very simple. Without any physical improvement on the land, an owner has made no contribution to the increases in land values. These are "unearned increments" that properly belong to the community and should be reaped by the community. But if every increase were to be returned to the community, what landowner would want to develop his land? Land assembly is a recognition that the best way to recapture increases in land values is for the government to become an owner.

Land assembly is seen as a tool to implement planning as well as to regulate land prices and recapture increases in land values for the community. But there are some practical problems — which land to acquire? who should have the power? how much should be paid for land acquisitions, and how much should be charged when selling off the land?

The answer to the first question is easy. Land acquisition should be guided by the land use plan.

The second question is the most difficult one. Land assembly is costly and requires great management skill if the government is to regulate the supply of land and at the same time recapture the increases in land values to the full. Traditionally, the land use planner is bypassed for this important job. Either the municipal government sets up its own corporation for land assembly or, as is often the case, a corporation is appointed and financed by a higher level government. Two considerations are relevant. First, as the mandate of a land assembly corporation is often more than just implementing the land use plan (which is often considered incidental), how can we ensure that the acquisition and release of land by the corporation will follow the guidance of the land use plan? The corporation is usually required by law to acquire only those lands identified in the land use plan, but the other mandates of the corporation, especially the supply of land to the development industry and the recapture of land value increases, may dictate different acquisition and release strategies. A tug-of-war then develops between the politically and financially strong corporation on the one side and the planning department with its implicit veto on the other. This is not a congenial or an effective way to implement a land use plan. The second consideration is profit sharing and, of course, loss absorption. This is a particularly difficult question if the corporation is set up and financed by a higher level government. Since the profit is incurred on land in the city, it seems logical that the city should have its fair share. This raises a very interesting point about the definition of "community." What is this community which has contributed to the rise in land values? Is it the city, the province or state, or beyond? After all, land prices are affected as much by development control as by the world economy. There are no satisfactory answers. Successful land assembly operations, defined as those which can maintain a steady supply of land for development and/or are financially successful, tend to be region-wide operations as in the case of the land assembly corporation in Saskatchewan, Canada.

The third question is about what price to pay for land and what price to charge for the release of land. From an entrepreneurial point of view, land should be acquired at a time when the market value is low, but in practice it is only when market values are high that there is political pressure for public land assembly. Most land assembly operations are money losers.

Unless and until land assembly becomes an integral part of planning, it will continue to serve primarily those other purposes which may be at odds with planning goals. So far, land use planning has only played a passive role in providing a justification for land assembly. Instead, land assembly should be the servant rather than the master of planning. The more successful land assembly for planning purposes occurs in the area of small-scale, strategic acquisitions such as urban open spaces. It would seem that the recipe for success is a carefully researched and convincing argument which has public support and acquisition that requires only limited funds. This kind of concrete, small-scale achievement is better than the empty promise of more glamourous schemes.

One such practical approach is the "land trust". Land trusts are non-profit, voluntary organizations created specifically to hold land for the benefit of the community. Most operate at the local and regional levels. Many are community based with memberships from the general public. There are several types of land trusts: community land trusts deal with the provision of affordable housing and community development; conservancy land trusts deal with the conservation of open space, agricultural land, historic buildings, or natural areas; land stewardship trusts often encompass the goals of both conservancy and community trusts (Hills and Reid, 1993). Land trusts can also manage bicycle paths, conservation areas and community gardens, or work with government agencies on specific programs such as documenting and developing inventories of significant natural and cultural heritage areas.

Land trusts can be called a Conservancy, a Foundation, an Association, or a Society. Their most distinctive characteristics are their grassroots and voluntary approaches to land management, and they have grown into an important component of the North American land management system. Their strengths lie in their responsiveness to local needs, the clarity of their mission, the emphasis of partnership building, the sense of community ownership, and their flexibility on account of the lack of bureaucratic constraints. Governments are willing to build partnerships with land trusts. For example, a planning department can deliver land use information that is of interest to a land trust, municipal zoning powers can be used to negotiate commitments from developers to make donations of land and to build affordable housing for a land trust. A government may also help fund a land trust to establish a formal cooperative relationship. As well, government agencies may benefit from the technical expertise and local experience of land trusts, especially in areas involving conservation easements, land stewardship, partial donation of properties, and other techniques of land protection.

A land trust acquires land mainly through three mechanisms. (i) It can purchase threatened lands, often at less than its full market value, because the seller can receive tax benefits in return. (ii) It can encourage the donation of lands which can either be held as trust properties or sold to raise funds. The donor can request that the land use or certain characteristics of the property be maintained, or receive a stream of payments. (iii) It can acquire conservation easements (i.e., a legal agreement between a landowner and the land trust or a government agency, that restricts the development, management or use of the land while allowing the owner to own it) or other limited interests in land. Therefore, land trusts rely very much on their tax-exempt status to attract donations, such as the tax deductibility of conservation easement donations. But this status depends on government policy. Also, land trusts can be easily hampered by landowners who own critical land parcels and who refuse to participate. They also lack big budgets to support a permanent staff, which is needed in order to compete with developers and to develop and implement a strategic acquisition plan. Often they end up acquiring a scattered pattern of lands.

DEVELOPMENT CORPORATIONS AND PUBLIC-PRIVATE PARTNERSHIPS

Development corporations are usually project-oriented corporations, although these projects may be huge, such as urban renewal, waterfront redevelopment, and industrial park development. A development corporation may involve some or all of the following functions: planning and design, land acquisition and preparation, construction operation and maintenance, financing, marketing, and management. It can be a municipal corporation or a corporation involving different levels of government, and it can be a public enterprise or a public-private joint venture. Different participants may contribute in different ways such as land, finance, and marketing skills.

The municipal government usually owns tracts of land but lacks the finances to develop them or the skill to market the development. It can enter into some form of partnership with a private developer, from granting of a lease on the land and providing it with infrastructure and a specific development brief to forming a development corporation for a specific purpose. In this way, the municipal government can control the development more closely, recover part of the "profit" for the community, obtain a contribution towards the cost of infrastructure, and raise finances outside of senior government control. On the other hand, the developer gets land, part of which he/she might not have had to pay for, compulsory purchase powers from the government, for land assembly, assistance in planning and development approval, and an asset he/she can subsequently sell. For both sides, the main advantage is the fact that the development actually takes place. But there are commercial risks inherent in such an operation and there may be conflicts between public and private goals. Social goals and accountability to ratepayers are different from commercial goals and responsibility to shareholders. Therefore, the question of control is very important in a public-private partnership. The same concern about control and responsibility applies to partnership between a public authority and a nonprofit organization or cooperative (often referred to as the third sector).

Since the late 1970s, many cities have placed economic development as their top priority, and planning has turned from regulating urban growth to encouraging it, especially in revitalizing the older city districts. Increasingly, planners are identifying with the development industry. Notwithstanding the moral dilemma (Can a city serve as both a partner and regulator at the same time?) a new kind of "creative partnership" has emerged. The earlier examples were Boston's waterfront and the Inner Harbour of Baltimore — showcases of urban revitalization through public-private partnerships. Then, there are the high profile cases of London's Docklands and Toronto's Harbourfront. My colleague, David Gordon's (1997) study of New York's Battery Park City illustrates the macro-conditions and inner-dynamics that can make or break a development corporation. Essentially, a development corporation is a centralized, top-down, appointed body which can act quickly and decisively (often bypassing the democratic processes of local government). It can undertake market analysis, request for proposals, negotiate contracts and manage the assets. Its biggest draw, for a city government, is that it can use public funds to "leverage" a much larger amount of private investment. But it must be pointed out that private investors are attracted only because there are a number of public "subsidies": tax-exempt municipal bonds, "moral guarantees" of the corporation's bonds by a senior government, mortgage insurance by a senior government, payment in lieu of property taxes, property tax abatements, etc.

As a tool to implement the land use plan, the development corporation derives its strengths and weaknesses from the same source. Its mandates are usually very clear and the integration of functions enables it to pursue its mandate efficiently. As long as the municipal government retains a reasonable level of control, a development corporation is a powerful instrument. Experience has shown, however, that a municipal government usually has to concede much of its control when it enters into partnerships with senior governments and the private sector. Moreover, a successful corporation becomes so powerful that it breaks out of municipal government control. There is also the question of single-mindedness in the fulfilment of its mandate. Land use planning is not just urban renewal or waterfront development, although these may be of strategic importance. A successful development corporation may be tempted to exploit its success to perpetuate itself even after the task for which it was created has been fulfilled, or to expand its mandate as an effort of empire building. It is difficult to argue with success.

It is unlikely that a development corporation will be created as a servant to the planning department but its mandate should be to serve the plan. Once created, it is difficult and unwise for the government to meddle too much in its affairs; therefore, its powers and responsibilities should be set out judiciously at its inception. Most important of all is that it should be dissolved once its task is fulfilled. Some successful development corporations are organized in the form of a task force with expertise seconded from existing departments, including the planning department. Once the project is done, these people return to their earlier jobs. This is often better than creating an entirely new bureaucracy.

COMMUNITY IMPROVEMENT

As opposed to new development, redevelopment, or renewal, community improvement assumes that conservation and enhancement of the existing building stock and/or urban infrastructure is a more appropriate way to implement the plan. Instead of introducing new uses to an area or relocating its existing uses, community improvement efforts aim at enhancing the locational and spatial quality for existing uses by improving the quality of the building stock and of the physical and social infrastructure and amenities.

To qualify for such efforts an area must demonstrate that it is both deserving and capable of conservation and improvement. It has to be an area with relative stability and homogeneity in its use, but one that is suffering a decline in its vitality and yet the decline is not yet irreversible. The usual indicators are: age and condition of building stock; existence of incompatible uses; changes in demographic and familial structure, especially the proportion of elderly and young children; changing socioeconomic status and income of the residents, or the types of shops and sales revenue in the case of a commercial area; the quality and upkeep of the environment including streets and open space; the pattern of property ownership, especially absentee owners; traffic and parking conditions; and the availability of community facilities and services. No wonder that most of the areas chosen for community improvement efforts have been inner city neighbourhoods and main street commercial areas.

Community improvement involves a combination of tools, from regulation to public investment. For instance, building stocks, especially in residential areas, are improved through the enforcement of property maintenance standards, loans (forgivable or otherwise) for minor and major repair work, and subsidies for installing insulation. Upgrading of physical infrastructure is an important item, which includes drainage works, road works, and sidewalk repairs. A special consideration is accessibility for the handicapped, from ramps to audio traffic signals. Perhaps the most innovative use of community improvement efforts is in the area of soft services from tot lots to library facilities, and from soccer fields to street lighting. Soft services, that is, community facilities and services, get a lot of intellectual discussion but very little practical action in land use planning. But, with the conservation and enhancement emphasis in most community improvement programmes, soft services become very legitimate improvement items. Another emphasis is "beautification" of commercial areas, from sidewalk paving to street planting, and from street signage to weather protection.

Most community improvement efforts are directed towards residential areas. The chosen area is usually an area which offers scope for creating a better environment and which contains stable communities. There is a built-in bias toward improving areas which have predominantly owner-occupied housing, in the belief that these are more stable areas and that owner-occupiers would invest in improving their houses parallel to public efforts in improving the environment.

Areas adjacent to the chosen area for community improvement may be affected by the programme, positively or negatively. It is important that the situation should be monitored and the boundaries of the area adjusted to respond to changing conditions. The delineation of the boundary of a community improvement area is a highly political issue.

There are a number of problems about community improvement programmes that should be noted. Most of the thrust for this approach has come from senior levels of government. This is part of the "inner city problem" syndrome of recent years. Like all fashionable ideas, this may change with the political agenda of the day leaving a lot of unfulfilled expectations. More troublesome is the fact that programmes of this kind are usually one-off efforts with no follow-up or continuous attention. As an area's environment is improved, housing prices go up and the existing residents, especially renters, are replaced by people who can afford the increased housing prices in the area. In the end, landlords of rental housing benefit most from the programme. Land use planning is the pursuit of congruence between user needs and land supply. This can be achieved by locating the user on the appropriate land or by changing the land to suit the user. Community improvement aims at improving the environment rather than relocating the user but if the improved environment leads to a change of user, then we may have to rethink the appropriateness of the tool in terms of the community goals to be served.

Even when the improvements are to benefit local residents, the programme has to ensure that these are the improvements the local residents want. These programmes should not end with the planting of trees, because trees have to be watered and maintained as well, usually by the local residents themselves. Therefore, if the intention of community improvement is to improve the environment for the local people, it is important that they are convinced that they are the real beneficiaries of the effort.

DEVELOPMENT FEES

These are lot levies, impact fees, cash contributions, development charges, and so on, which are charged to a developer at a flat rate or variable rates. They can serve a number of purposes.

Beginning in the 1960s, senior level government contributions to the finance of community facilities have gradually been declining. As a result, many rapidly growing communities turned to other sources to fund public facilities for new development. Today, development fees are used to finance a variety of facilities such as water and sewer drainage, roads, parks, fire and police, libraries, museums, and even government offices. Frank and Downing (1987) have identified five objectives for the use of development fees in the United States: (i) to shift the new capital financing burden from the existing users to the new development; (ii) to synchronize new development with the installation of new facilities; (iii) to impose economic discipline on land development decisions, especially those that contribute to urban sprawl, by requiring development to absorb the costs of providing new services and facilities; (iv) to enhance the quality of life for existing users as well as those of the new development with special emphasis on remedying deficiencies in parks and streets; and (v) to appease the anti- or slow-growth sentiment of local, vocal interest groups.

The determination of the fees is a very intricate matter. In theory, the "rational-nexus test" is used as a guide, which simply means that in the determination of fees a reasonable and clear connection has to be established between community growth that the new development generates and the need for additional facilities to serve that growth. There must also be a substantial connection between the expenditure of the fees collected from the contributing development and the benefit the development will enjoy (Nicholas and Nelson, 1988). These principles try to deal with two major contentious issues: (i) the suspicion that development impact fees are used for facilities that benefit the entire community or some special groups and not the residents or users of the proposed development; and (ii) the argument that such fees will eventually be passed on to residents and users of the proposed project who will be paying the same taxes and fees for infrastructure, that all community residents pay, thus amounting to double payment. Some of the fees are particularly contentious such as requiring a developer of downtown offices to contribute to a housing fee. Given the successful lobbying of governments by environmental, energy and housing groups and the inclination of many communities to control or even exclude growth, developers are reluctantly accepting this imposition but they want to make sure that it is administered clearly and fairly.

To work out these fees for various facilities, the planner has to go back to the basis of the land use plan. The municipality must show established facility standards and capital improvement programmes in order to justify any imposition of development fees. Furthermore, the relationship between existing and estimated changes in population, employment, economic activities, and land uses has to be investigated; and a base line has to be set up to measure the level of services and the adequacy of facilities at present and those aimed at for the future. Only on this basis can the impact of the proposed development and the amount of contribution from the developer be worked out.

The following considerations are important in determining the share of facilities' cost that must be borne by a development.

(i) The cost of existing facilities, which is usually expressed in terms of cost per capita, per dwelling unit, or per floor space to be served.

(ii) The method of financing of existing facilities. If property tax is the main source of municipal finance, then the property tax paid on the land in the past would have contributed to the cost of the existing facilities. Any future property tax after the development would continue to make that contribution. It is therefore important to avoid double taxation.

(iii) Certain on-site and off-site facilities which the developer is required to install may benefit the community at large, such as roads, rights-of-way, traffic signs, signals, and turn lanes. These may be used to offset the development fees.

All these are to ensure that the additional facilities that will be financed by the development fees result from the new development rather than from addressing existing deficiencies; that the fees represent a proportionate share of the cost of providing the facilities to serve the new development; and that the new development will benefit substantially from the payment of fees. For this last point, location and time criteria are normally used; for instance, a park has to be no more than two miles away, or the fees for an intended facility will be refunded with interest if the city fails to construct the planned facility within a specific time. It is more appropriate to separate the funds generated by these fees from the municipality's general revenue, provided that the accounts are substantial enough to justify the administrative costs.

It is important to note that although development fees have been used to raise finance for community facilities, they are a legitimate land use implementation tool. Their operation requires a plan and a capital works programme. The way they are determined is guided by the facility standards set out in the plan, the plan's estimate about deficiencies and needs, and the plan's strategies about how these needs are to be fulfilled.

The impacts of these fees on the development pattern of the city must be monitored. The fees may result in higher priced housing units, lower housing quality, or no new housing until reduced supply and increased demand raise the price of housing to a level that is acceptable to the developers. This means that low- to moderate-income housing would suffer. The fees may also force lower income households into other less well-prepared communities. In the situation where new office buildings are linked to the provision of affordable housing through the use of this instrument, office rents would rise as a result, and new office development may be pushed to other locations.

Higher housing prices may also lead to reduced consumption. This means smaller homes and smaller lots. Singell and Lillydahl (1990) find that the average residential lot size in their Colorado case study decreased by 10% after the introduction of development impact fees. Of course, such a shift in demand may also encourage developers to innovate and to build medium and higher density housing. Skaburskis and Tomalty (1998) offer some interesting initial findings from their survey of developers. (i) When market demands are comparable across different municipalities, most developers consider municipal differences in development fees when making location decision. (ii) Developers believe that municipalities that use development fees encourage or discourage certain housing types. (iii) Developers also believe that development fees could delay development when the market is weak, but would not have any effect if the market were strong.

To conclude, development fees are determined by local situations. Their amounts and the way they are calculated and used will change the attractiveness of the community to developers and to particular kinds of development. This may bring unintended social, economic, and development outcomes. Connerly (1988) observes that, while this tool enables the planner to play an important role in the fiscal affairs of the city, it also lures him/her into defining the public interest to include only the needs of the community which he/she currently serves. This, he argues, enhances the idea of "the city selfish" and narrows the focus of the profession to helping existing community residents save money. The result is a profession which is reduced to a rather technical role. This in turn reinforces a status quo characterized by unequal access to good housing and communities.

CONCLUSION

Many government policies and programmes affect land use but only a few are within the planner's power to use or influence in order to implement the land use plan. Certainly, senior level government policies on employment, industrial and office locations, transportation, and so on, affect urban land use, but even local government policies such as housing, recreation, police and traffic management will also affect the land use pattern. Taxation of various kinds have intended or unintended consequences on land use. For instance, income tax giving special exemptions to housing investment and mortgage interest payment may influence the supply of certain housing types, capital gains tax may serve as incentive or disincentive for housing or other building investment, and even a sales tax such as that on building supplies and materials affects development activity. Certainly, property tax and the way that property values are assessed have significant implications on the development and maintenance of land. In fact, a vacant land tax assessed on the basis of development potential rather than existing use has been employed to discourage the withholding of land which has been approved for development. Finally, there are direct and indirect subsidies of various kinds, from housing to infrastructure and from financial assistance in preparing plans to housing allowance for low-income households, which all contribute to the supply or demand of certain development.

However, the land use planner's contributions to the formulation and implementation of these policies and programmes have been insignificant and with maybe a few exceptions, such as land taxation and infrastructure programming, they will remain so. Given the dearth of action-oriented implementation tools available to the planner it is particularly important that those which he/she has should be used more effectively. In this chapter we have discussed five such tools which can be used separately or in various combinations. They are capital programming, land acquisition and assembly, development corporations and public-private partnerships, community improvement, and development fees. Planners' track record in using these tools is at best checkered. There can be a number of reasons. Plans may be too vague to give any useful direction as to how these tools may be applied. They may lack the vision or conviction to excite the political will needed to call up these tools. Planners may lack the knowledge and appreciation of the skills needed to use these tools effectively, such as engineering, systems programming, financing, marketing, negotiation, and management. The institutional division of labour in local government and between different levels of government also limits the contribution that the land use planner can make. But the most important reason for the apparent lack of success is perhaps that these tools have either been designed or used for purposes which are different from, or at times in conflict with, those of land use planning.

Planners may perhaps need to consider the following if they want to be more effective in using the action-oriented measures to implement their plans.

(i) Expand their knowledge base so that they can appreciate and dialogue with other professionals in their respective language, particularly engineering, finance, and management.

(ii) Encourage other people to recognize the planner's expertise and the values of a planner's involvement in their decision-making process. Institutionally the land use plan is needed for all the tools described in this chapter, but planners should demonstrate to others that the land use plan is not an obstacle nor a nuisance to their operation, but rather a meaningful and profitable vehicle to serve their interests, either in terms creating revenue or saving cost for them.

(iii) Most important of all is that planners must demonstrate competence and intelligence. Plans must offer a convincing and attractive vision of the future, and provide workable prescriptions as to how the future can be attained through the various tools of implementation. Only then can planners hope to be the master of these and other powerful tools.

CHAPTER NINE

THE LAND USE PLANNER

T he land use planning profession is plagued by unrealistic expectations and sloppy execution on the part of planners and by cynicism and expedience on the part of those they serve. The following are the major problems encountered by planners.

(i) There are no uniform definitions of what constitutes land use planning. The contents and scope of plans vary, often exceeding what can be realistically pursued. The analyses are uneven in depth and sophistication. As a result, both governments and the public are confused about what land use planning is and what it can do for them.

(ii) Land use planning principles are based on outmoded idealism and romanticism used to protect the status quo while ignoring the disparate social needs of a pluralistic society. Many planning decisions have yielded more adverse than beneficial impacts. For instance, environmental protection measures such as the greenbelt have brought about land shortage and high land prices, hurting those who are least able to pay.

(iii) Because of the confusion between land use planning and development control, many municipalities have opted to do plans only on an area-by-area or use-by-use basis, thus losing sight of the geographic comprehensiveness and functional integration needed for good planning. Worse still, since most development control decisions involve specific land parcels or proposals which are not apparently related to any overall development pattern of the city and can thus be made without reference to a plan, governments do not feel the pressure to make plans. The piecemeal and "muddling through" approach is good enough until the cumulative effect of inappropriate individual decisions manifests itself in some dramatic crisis. It has been difficult to convince governments to pay sufficient attention and devote enough resources to planning until it is too late.

(iv) On the other hand, comprehensiveness and integration have been taken by some to mean planning in minute detail and with paralyzing caution. Many municipal governments simply do not have the time or the resources and have simply given up planning.

(v) Many plans are unimaginative copies of other plans. As a result, they are often unrelated to what the community needs or can afford. These plans are often abused or used to pursue individual or special interests.

(vi) As a legal basis for development control, the land use plan should be clear, detailed, and firm. As a policy statement, it should be comprehensive, general, long-term, and visionary. As an educational document for public involvement and discussion, it should be easy to understand, attractive, and topical. As a programming device, it should focus on the medium/short-term specific functions and implementation strategies. These different needs and considerations often conflict with one another. It is not always possible to include everything.

(vii) The long-term perspective and the integrated approach necessary for good planning conflict with short-term political expedience. Politicians do not like to be embarrassed.

(viii) Institutionally, land use planning does not dovetail well with the planning and programming by other government bodies. Yet, the land use plan has to coordinate, or at least reflect, the myriad of other plans and programmes. The inadequacy of land use planning to do so has eroded confidence about what it can deliver.

(ix) Planning education emphasizes survey and analysis of various social, economic, and environmental problems. Some governments find such expertise useful for other kinds of "planning." At the same time, some planners want to gain more power and expand their influence by encouraging this perception. This has led to unrealistic expectations of what a planner can do. Once it is discovered that there is discrepancy between expectation and ability, the credibility of the profession to handle its proper task, that is, land use planning, is eroded.

We have gone some way in this book to describe what competent planning requires. But success depends much on the skills and emotions of the practitioners. We will devote the last chapter to them.

WHO IS THE LAND USE PLANNER?

Can we say that those people who work in municipal planning departments are land use planners? This will be over-inclusive because many of them consider themselves to be health planners, or social planners, and that their work will neither require expertise in, nor contribute to, land use planning. At the same time, this will be under-inclusive because land use planning is done by other government departments or agencies, such as transportation and parks and open space, as well as at various levels of government. A land use planner is perhaps best defined as one whose job it is to ensure the congruence between the activities of people, firms and institutions and the physical setting in which these take place.

It is necessary to distinguish between contributors to land use planning and specialists within land use planning. According to Keeble (1983: 167-168), contributors to land use planning are people whose expertise and experience in certain matters are of special importance to land use planning, such as education planners and health planners. It is important for the land use planner to be able to brief these contributors effectively in relation to the contributions they can make to land use planning. Specialists within land use planning have special expertise and experience in certain land use types such as open space and industrial park, or in certain planning functions such as citizen participation and negotiation with developers, or in certain analytic tasks such as urban economics, urban sociology, and planning law. At the same time, a land use planner would, through training and experience, have acquired some skills in one or more of the above areas, but it is more important that a planner should know and understand the basic principles of each discipline involved in land use planning rather than trying to be an expert in all areas. In this way, a planner is a generalist who has to call on a very great deal of specialist information and advice from a variety of fields and then to coordinate, compare, and evaluate their importance, finally melding them with his/her own ideas and skills to create a dynamic plan, disciplined by the limitations imposed from other fields of knowledge.

Of special importance is the relationship between plan making and development control. At present these are the two major tasks assigned to planning at the municipal government level. Conceptually they are integrated but in practice they are often two separate bureaucracies within the same department, with very little dialogue, and almost no cross-over of personnel.

Figure 9-1
Planner's Roles and Strategic Questions

Strategies	Roles
	Manager, Advocate, Controller, Designer, Evaluator or Negotiator
Client Professional Relationship	• To whom do I owe my loyalty?
	• What responsibilities do I have to my client?
Time Horizon	• What are my short-term and long-term objectives?
	• How do these mesh or conflict?
	• What range of predictable futures will I be held accountable for?
Institutional Constraints	• What variables can I manipulate or cause to be manipulated in the way I want?
Outputs	• What products must my actions yeild in order for me to maintain my credibility?
Measure of Success	• Who will judge my performance, what standards will they use, and what risks am I prepared to take in regard to their evaluation of my effectiveness?

Note: Different roles require different answers to the strategic questions.
Adapted from Susskind (1974)

Larry Susskind (1974) was perhaps the first planner who made serious enquiry into the various professional roles that planners can be called upon to perform and the principles they can use to guide their actions within each of the roles. The roles include those of a manager, designer, advocate, evaluator, controller, and negotiator. For each of these roles, and often a planner may be involved in more than one, he/she has to define the function and mood associated with the role, client-professional relationship, time horizon, institutional constraints and leverages, outputs, and measure of success. Take, for instance, the role of a manager. The function of a manager is to manipulate the flow and timing of resources, that is making resource-allocation decisions and maintaining the equilibrium of the organization. A manager's attitude, therefore, is usually cautious and skeptical towards innovation. In terms of client-professional relationship, a manager is often working for an agency at the municipal, provincial/state, regional or national level. A manager can also work for a board or commission or for elected officials. Loyalty here is towards the council or mayor, or the director of the agency. This means that a manager would try to protect the organization from internal and external pressure through maintaining the status quo, which is different from, say, the role of an advocate who creates pressure and disequilibrium. The time horizon for a manager is usually short and may even be day-to-day. The institutional constraints and leverages that a manager has include the budgetary processes and political and institutional relations. The expected output in this case is usually in the form of a decision, as opposed to a scheme or a design. The measure of success is the most difficult part for any role. In the case of the manager it may be his/her performance in securing funding, obtaining political support, or maintaining the equilibrium or credibility of the organization.

PLANNING EDUCATION

Much has been said about planning education by very qualified people. The debate about what planning education should be follows essentially the debate about what planning is or should be.

In the early days of modern city planning when it was primarily land use and transportation planning, planning education was a subdiscipline in architecture. In the first quarter of this century architecture, including planning, embarked on the "modernist" movement which was to influence architecture and city planning to the present day. The emphatic argument of the "modernist" approach, as opposed to the "artistic" approach, was that architecture and city planning should reflect the efficiency of modern construction materials and techniques on the one hand, and the importance of the "ordinary people" (meaning the working class) on the other. The approach was therefore at once mechanistic and humanistic. This was the theoretic basis of "functionalism" — the integration of technology with society. The mainstream of this "modernist" movement was in Europe but in the 1920s and 1930s the political climate in Europe worsened and many progressive architects

Hok-Lin Leung

and planners left for America, especially the United States. In the same period, the Great Depression in America prompted national programmes of huge public works projects and city renewal programmes, bringing a sense of urgency and professionalism to city planning. As a result of these push and pull factors, America absorbed both the people and ideas of "functionalism" from Europe.

Rapid economic expansion and population growth after the Second World War led to unprecedented expansion of the cities. City planning, still primarily in the land use and transportation sense, was also an expanding profession. Planning departments in Canada and the United States needed qualified personnel urgently. Traditionally, the supply of planning professionals came from the architecture and engineering disciplines. Most of these acquired planning expertise while on the job and some did graduate education in planning before entering the profession. However, this traditional source of supply was very inadequate for the great demand. Besides, it was drying up quickly because it was easy for most architecture and engineering graduates to find work and there was little financial incentive for them to do graduate training in planning. As a result, a new generation of planners and planning academics came from the social sciences disciplines. Their views on city planning and planning education raised questions about the validity and efficacy of "functionalism." This was the first soul-searching: whose function should the planner consider?

Most of the impetus of this self-examination came from social/behavioural scientists. They argued that economic developments had brought about social pluralism. The production of wealth had led to the question of the distribution of wealth because different social/economic groups had different contributions to make and needs to be fulfilled. This raised the question: Whose needs were more important? Whose environment needed more attention and improvement? Whose "functions" should city planning serve? For example, should the land use pattern and transportation network favour industrial and commercial development or should they protect residential environment? Should the amount of residential land be calculated and its layout be designed to satisfy the needs of the middle income young households or to cater to the needs of the elderly, the handicapped and the poor? Should urban renewal be used to provide space for offices or to preserve the characteristics of the mixed-use inner city neighbourhoods? In short, it was a debate of efficiency versus equity.

While these questions were being raised in the 1950s and 1960s, especially in North America, planning practice still emphasized economic and technical efficiency. The predominant planning theories were still those borrowed from architecture, engineering, and economics, the focus was still the physical aspect of land use and transportation, and the approach used was still the comprehensive land use plan. But by this time the earlier ideals and energy of the "modernist" movement had waned. Most practitioners had already lost sight of the challenge of integrating technology with society, or had ignored the societal changes which had taken place since the 1920s and 1930s. The "modernist" movement had lost its vitality and had become a style both in planning and architecture. The copybook approach in architecture had produced monstrous concrete jungles or monotonous matchbox suburbs, and land use planning had come to mean endless expansion of urban areas based on the private automobile as the only viable mode of transportation. All these led to tremendous waste of land and other resources and a complete disregard for the essential human element in the cities.

Figure 9-2: Locus of Planning Education

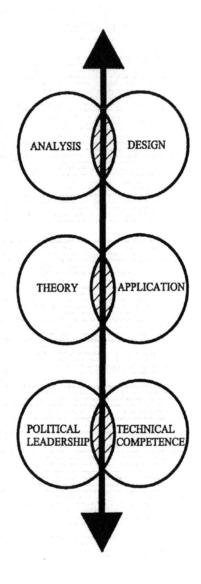

This unsatisfactory situation could no longer be tolerated. The battle cry was that "modernism" and "physical determinism" had to be discarded. The new philosophy emphasized processes and procedures of planning decision-making in order to accommodate the multiple interests in a pluralistic society. The new focus was critical analysis and not creative design. Planning schools "taught" citizen participation, conflict resolution, and various sociological studies while reducing or sometimes eliminating topics such as physical design, traffic studies, and infrastructure analysis.

As more and more planning offices began to be staffed by people trained in the social sciences and critical analysis, events took an interesting turn. Since the mid-1970s, slower economic growth has brought about a recognition that, after all, equity in the distribution of wealth required that wealth be created first. Since the 1980s we have seen a change in society's attitude. New conservatism means there will be far less wealth for the planners to redistribute.

Cities are now going through a mid-age crisis with slower growth and many more needs. Efficiency considerations have made a come-back. Of course, "functions" and "efficiency" are now more complex concepts than those used in the 1950s. The new challenge is to define the community's good in a pluralistic society, to reconcile efficiency and equity, and to invent techniques which can usefully incorporate sociological analyses into physical design. But above all, planning education has to infuse its graduates with a sense of mission and purpose tempered by sensitivity and realism.

Planning education should focus on the middle ground, emphasizing the integration of critical analysis with creative design, and the complementary between the design professions and the social sciences. In fact, there are three middle grounds to be sought: between analysis and design; between theories and applications; and between political leadership and professional competence.

Planning requires a special way of thinking. It has to break through the traditional mystique of design and to establish logical, systematic, and demonstrable methods and procedures of planning synthesis. At the same time, it has to discard irrelevant and hair-splitting analyses and to pursue clear-sighted and practice-oriented analyses. Analyses should be guided by design needs and design should be supported by analytic findings.

Planning needs practical and specific theories and techniques. Land use planning deals with the concrete problems of the use of land, and focuses on its physical dimensions, that is, what, where, how much, and when. But in order that its prognosis and prescriptions are practical and practicable, it has to establish purpose, explanation and causation, that is, why, how and wherefore. For these reasons, the planning profession has to develop its special repertoire of physical design theories and techniques from those of architecture and engineering, and social, economic, and behavioural theories and techniques from those of the social and behavioural sciences.

To be successful, a land use planner must reinforce the link between political leadership and professional competence. Planning without professional competence is ignorant. Planning without political leadership is impotent. Politicians and professionals do not necessarily think alike but they can share the fundamental recognition of the purpose, conditions, and logic of planning.

The land use planner is always a generalist and a bridge linking analysis to design, user needs to land conditions, and political sensitivity to technical knowledge. The planner may also develop special expertise and experience in certain land use types such as residential and commercial, or certain functions such as transportation and heritage preservation. However there is a core of knowledge that all land use planners should have. This includes the following.

(i) Foundation Knowledge.

(a) Activities of the urban population and the processes and problems of urbanization.

(b) Planning history, and history of planning ideas.

(c) The physical, spatial and environmental elements that constitute land and its use.

(d) The social, economic, and behavioural factors that explain and help to predict how land is related to its users.

(ii) Basic Techniques.

(a) Methods and tools of physical analysis of land and activity analysis of users.

(b) Methods and techniques of planning synthesis and physical design.

(c) Laws and procedures pertaining to land use planning, control, and administration.

(d) Techniques of communication.

(iii)Problem Solving Ability.

(a) Repertoire of real and hypothetical cases in land use planning.

(b) Design synthesis skills.

In other words, a qualified land use planner should know most, if not all, of the materials covered in this book. He/she can then choose to specialize in particular land use types or functions.

With this generalist training, the planner is able to appreciate, solicit, and coordinate the expertise from the various professions in analyzing land use issues, designing proposals, and implementing decisions.

I want to put in a special note on "communication". There is a lot of interest in the techniques of negotiation, consensus building, alternative dispute resolution, etc. Although these are not strictly·"communication" techniques, they are often touted as such. But ethical integrity and political sensitivity are about "character"; and people skills and public presence are essentially about "personality". They are not "techniques". A planner's task is not to "communicate" for its own sake, but to interpret and translate the political and technical languages that different stakeholders use, search and create viable options and, if need be, arbitrate with authority. Communication techniques are useful, but they are no substitute for substantive knowledge.

PLANNING BELIEFS

Most planners work in public or private organizations where bureaucratic routines take up a very significant portion of the day. They act more out of reflex action than reflections. Schon's Knowing-in-Practice (1982) is probably a good approach for analyzing and learning from practice, but there is often no time or space for practitioners to think aloud while going about their daily business. Practitioners, therefore, work from simple principles, norms, and the notorious rules-of-thumb. These may be crude or sophisticated, general or specific, but they represent the beliefs which a practitioner has acquired through training and indoctrination at school, as well as experience and reflection at work.

Most practitioners do not have "systems" of beliefs because many of their beliefs are incoherent and contradictory. Many of the beliefs of a new graduate are really dogmas and axioms representing at least as many points of view as the number of professors he/she has had. Planning beliefs are usually normative and prescriptive and can be about good city government and planning processes as well as about city form and urban environment. They determine behaviour and guide action. In practice, which is used here to mean bureaucratized and routinized professional activities, these beliefs are being continuously reaffirmed and changed by personal experience and objective evidence. The reflective practitioner learns to relate beliefs to practice. The happy practitioner is one who achieves congruence between them, that is, between his/her conception of the world and his/her perception of it.

So, practitioners are constantly searching, consciously or unconsciously, for the relationship between their beliefs and the practice in which they are involved. There can be five types of such relationships, all of which are characterized by the nature, degree, and the dynamics of the congruence between the practitioners' beliefs and the bureaucratic practice with which they are involved (Leung, 1988).

(i) **Beliefs Internalized in Practice.** This is like "reinventing the wheel" in practice, and is a humbling and enlightening experience. A practitioner may discover that a seemingly simplistic or even strange bureaucratic routine has actually and efficiently incorporated sound planning principles. There are numerous bureaucratic routines and rules-of-thumb which are the product of years of institutional learning and accumulated wisdom. To reject them without examination is cynical, but to accept them without questioning is unconscionable. A newcomer to a bureaucracy has a duty to examine the logic of bureaucratic practices. He/she also represents a catalytic opportunity for the bureaucracy to do some reexamination and renewal of its own.

(ii) **Beliefs Questioning Practice.** A bureaucracy measures success often in terms of "what works," that is, whatever routine that enables the bureaucracy to discharge its duties with the least fuss and disruption. It is only when a routine fails that the bureaucracy is jolted into rethinking the underlying purpose and justification of the routine. When this happens, a practitioner will be guided by his/her own beliefs in the search for explanation and remedy. If one's beliefs are robust and convincing enough it is possible to move practice closer to one's beliefs.

(iii) Beliefs Changing Practice. Bureaucracies are inherently conservative. They do not experiment with new ideas unless forced to do so. It is usually the emergence of a new situation to which the existing routine does not apply that precipitates the search for new ways of doing things. When this happens, the "creative" practitioner can examine the new situation against his/her beliefs and ask "why not?" In this way, a practitioner's beliefs may be extended and incorporated as an integral part in the new routine thus making practice congruent with beliefs.

(iv) Beliefs Bounded by Practice. A practitioner does not carry his/her beliefs as one would carry a dictionary to which one can refer for a definitive guide for actions. It is specific practice that confers relevance, meaning, and boundary to a belief. Practice sets limits to the pursuit of one's beliefs. Much of planning practitioners' learning about their professional mandates and their relation with the bureaucracy is focused on this boundary. They have to discover when the pursuit of their beliefs is circumscribed by the political, cultural, and economic context of practice. That is, when do their beliefs become "irrelevant" and/or "impractical"? For example, how far can they pursue rational analysis before it is considered hair-splitting? When does their insistence on orderly growth mark them as an obstructionist? How responsive can they be in controlling development before they lose control? The actual boundary depends on their relation with the bureaucracy, their understanding and appreciation of their mandate, and their expectations and abilities.

(v) Beliefs Change by Practice. At school and in work one acquires beliefs which are continuously being tested in practice. Some will be reaffirmed, some checked, and others changed. This may not necessarily be a compromise but could be an enlightenment. In this type of relation, the tension between beliefs and practice is resolved through "delearning" one's preconceptions and appreciating the accumulated "wisdom" of the bureaucratic practice. Modified, or even new beliefs, can emerge as the result of social learning and reflection on practice.

A professional needs to learn from practice. A land use planner, especially when he/she is placed at the front line of development control, can have a very hectic and frustrating existence but it is important to find time and space to reflect so that a state of enlightened congruence emerges between beliefs and practice.

PLANNERS AND CITY FUTURE

Futurists give us two scenarios of the post-industrial society: a service or an information society of high technology, global interdependence, wealth and leisure; or a society which is decentralized, ecologically-oriented and employing human-scale technology. These represent the opposing ideologies in planning: interdependence and self-sufficiency. Can cities and city parts be at once interdependent and self-sufficient? Jane Jacobs (1984) makes a good case in her Cities and the Wealth of Nations where she argues that cities are unique in their abilities to shape and reshape the economies of other settlements, including those far removed from them geographically. The strengths and wonders of the creative city lie in the huge collection of little firms--concentration of diversities. The symbiosis, the ease of breakaways and the flexibilities are city realities. Diversity gives it the versatility to adjust; concentration gives it the critical masses and the economies of scale.

The vibrant city is a contradiction; it is both diversity and concentration. But the concentration of diversities, by itself, does not create vibrancy. Nowhere is there a greater concentration of diverse individuals than in a crowded cinema. It is connectedness that provides the spark for growth in autonomous individuals and communities.

Christopher Alexander (1982: 22) proposes the idea of the city as a "growing whole" where "every increment of construction [I take this to include physical and social acts] must be made in such a way as to heal the city....Every new act of construction has just one basic obligation: it must create a continuous structure of whole around itself." Thus, for Alexander, city growth becomes "the creation of a loosely connected system of local symmetries, always relaxed, always allowing necessity to guide it, in such a way as to produce the deepest possible structure of centers at every scale." (ibid: 95) What does he mean by wholeness? "When we say that something grows as a whole, we mean that its own wholeness is the birthplace, the origin and the continuous creator of its on-going growth. That its new growth emerges from the specific, peculiar structural nature of its past. That it is an autonomous whole, whose internal laws and whose emergence govern its continuation, govern what emerges next." (ibid: 10)

A successful city grows in a continuous life process of nucleating and reproducing self-determined, inward-governed, growing wholes. Each part is a whole; together they form a whole — exactly the interplay of self-sufficiency and interdependence in Jacobs' economic city. The spark for growth comes through connecting; the purpose of growth is wholeness. I believe we can begin with the neighbourhood.

The neighourhood is the smallest coherent agent of human continuity in a city, in space and time. Its living memory binds together generations of inhabitants. Its spatial boundaries bind the economic and social synergies. It is at this level that the urban cycle of growth, expansion and decay will be experienced firsthand. What is a neighbourhood? This question can never be answered in ways that would please a theoretical purist. The dynamics of urban growth and the creative contradictions of urban life insist that neighbourhood boundaries are fuzzy and changing — distinct enough to give cultural and economic identities yet seamless enough to allow interpenetration and symbiosis. It cannot be defined for bureaucratic convenience but is nevertheless clearly "perceived" by its inhabitants according to the particular purpose or issue at hand. There is a kind of "duck-test." Like in Steven Segal's movie Out for Justice, where Arthur Miller's definition is quoted: "While to the stranger's eye one street was no different from another, we all knew where our 'neighborhood' somehow ended. Beyond that, a person was ... a stranger."

An even more vexing question is, "What is a good neighbourhood?" Jane Jacobs has argued for mixed land uses and diverse cultural groups within a residential neighbourhood, Her model was Greenwich Village, New York, of the 1950s, where her experience was one of vibrancy and colour. Herbert Gans modelled his after Boston's working-class west-end, before urban renewal in the 1960s "destroyed" it. He saw it as a culturally homogeneous, socially compatible "urban village." If a good city is to have diversity and concentration, where interdependence and self-sufficiency complement each other, then what it needs is perhaps not more neighbourhood diversity but more diversity of neighbourhoods. To know the neighbourhood — to feel its pulse and work to harmonize its growth cycle — is a responsible first step toward healing our cities.

But this healing is to be done in the context of tomorrow's city. The operative word for the successful city of the future is adaptiveness, which is the antithesis of administration and control — the very stuff of conventional planning. Conventional planning began as an effort to sort out the chaos of the late nineteenth-century industrial cities through the mechanical segregation of the entangled functions of the city. We have been good at stopping things. Planning, especially the metropolitan type, tends to be an overkill that undermines the vitality and diversity that is the city. My colleague, Mohammad Qadeer, who has been a keen observer of cultural diversity, told this story. There was this municipality in the Toronto area, where its Muslim citizens wanted to build a mosque. The proposal, of course, did not fit in with the existing zoning and site plan requirements for religious uses, which were based on the requirements of "churches." The planning bureaucrats wanted to accommodate, but felt they were bound by the rules. The minarets and domes were a special headache. They had to be "designed as a clock tower" in order to comply with the codes. To carry the logic to its necessary conclusion, a miniature clock was required to be installed. On seeing the plans, the mayor said, "I have never seen such beautiful and inspired clock towers." It was unadulterated bureaucratic lunacy.

In the last thirty years or so, governments spent billions to revitalize the inner city to prevent further exodus and to attract people and businesses back. The structure of the urban economy has changed from predominantly manufacturing to services, creating millions of new jobs in the city, especially the professional type. New urban professionals, who are fed up with suburban living or who never liked the suburbs anyway, find the revived city centres attractive in terms of both quality of life and access to work. To cater to this new and affluent clientele, city governments and developers have combined forces to build luxury condominiums and other residential enclaves, renovate old houses, introduce mixed uses, upgrade infrastructure, enhance services and improve security — in short, to make the inner city match the environmental ideals of the new urbanites.

Thirty years is a generation. The post-war suburbs of the fifties and sixties have become today's inner suburbs. Across North America, the population has aged and the children have left home. What were once attractive features — large lots and homes — have become physical and financial burdens. What were once essential services — neighbourhood schools and children's playgrounds--have fallen into disuse. Additional, self-contained units are beginning to appear in these suburbs as granny flats and accessory apartments. With some reasonable safeguards of privacy, sunlighting, aesthetics and other community considerations, the renewed suburbs can accommodate many more second houses without seriously compromising their environmental quality. In fact, the newer and younger families, who are the most likely homebuyers, will help to revive the neighbourhood schools and other services that are presently underused. Higher-density reuse means less pressure for sprawl, less environmental degradation and greater infrastructure efficiency. Many old suburbanites are ready for new neighbours. But how about the planners?

Planners should, first and foremost, embrace city life. The beginning of life is usually tentative and fragile, easy to be overlooked or thwarted. City innovations (physical forms, economic institutions and social organizations) demand an inordinate amount of attention and nurturing, which can be inconvenient, annoying and disruptive of established routines. At best, we should foster innovations by providing the opportunities for interplay, and soothe the pangs and disruptions of change. But if we have no informed options to offer, we should do as little harm as possible. Trying to "co-ordinate" the creative processes of the city is akin to conducting a symphony without knowing the music. The following are some thoughts on the possible roles, or non-roles, of planners.

(i) **Lift the roadblocks to innovation.** Innovation is always provisional, often surreptitious and sly, pushing at the limit of acceptability or respect-ability and testing established norms and laws. Whether these are techno-logical, socio-economic or institutional innovations, their success depends on "seizing the moment." Delays close the window of opportunity.

Official sanction is neither sought nor conducive to the act of innovating. For instance, Ontario talks about a "one-window" approach to planning approval. One-window it may be; one-stop it certainly is not. Once a development application passes through the "window" of the planning department, it goes into the "foggy-bottom" of the review process — long paper trails to various departments, agencies and authorities at the federal, provincial and municipal levels. Beyond the narrow confines of the word-ings of the official plan and zoning by-laws (even that territory is syphoned off to the building inspector's office), planners contribute little to interpret, clarify or negotiate the substantive merits of the proposed development. Anybody can check a rulebook. The task is essentially "bureaucratic." The bureaucrats in the other departments and agencies will examine only those parts of the application that have an impact on their jurisdiction, such as transportation, conservation and the environment. They cannot be expected to do "planning". Planners are trained and paid to make professional judgments about a development proposal "as a whole" — that is, to consider all the relevant aspects of the application in relation to the city environment, specifically and coherently, in a kind of Christopher Alexander interconnected wholeness. Failing this, there is no social justification for planners.

If review is needed to minimize the disruptive effects of an innovation, the delay and uncertainty of the process must not overwhelm the innovator who, by definition, is taking a leap of faith. One good review is enough. Any more just serve to pass the buck. And, if we really believe in innovation, how about reversing the burden of proof a little by requiring the reviewer instead of the innovator to justify its case?

(ii) Don't punish failure, learn from it. Planners are afraid to innovate themselves, or "allow" others to do so, for fear of punishment for failures, career-wise. The perversion is that failures are often denied or passed off as successes in order to avoid penalties. Such resistance or denial reduces the ability of planners to learn from "failures."

The future will always remain uncertain. Planning should then become a learning process that continuously informs the next action. In that way, there are no failures but each experiment clearing the ground for the next. Take the zero-lot-line. The first such development in Canada was a flop. Why? Because the developer had made every parcel a zero-lot-line. The next developer made one-fifth of the parcels zero-lot-lines and the rest conventional layouts, and was a great success. Was the first zero-lot-line experiment a failure? The more readily and sympathetically planners are disposed toward experimentation, the more our cities will thrive. Planning officialdom cannot create city vibrancy, but it can certainly thwart it. The challenge is to develop flexibility within the bureaucracy, a contradiction in terms perhaps but a necessary condition to remove the paranoia that planners-bureaucrats have toward the occasional "unconventional" development proposals.

(iii) Does anybody know about the long term? Professional futurists were the first ones to give up a blueprint approach to the future because of lack of knowledge. Instead, they now use visioning and scenarios. Our knowledge about cumulative and indirect effects is equally sketchy. Insistence on knowing all the long-term consequences before taking action is a sure recipe for analysis paralysis. In general, and in the abstract, people can address the long term. But how does that guide local actions and satisfy immediate needs, which are site-, event- and time-specific? Sometimes it is more conscionable to make sure the roofs do not leak over the heads of some poor family than to be overly worried that by patching up the roof you may be increasing the property's value, and thereby chasing out the poor family because it can no longer afford the increased rent.

Planners have too often neglected the immediate, the peculiar and the contingent, the very stuff of life. Maybe it is time to focus a little more on the concrete and experiential, and aim at making daily life decent. Planners have to examine why they are so busy and to prioritize. Maybe it is worthwhile to spend more time on potentialities than problems. Get out of the office, walk the street and feel the pulse of city life.

(iv) Who wants co-ordination? Everybody wants to co-ordinate, but who wants to be co-ordinated? A planning department does not have the clout, budget or competence to co-ordinate other departments. More seriously, city life defies co-ordination. How do you co-ordinate diversity? To foster innovation means you have to allow for the unpredictable and unusual. Planners are not the only "good guys," and they are also not the only people who are "frustrated" by bureaucratic inertia. Co-operation is perhaps more useful.

Planners have to learn to appreciate the messiness and fuzziness about city dynamics. Jane Jacobs may have dramatized the case when she says that planners have "nothing but lies" to tell about how the city works and how it is perceived by its citizens. But it is true that planners have been telling partial truths because those are what they have been trained to see. The rhetorics of long-term, comprehensive and co-ordinated planning are the rhetorics of power — the top-down, bird's-eye view, big picture--literally and metaphorically. As Donald Appleyard (1976) so ably argues that seen from this top-down viewpoint the city is an extensive diagram of paths, sectors and boundaries, compact and coherent, thin in the center, yet bound by distinct outlines as etched out on a map. This view is powerful because it gives a sense of comprehension and control, but it makes no allowance for the ambiguities and contradictions that are vital ingredients of the living city.

Planners should not have extravagant expectations, but should be ready to take small steps and win small battles. In the end, how a city looks and functions should really be the choice of its citizens. But choice depends on the availability of options. If planners are serious, then they should begin to nurture diversity. Only then can there be real choice, and only with choice can we discover our future.

Hok-Lin Leung

CONVERSION TABLES

CONVERSION TABLE 1
Metric to Imperial

	Metric Unit	**Imperial Equivalent**
Length	1 centimetre (cm)	0.394 (inches) (in.)
	1 metre (m)	3.281 foot (ft.)
	1 kilometre (km)	0.621 mile (mi.)
Area	1 square metre (m^2)	10.764 square feet (ft^2)
	1 square kilometre (km^2)	0.386 square mile (mi^2)
	1 hectare (ha)	2.469 acres (ac)
Volume	1 cubic metre (m^3)	35.315 cubic feet (ft^3)
	1 litre (L)	0.264 gallons U.S. (gal.)
Weight	1 kilogram (kg)	2.205 pounds (lb.)
Speed	1 kilometre/hour (km/hr)	0.621 miles/hour (mi/hr)
Land Use Density	1 unit/hectare (unit/ha)	0.405 unit/acre (unit/ac)

CONVERSION TABLE 2
Imperial to Metric

	Imperial Unit	**Metric Unit**
Lengths	1 inch (in.)	2.54 centimetres (cm)
	1 foot (ft.)	0.305 metre (m)
	1 mile (mi.)	1.609 kilometres
Area	1 square foot (sq. ft. or f^2)	0.093 square metres (m^2)
	1 square mile (sq. mi. or mi^2)	2590 square kilometres (km^2)
	1 acre (ac)	0.405 hectare (ha)
Volume	1 cubic foot (ft^3)	0.028 cubic metres (m^3)
	1 gallon (gal.) U.S.	3.785 litres (L)
Weight	1 pound (lb)	0.454 kilogram (kg)
Speed	1 mile/hour (mi/hr)	1.609 kilometres/hour (km/hr)
Land use Density	1 unit/acre (unit/ac)	2.471 units/hectare (units/ha)

Hok-Lin Leung

REFERENCES

Alexander, C. (1982). *A New Theory of Urban Design. New York*: Oxford University Press.

Alexander, E.R. (1981). "If Planning Isn't Everything, Maybe It's Something." *Town Planning Review* 52(1): 131-142.

Allen, F. (1925). "Suburban Nightmare." *The Independent* Vol. 114: 670-672.

Allen, L. et al. (1987). *DRASTIC: A Standardized System for Evaluating Ground Water Pollution Potential Using Hydrogeologic Settings*. Ada, Oka: Robert S. Kerr Environmental Research Laboratory, U.S. Environmental Protection Agency.

Alonso, W. (1960). *A Theory of the Urban Land Market. Regional Science Association Papers 6*. Philadelphia: Wharton School of Finance and Commerce, University of Pennsylvania.

Alonso, W. (1964). *Location and Land Use: Toward a General Theory of Land Rent*. Cambridge, MA: Harvard University Press.

American Law Institute (1976). *A Model Land Development Code*. Philadelphia: The Institute.

American Public Health Association (1946). "Appraisal of Dwelling Conditions." *An Appraisal Method for Measuring the Quality of Housing, Part II*. Washington, D.C.: The Association.

American Public Health Association (1950). "Appraisal of Neighbourhood Environment." *An Appraisal Method for Measuring the Quality of Housing, Part III*. Washington, D.C.: The Association.

American Public Health Association, Committee on the Hygiene of Housing (1960). *Planning the Neighborhood*. Chicago: Public Administration Service.

American Society of Planning Officials, Planning Advisory Service (1963). *School Site Selection*. Information Report 175. Chicago: The Society.

Andrew, C. (1992). "The Feminist City." *Political Arrangements: Power and the City*. Ed. L. Henri. Montreal: Black Rose Books.

Andrew, C. and B. M. Milroy (1988). *Life Spaces*. Vancouver; UBC Press.

Appleyard, D. (1976). *Planning a Pluralist City*. Cambridge, MA: MIT Press.

Arnstein, S.R. (1969). "A Ladder of Citizen Participation." *Journal of the American Institute of Planners* 35: 216-224.

Babbie, E.R. (1973). *Survey Research Methods*. Belmont,CA.: Wadsworth.

Bacon, E.N. (1974). *Design of Cities*. New York: Viking Press.

Bartsch, C. and E. Collation (1997). *Brownfields: Cleaning and Reusing Contaminated Properties.* Westport, CN: Praeger.

Batty, M. (1993). "Using Geographic Information Systems in Urban Planning and Policy Making." *Geographic Information Systems, Spatial Modelling and Policy Evaluation.* Eds. M.M. Fischer and P. Nijkamp. Berlin: Spring-Verlag.

Bendavid, A. (1974). *Regional Economic Analysis for Practitioners: An Introduction to Common Descriptive Methods.* New York: Praeger.

Berry, B.J.L. (1972). "Population Growth in the Daily Urban Systems of the United States." *Population Distribution and Policy.* Ed. S.M. Mazie. Vol. 5 of Research Reports of the U.S. Commission on Population Growth and the American Future. Washington, D.C.: GPO. 229-270.

Black, A. (1995). *Urban Mass Transportation Planning.* New York: McGraw-Hill.

Blakely, E.J. and D. Deka (1996). "'The Space Lock' and Urban Policy in the U.S. and U.K." *Multiculturalism in a Cross-National Perspective.* Ed. M.A. Burayidi. New York: University Press of America, Inc.

Brett, D.L. (1982). "Assessing the Feasibility of Infill Development." *Urban Land* 41(4): 3-9.

Broady, M. (1968). *Planning for People.* London: National Council of Social Service, Bedford Square Press.

Brooks, D.B. and R. Peters (1988). *Water: The Potential for Demand Management in Canada.* For Science Council of Canada. Ottawa: Marbek Resource Consultants.

Brooks, M. P. (1988). "Four Critical Junctures in the History of the Urban Planning Profession: An Exercise in Hind-Sight." *Journal of the American Planning Association* 54(2): 241-248.

Brown, D.F. and D.A. Schoen (1987). "Using Micro-Computer CAD Packages in Planning." *Journal of the American Planning Association* 53(2): 249-258.

Braybrooke, D. and C. Lindblom (1963). *A Strategy of Decisions.* New York: Free Press of Glencoe.

Bruce-Briggs, B. (1977). *The War Against the Automobile.* New York: E. P. Dutton.

Bryson, J. (1988). *Strategic Planning for Public and Nonprofit Organizations.* San Francisco: Jossey-Bass.

Buechner, R.D. (1971). *National Park Recreation and Open Space Standards.* Washington, D.C.: National Recreation and Park Association.

Burgess, E.W. (1925). "The Growth of the City." *The City.* Eds. R.E. Park et al. Chicago: Chicago University Press.

Burke, G. (1976). *Townscapes.* New York: Penguin Books.

Calthorpe, P. (1993). *The Next American Metropolis: Ecology, Community, and the American Dream.* New York: Princeton Architectural Press.

Hok-Lin Leung

Canada Mortgage and Housing Corporation (1998). *Multifamily Housing for Community Sustainability*. Ottawa: Canada Mortgage and Housing Corporation.

Carrothers, G.A.P. (1956). "An Historical Review of the Gravity and Potential Concepts of Human Interaction." *Journal of the American Institute of Planners* 22(2): 94-102.

Cervero, R. (1984). "Light Rail Transit and Urban Development." *Journal of the American Planning Association* 50(2):133-147.

Cervero, R. (1996). "Mixed Land-Use and Commuting: Evidence from the American Housing Survey." *Transportation Research. Part A: Policy and Practice* 30(5): 361-377.

Chadwick, G. (1971). *A Systems View of Planning: Towards a Theory of the Urban and Regional Planning Process*. Oxford: Pergamon Press.

Chapin, F.S. and E.J. Kaiser (1979). *Urban Land Use Planning*. Urbana: University of Illinois Press.

Chesterton, G.K. (1978). *The Napoleon of Notting Hill*. New York: Paulist Press.

Christoforidis, A. (1994). "New Alternatives to the Suburb: Neo-Traditional Developments." *Journal of Planning Literature* 8(4): 429-440.

Connerly, C.E. (1988). "The Social Implication of Impact Fees." *Journal of the American Planning Association* 54(1): 75-78.

Constant, C.K. and L.L. Wiggins (1990). "Toward Defining and Assessing Cumulative Impacts: Practical and Theoretical Considerations." *The Scientific Challenges of NEPA: Future Directions Based on Twenty Years of Experience*. Ann Arbor: Lewis Publishers.

Converse, J.M. and S. Presser (1986). *Survey Questions: Handcrafting the Standardized Questionnaire*. Sage University Paper series on Quantitative Application in the Social Sciences, 07-063. Thousand Oaks, CA: Sage Publications.

Cooper, C. (1972). "Resident Dissatisfaction in Multi-Family Housing." *Behaviour, Design and Policy Aspects of Human Habitats*. Ed. W.M. Smith. Green Bay, WI: University of Wisconsin.

Crowe, W.A. and M.E. Siemonsen (1996). *Canadian Retailing Development Trends in Canada*. Toronto: Nelson Canada.

Dasgupta, A.K. and D.W. Pearce (1979). *Cost-Benefit Analysis: Theory and Practice*. London: Macmillan.

Davies, L. (1996). "Equity and Planning: Race." *Implementing Town Planning: The Role of Town Planning in the Development Process*. Ed. C. Greed. Harlow, UK: Longman.

Delcan Corporation, Golden Associates and McCarthy-Tétrault (1997a). *Removing Barriers: Redeveloping Contaminated Sites for Housing*. Ottawa: Revouf Publishing Co. Ltd.

Delcan Corporation, Golden Associates and McCarthy-Tétrault. (1997b). *Urban Brownfields: Case Studies for Sustainable Economic Development*. Ottawa: Canada Mortgage and Housing Corporation.

Dennis, M.M. and S. Fish (1972). *Programs in Search of a Policy: Low Income Housing in Canada*. Toronto: Hakkert.

Dunphy, R.T. (1994). "Federal Transportaion Policy and Land Use: A New Ball Game?" *Urban Growth Development Prospects and Issues*. Washington, D.C.: Urban Land Institute.

Ervin, D.E., et al. (1977). *Land Use Control: Evaluating Economic and Political Effects*. Cambridge, MA: Bollinger.

Erwin, S.M. (1998). "Designing with Maps: Integrating GIS and CAD." Internet site: http://www.gsd.harvrd.edu/~servin/giscad/giscad.html

Essiambre-Phillips-Desjardine Associates Ltd., *et al.* (1997). *Conventional and Alternative Development Patterns: Phase 1: Infrastructure Costs*. Ottawa: Canada Mortgage and Housing Corporation.

Ewing, R. (1995). "Beyond Density, Mode Choice and Single-Purpose Trips." *Transportation Quarterly* 49(4): 15-24.

Ewing, R. (1996). *Best Development Practices*. Chicago: Planners Press.

Faludi, R. (1992) "Emerging Retail Development Trends in Canada." *Plan Canada* 32(6): 30-34.

Fegan, J.C. (1992). "National Bicycle and Walking Study - Results and Recommended Actions." *The Bicycle: Global Perspectives*. Eds. R. Boivin and J-F. Pronovost. Montreal: A Vélo Québec Publication.

Fields, T. (1992). "Municipal Infrastructure: Scope for Achieving Cost Efficiency/Effectiveness Through Technical Innovations." Paper Presented at the Canada Mortgage and Housing Corporation and Canadian Home Builders Association Workshop "Infrastructure and Housing: Challenges and Opportunities." Ottawa: Canada Mortgage and Housing Corporation.

Fischer, M.M. and P. Nijkamp (1993). *Geographic Information Systems, Spatial Modelling and Policy Evaluation*. Berlin: Springer-Verlag.

Fisher, R., W. Ury and B. Patton (1991). *Getting to Yes: Negotiating Agreement Without Giving In. 2nd ed*. New York: Penguin Books.

Forester, J. (1989). *Planning in the Face of Power*. Berkeley, CA: University of California Press.

Frank, J.E. and P.B. Downing (1987). "Patterns of Impact Fee Usage." Paper presented to the Conference of the American Planning Association, April 1987.

Franzese, P.A. (1991). "Mount Laurel and the Fair Housing Act: Success or Failure?" *Fordham Urban Law Journal* 19(1): 60-85.

Friedmann, J. (1966). "Planning as Innovation: The Chilean Case." *Journal of the American Institute of Planners* 32(1).

Friedmann, J. (1973). "The Future of the Urban Habitat." *Environment: A New Focus for Land Use Planning*. Ed. D.M. McAllister. Washington, D.C.: GPO. 57-82.

Hok-Lin Leung

Fulton, W. (1996) *The New Urbanism: Hope or Hype for American Communities?* Cambridge, MA: Lincoln Institute of Land Policy.

Gallion, A.B. and S. Eisner (1986). *The Urban Pattern: City Planning and Design.* New York: Van Nostrand Reinhold.

Gans, H. J. (1968). *People and Plans.* New York: Basic Books.

Gomez-Ibenez, J.A. (1991). "A Global View of Automobile Dependence: A Review of Cities and Automobile Dependence: An International Sourcebook." *Journal of the American Planning Association* 57(3): 376-379.

Gordon, D.L.A. (1997). *Battery Park City: Politics and Planning on the New York Waterfront.* Amsterdam, The Netherlands: Gordon and Breach Publishers.

Gordon, P. and H. Richardson (1989). "Gasoline Consumption and Cities: A Reply." *Journal of the American Planning Association* 55(3): 342-345.

Grant, J., J. Darrell, and P. Manuel (1993). *Sustainable Development in Residential Land Use Planning.* Halifax, NS: Canada Mortgage and Housing Corporation.

Great Britain. Expert Committee on Compensation and Betterment (1942). *Final Report.* (The Uthwatt Report). London: HMSO.

Greed, C. (1994). *Women and Planning: Creating Gendered Realities.* London: Routledge.

Greenberg, R. and J. Hecimocvich (1984). *Traffic Impact Analysis.* APA PAS Report 387. Chicago: American Planning Association.

Haggett, P. (1977). *Locational Analysis in Human Geography.* London: Edward Arnold.

Hagman, D.G. and D.J. Misczynski (1978). *Windfalls for Wipeouts: Land Value Capture and Compensation.* Chicago: American Society of Planning Officials.

Handy, S.L. and P.L. Mokhtarian (1995). "Planning for Telecommuting: Measurement and Policy Issues." *Journal of the American Planning Association* 61(1): 99-111.

Harris, C.D. and E.L. Ullman (1945). "The Nature of Cities." *Annals of the American Academy of Political and Social Science* 242(6): 7-14.

Hawley, A. (1950). *Human Ecology: A Theory of Community Structure.* New York: Ronald Press.

Hayden, D. (1984). *Redesigning the American Dream: The Future of Housing, Work and Family Life.* New York: W.W. Norton.

Headicar, P. (1974). "Town Centre Planning: A New Style." The Planner 60(8): 835-838.

Hill, M. (1968). "A Goals-Achievement Matrix for Evaluating Alternative Plans." *Journal of the American Institute of Planners* 34(1): 19-29.

Hills, S. and R. Reid (1993). *Creative Conservation: A Handbook for Ontario Land Trusts.* Don Mills, ON: Federation of Ontario Naturalists.

Hird, J.A. (1994). *Superfund: The Political Economy of Environmental Risk*. Baltimore, MD: Johns Hopkins University Press.

Hitchcock, J. (1994). *A Primer on the Use of Density in Land Use Planning*. Paper #41, Papers on Planning and Design. Program in Planning, University of Toronto. Toronto: Program in Planning, University of Toronto.

Hodge, G. (1986). *Planning Canadian Communities: An Introduction to the Principles, Practice and Participants*. Toronto: Methuen.

Hough, M. (1995). *Cities and Natural Processes*. London: Routledge.

Howard, A. (1976). "The Great Participation Fallacy." *The Planner* 62(6): 163-164.

Hoyt, H. (1939). *The Structure and Growth of Residential Neighborhoods in American Cities*. Washington, D.C.: Federal Housing Administration.

Innes, J. (1998). "Information in Communicative Planning." *Journal of the American Planning Association* 64(1): 52-63.

Institute of Transportation Engineers (1991). *Trip Generation. 5th Edition*. Washington, D.C: Institute of Transportation Engineers.

International Council for Local Environment (ICLEI), The International Development Research Centre (IDRC) and the United Nation's Environment Programme (UNEP) (1996). *The Local Agenda 21 Planning Guide: An Introduction to Sustainable Development Planning*. Toronto: ICLEI and IDRC.

Jacobs, J. (1972). *The Death and Life of Great American Cities*. London: Penguin.

Jacobs, J. (1984). *Cities and the Wealth of Nations: Principles of Economic Life*. New York: Random House

Kaiser, E.J. (1966). "Towards a Model of Residential Developer Location Behavior." Diss. U. of North Carolina.

Kaiser, E.J. , D.R. Godschalk and F.S. Chapin Jr. (1995). *Urban Land Use Planning*. Urbana, IL: University of Illinois Press.

Keeble, L. B. (1983). *Town Planning Made Plain*. London; New York: Construction Press.

Kelbaugh, D. (1997). *Common Place: Toward Neighborhood and Regional Design*. Seattle: University of Washington Press.

Kelly, E.D. (1994). "The Transportation-Land Use Link." *Journal of Planning Literature* 9(2): 128-145.

Kendig, L. (1980). *Performance Zoning*. Chicago: Planners Press, American Planning Association.

Kent, T.J. (1964). *The Urban General Plan*. San Francisco: Chandler.

Hok-Lin Leung

Kenworthy, J.R. and F.B. Laube (1996). "Automobile Dependence in Cities: An International Comparison of Urban Transport and Land Use Patterns with Implications for Sustainability." *Environmental Impact Assessment Review* 16(4-6): 279-308.

Knack, R.E. (1991). "Tony Nelessen's Do-It-Yourself Neotraditionalism." *Planning* 57(12): 18-22.

Knight, R.L. and L.L. Trygg (1977). "Evidence of Land Use Impacts of Rapid Transit Systems." *Transportation* 6(3), September:231-247.

Koppelman, L. and J. DeChiara (1975). *Urban Planning and Design Criteria*. New York: Van Nostrand Reinhold.

Koppelman, L. and J. DeChiara (1978). *Site Planning Standards*. New York: McGraw-Hill.

Kozlowski, J. and J.T. Hughes (1972). Threshold Analysis. London: Architectural Press.

Krieger, A. and W. Lennertz (1991). *Andres Duany and Elizabeth-Plater-Zyberk: Towns and Town-Making Principles*. Cambridge, MA: Harvard University Graduate School of Design.

Krueckeberg, Donald A., ed. (1983). *The American Planner: Biographies and Recollections*. New York: Methuen.

Lee, C. (1973). *Models in Planning*. Oxford: Pergamon Press.

Leung, H-L. (1979). Redistribution of Land Values. Occasional Paper 11. Cambridge, UK: Department of Land Economy, Cambridge University.

Leung, H-L. (1985). *Towards a Subjective Approach to Policy Planning and Evaluation: Common-Sense Structured*. Winnipeg, Man.: Ronald P. Frye & Co.

Leung, H-L. (1987a). "Developer Behaviour and Development Control." *Land Development Studies* 4(1): 17-34.

Leung, H-L. (1987b). "Routes and Perceptions." *Landscape Architecture* 75(3): 77-81.

Leung, H-L. (1988). "Reflection on Planning Beliefs and Practice." *Urban Design and Preservation Quarterly* 11(2/3): 9-15.

Leung, H-L. (1993). *Residential Density and Quality of Life*. Research Report. Ottawa: Canada Mortgage and Housing Corporation.

Leung, H-L. (1995). "A New Kind of Sprawl." *Plan Canada* September: 3-4.

Leung, H-L. (1998). *Regulating Processes and Timeframes for Residential Development in Ten Canadian Cities: An Update*. Toronto: Intergovernmental Committee on Urban and Regional Research.

Levine, N. (1996). "Spatial Statistics and GIS: Software Tools to Quantify Spatial Patterns." *Journal of American Planning Association* 62(3): 381-391.

Lewis, P. (1969). *Mis-Used Techniques in Planning*. Occasional Papers 1. Manchester, UK: Center for Urban and Regional Research, University of Manchester.

Lichfield, N., P. Kettle, and M. Whitbread (1975). *Evaluation in the Planning Process*. Oxford: Pergamon Press.

Little, J. (1994). *Gender, Planning and the Policy Process*. Bristol, UK: Pergamon.

Llewelyn-Davies, R., Baron (1972). "Changing Goals in Design: The Milton Keynes Example." *New Towns: The British Experience*. Ed. H. Evans. London: Charles Knight. 102-116.

Loew, S. (1979). *Local Planning. London*: Pembridge Press.

Lovejoy, E. (1992). "Mount Laurel Scoreboard." *American Planning Journal* May:10-14.

Lowry, I.S. (1964). *A Model Metropolis*. Memorandum RM-4035-RC. Santa Monica, CA: Rand Corporation.

Lupa, M.R. et al. (1995). "Transportation Sketch Planning with Land Use Inputs." *Transportation Research Record* 1499: 83-94.

Lynch, K. (1960). *The Image of the City*. Cambridge, MA: Harvard University Press and Technology Press.

Lynch, K. (1971). *Site Planning 2d ed*. Cambridge, MA: MIT Press.

Lynch, K. (1981). *A Theory of Good City Form*. Cambridge, MA: MIT Press.

Lynch, K. and G. Hack (1984). *Site Planning*. 3d ed. Cambridge, MA: MIT Press.

MacBurnie, I. (1992). "Reconsidering the Dream: Alternative Design for Sustainable Developments." *Plan Canada* September: 19-23.

Mackaye, B. (1930). "The Townless Highway." *The New Republic* 62: 93-95.

Maclaren, V.W. (1996). *Developing Indicators of Urban Sustainability: A Focus on the Canadian Experience*. Toronto: Intergovernmental Committee on Urban and Regional Research.

Marans, R.W. and W. Rodgers (1973). "Evaluating Resident Satisfaction in Established and New Communities." *Frontiers of Planned Unit Development: A Synthesis of Expert Opinion*. Ed. R.W. Burchell. New Brunswick, NJ: Center for Urban Policy Research, Rutgers University.

Mars, J. and M.I. Kyriakides (1986). *Riders, Reasons and Recommendations: A Profile of Adult Cyclists in Toronto*. Toronto: City of Toronto, Planning and Development Department.

Martin, M. (1996). "Back-Alley as Community Landscape." *Landscape Journal* 15(22): 138-153.

McHarg, I. (1969). *Design with Nature*. Garden City, NY: Natural History Press.

McKenzie, R.D. (1933). *The Metropolitan Community*. New York: McGraw-Hill.

McLoughlin, J.B. (1969). *Urban and Regional Planning*: A Systems Approach. London: Faber.

McRae, R.J. (1987). "Balancing New Road Construction with Road Maintenance Needs." Paper presented at the Federation of Canadian Municipalities "First Canadian Conference on Urban Infrastructure." Edmonton: Sodanell Canada Inc.

Messenger, T. and R. Ewing (1996). "Transit-Oriented Development in the Sun Belt." *Transportation Research Record* 1552: 145-153.

Metcalf and Eddy, Inc. (1991). *Wastewater Engineering: Treatment, Disposal and Reuse*. New York: McGraw-Hill.

Mokhtarian, P.L. (1994). "Modeling the Choice of Telecommuting: Setting the Context." *Environmental and Planning* A 26: 749-766.

Mokhtarian, P.L. (1998). "A Synthetic Approach to Estimating the Impacts of Telecommuting on Travel." *Urban Studies* 35(2): 215-241.

Mumford, L. (1961). *Cities in History: Its Origins, its Transformations, and its Prospects*. New York: Harcourt, Brace & World.

Mumford, L. (1963). *The Highway and the City*. New York: Harcourt, Brace and World.

Muth, R.F. (1969). *Cities and Housing*. Chicago: University of Chicago Press.

Myrdal, G. (1944). *An American Dilemma*. New York: Harper.

National Round Table on the Environment and the Economy (1997). *State of the Debate on the Environment and the Economy: Greening Canada's Brownfield Sites*. Ottawa, ON: National Round Table on the Environment and the Economy.

Newman, P.W.G. and J.R. Kenworthy (1996). "The Land Use - Transportation Connection." *Land Use Policy* 13(1): 1-22.

Nicholas, J.C. and A.C. Nelson (1988). "Determining the Appropriate Development Impact Fee Using the Rational Nexus Test." *Journal of the American Planning Association* 54(1): 56-66.

O'Mara, W.P. (1982). *Office Development Handbook*. Washington, D.C.: The Urban Land Institute.

Ontario Ministry of Housing (1980). *A Guide to Residential Planning and Design in Small Communities*. Toronto: Ontario Ministry of Housing.

Ontario Ministry of Municipal Affairs and Housing (1983). *Urban Development Standards: A Demonstration of the Potential for Reducing Costs*. Toronto: Ontario Ministry of Municipal Affairs and Housing.

Ontario Ministry of Transportation and Ministry of Municipal Affairs (1992). *Transit-Supportive Land Use Planning Guidelines*. Toronto: Ontario Ministry of Transportation.

Oppenheim, A.N. (1966). *Questionnaire Design and Attitude Measurement*. New York: Basic Books.

Owen, W. (1968). "The New Highways: Challenges to the Metropolitan Region." *Readings in Urban Transportation*. Ed. G.M. Smerk. Bloomington:Indiana University Press.

Hok-Lin Leung

Perloff, H.S. (1980). *Planning the Post-Industrial City*. Chicago: Planners Press.

Perry, C. (1966). "The Neighborhood Unit Formula." *Urban Housing*. Eds. W.L.C. Wheaton, et al. New York: Free Press.

Phillips, M.R. et al. (1991). "Management of Urban Drainage: Challenges and Trends." Paper presented at the Federation of Canadian Municipalities "Second Canadian Conference on Urban Infrastructure." Ottawa: Federation of Canadian Municipalities.

Pickard, J.P. (1972). "U.S. Metropolitan Growth and Expansion, 1970-2000, With Population Projections." *Population Distribution and Policy*. Ed. S.M. Mazie. Vol. 5 of Research Reports of U.S. Commission on Population Growth and the American Future. Washington, D.C.: GPO.

Porter, D. R. (1998). "Transit-Focused Development: A Progress Report." *Journal of the American Planning Association* 64(4): 475-488.

Qadeer, M. (1994). "Urban Planning and Multiculturalism in Ontario, Canada." *Race Equity and Planning: Policies and Procedures*. Eds. H. Thomas and V. Krishnarayan. Aldershot, UK: Avebury.

Qadeer, M. (1997). "Pluralistic Planning for Multicultural Cities: The Canadian Practice." *Journal of the American Planning Association* 63(4): 481-494.

Raskin, E. (1974). *Architecture and People*. Englewood Cliffs, NJ.: Prentice-Hall.

Real Estate Research Corporation (1982). *Infill Development Strategies*. Washington, D.C.: The Urban Land Institute and the American Planning Association.

Reilly, W.J. (1931). *The Law of Retail Gravitation*. New York: Putnam.

Rittel, H.W.J. and M.M. Webber (1973). "Dilemmas in a General Theory of Planning." *Policy Sciences* 4(2): 155-169.

Royal Commission on National Passenger Transportation (1992). *Analysis of National Highway System Proposals*. Ottawa: Ministry of Supply and Services Canada.

Rubinstein, H.M. (1980). *A Guide to Site and Environmental Planning*. New York: Wiley.

Rudel, T.K. (1989). *Situations and Strategies in American Land-Use Planning*. Cambridge: Cambridge University Press.

Schon, D. (1982). "Some of What a Planner Knows: A Case Study of Knowing-in-Practice." *Journal of the American Planning Association* 48(3): 351-364.

Seelig, M.Y. (1972). "School Site Selection in the Inner-city: An Evaluation of Planning Standards." *Journal of the American Institute of Planners* 38(5): 308-317.

Selltiz, C., L.S. Wrightsman, and S.W. Cook (1976). *Research Methods in Social Relations*. New York: Holt Rinehart and Winston.

Sert, J.L. (1942). *Can Our Cities Survive?* Cambridge, MA: Harvard University Press.

Singell, L. and J. Lillydahl (1990). "An Empirical Examination of the Effects of Impact Fees on the Housing Market." *Land Economics* 66(7): 82-92.

Skaburskis, A. and R. Tomalty (1998). *How Can Property Taxes and Development Charges be Used to Shape Cities: The Views of Ottawa and Toronto Area Developers*. Unpublished study Kingston, ON: School of Urban and Regional Planning, Queen's University.

Soberman, R.M. (1987). "Renewing Urban Transportation Infrastructure." Paper presented at the Federation of Canadian Municipalities "First Canadian Conference on Urban Infrastructure." Edmonton: Sodanell Canada Inc.

Southworth, M. (1997). "Walkable Suburbs? An Evaluation of Neotraditional Communities at the Urban Edge." *Journal of the American Planning Association* 63(1): 28-44.

Squires, G.D. (1994) *Capital and Communities in Black and White: The Intersections of Race, Class, and Uneven Employment*. Albany, NY: State University of New York Press.

Star, J. and J. Estes (1990). *Geographic Information Systems: An Introduction*. Englewood Cliffs: Prentice-Hall.

Stover, V.G. and F.J. Koepke (1988). *Transportation and Land Development*. Englewood Cliffs: Prentice-hall.

Strauss, A. ed. (1968). *The American City: A Source Book of Urban Imagery*. Chicago: Aldine Publishing.

Susskind, L.E. (1974). "The Logic of Planning Practice: A New Focus for the Teaching of Planning Theory." Paper presented at the Symposium on Planning Theory, Association of Collegiate Schools of Planning and the American Institute of Planners, Denver, Colorado, October 29.

Susskind, L. and J. Cruikshank (1987). *Breaking the Impasse: Consensual Approaches to Resolving Public Disputes*. New York: Basic Books.

Tacken, M. (1990). "Effects of Teleshopping on the Use of Time and Space." *Transportation Research Record* 1285: 89-91.

Tate, D. (1990). *Water Demand Management in Canada: A State-of-the-Art Review. Environment Canada Social Science Series No. 23*. Ottawa: Ministry of Supply and Services Canada.

Thompson, J.S. (1986). *Site Selection*. New York: Chain Store Publishing Corp.

Thorpe, P. (1998). "Top Ten Tips and Tricks for Selecting and Implementing GIS." Internet site: http://www.planweb.co.uk/tip/htm#top

Tobias, S. (1997). *Faces of Feminism*. Boulder, CO: Westview Press.

Toderian, B. (1996). "Big-Box Retailing: How Are Municipalities Reacting?" *Plan Canada* 36(6): 25-28.

Tolley, R., ed. (1990). *The Greening of Urban Transport: Planning for Walking and Cycling in Western Cities*. London: Belhaven Press.

Transportation Research Board (1985). *Highway Capacity Manual. Special Report 209*. Washington, D.C.: Transportation Research Board.

Ullman, E.L. (1962). *The Nature of Cities Reconsidered*. Regional Science Association Papers 9. Philadelphia: Wharton School of Finance and Commerce, University of Pennsylvania.

University of Michigan. Survey Research Center (1976). *Interviewer's Manual*. Ann Arbor: Institute for *Social Research*.

Untermann, R.K. (1984). Accommodating the Pedestrian: Adapting Towns and Neighborhoods for Walking and Bicycling. New York: Van Nostrand Reinhold.

Urban Land Institute (1960). *Community Builder's Handbook*. Washington, D.C.: The Institute.

Urban Land Institute (1975). *Industrial Development Handbook*. Washington, D.C.: The Institute.

Urban Land Institute (1978). *Residential Development Handbook*. Washington, D.C.: The Institute.

Urban Land Institute (1982a). *Office Development Handbook*. Washington, D.C.: The Institute.

Urban Land Institute (1982b). *Shopping Center Development Handbook*. Washington, D.C.: The Institute.

Urban Land Institute (1987). *Mixed-Use Development Handbook*. Washington, D.C.: The Institute.

Urban Land Institute (1988). *Business and Industrial Park Development Handbook*. Washington, DC.: The Institute.

Urban Land Institute (1990). *Residential Development Handbook*. Washington, DC.: The Institute.

Vélo Quebec (1992). *Technical Handbook of Bikeway Design*. Montreal, QU: Vélo Quebec.

Vickers, G. (1965). *The Art of Judgment: A Study of Policy Making*. New York: Basic Books.

Vrijlandt, P. and K. Kerkstra (1994). "A Strategy for Ecological and Urban Development." *Landscape Planning and Ecological Networks*. Eds. E.A. Cook and H.N. van Lier. Amsterdam, Neth: Elsevier.

Wachs, M. (1976). "Consumer Attitudes Toward Transit Service: An Interpretive Review." *Journal of American Institute of Planners* 42(1), January:96-104.

Webber, M.M. (1964). *Explorations into Urban Space*. Philadelphia: University of Pennsylvania Press.

Wekerle, G.R. and C. Whitzman (1995). *Safe Cities: Guidelines for Planning, Design and Management*. New York: Van Nostrand Reinhold.

Whyte, W.H. Jr. (1958). "Urban Sprawl." *The Exploding Metropolis*. Eds. Editors of Fortune. New York: Doubleday.

Whyte, W.H. Jr. (1980). *The Social Life of Small Urban Spaces*. Washington, D.C.: Conservation Foundation.

Wildavsky, A. (1973). "If Planning Is Everything, Maybe It Is Nothing." *Policy Sciences* 4(2): 127-153.

Wilson, R.L. (1962). "Liveability of the City: Attitudes and Urban Development." *Urban Growth Dynamics in a Regional Cluster of Cities*. Eds. F.S. Chapin Jr. and S.F. Weiss. New York: Wiley.

Wingo, L. (1961). *Transportation and Urban Land*. Washington D.C.: Resources for the Future.

Wright, J.B. (1992). "Land Trusts in the USA." Land Use Policy April: 83-86.

Wright, J.G. (1997). *Risks and Rewards of Brownfield Redevelopment*. Cambridge, MA: Lincoln Institute of Land Policy.

Yinger, J. (1979). "Prejudice and Discrimination in the Urban Housing Market." *Current Issues in Urban Economics*. Eds. P. Mieszkowski and M. Straszheim. Baltimore: Johns Hopkins University Press.

AUTHOR INDEX

SUBJECT INDEX

Hok Lin Leung